Parenting with Kindness
and Consequences

Barbara Frandsen

Parenting with Kindness and Consequences

An Intimate Guide
for Parents and Grandparents

Barbara Frandsen

Tranquility Press, 2022

Tranquility Press
723 W University Ave #234
Georgetown TX 78626
www.tranquilitypress.com

Teresa Lynn (www.TeresaLynnEditor.com) tackled the tedious details with amazing expertise. The book is better because of her input.

ISBN 978-1-950481-41-5

Library of Congress Control Number: 2022946328

Praise for

Parenting with Kindness & Consequences

An insightful and inspiring parents' guide to raising healthy, confident, and happy children.

~Cassandra S. Pete, M.Ed., MA

This breadth of expertise and wisdom is a rare find for caring parents trying their best to raise compassionate, thriving children while finding joy in the process.

~David L. Williams, bestselling author of *Fighting For Her Life: What to Do When Someone You Know Is Being Abused*

Her practical advice will easily guide parents in creating joyful families and facilitating the development of children who will grow into confident, competent adults. A perfect gift for new parents!

~Joy Holly, Certified Academic Language Therapist and Dyslexia Specialist

This is the book that new parents have been waiting for! A well-researched guide full of practical advice and empowering wisdom.

~Kirsten Brunner, Licensed Professional Counselor, co-author of *The Go-To Guide for New Dads*

More Praise for

Parenting with Kindness & Consequences

This is a book that ALL parents should keep close at hand and refer to often!
~Tammy Cox, LMSW and Certified Parent Educator

I find this book most helpful as we venture into our challenging post-COVID time. Educating and parenting have been turned upside down—thank you for this resource.
~Claudia Kramer Santamaria, retired principal

This tried-and-true guide presents easy to read insightful information and research, strategies, and tips to promote successful parenting during the formative years of your child's life. Each chapter provides topics that address ways to impact mental and physical development in children which leads to success in life.
~Linda Burleson, Administrative Supervisor of Elementary PK-5

Wise and easy guidance through the often-frightening maze of raising children today.
~Sharon Stidham Smith, Ph.D.

Parenting with Kindness and Consequences advocates for children, including those considered gifted and those with learning challenges.
~Suzy Hagar, M.A. M.Ed., Texas Gifted Education Endorsed, former Executive Director of Advanced Academic and Gifted Education Services at Dallas ISD, Texas Association for Gifted and Talented Administrator of the Year

I dedicate this book to my great-grandchildren,
DAISY and WREN,
who represent the future.

Although I cannot go there with them, I hope my love for them will shine through the pages of this book. I am convinced that when children grow up knowing they are loved, they will become strong enough to eventually take the reins with boldness guided by compassion.

Contents

Preface

While writing this book, major stress from COVID and the resulting pandemic became increasingly destructive to families. Even though we hope the worst is over, many parents and grandparents remain challenged by the damages and losses families continue to experience. Perhaps now more than at any other time in recent history, parents and grandparents need ways to guide children.

With continuing stress due to virus variations, global warming, excessive use of technology devices, uncertainty about schools, and a war abroad, the potential for frustration continues to be concerning. In every situation, my goal is to support those who parent as well as their children.

Introduction for Parents and Grandparents

After a lifetime of parenting and teaching, I am convinced that being a good parent must be the most challenging and important job any human can assume. The good news is that parents can continue to evolve and to learn. All of us can improve.

I made more mistakes than I want to remember. As a young mother, I knew almost nothing about raising children. Recognizing that no one does this job perfectly, I feel confident that, in the end, the most important goal is to provide loving acceptance. Our kids will forgive a lot of our messes if they know we absolutely love them.

My life experiences with children include:

- Teaching almost every age from preschool children with disabilities through the university level;
- Teaching at Stonegate Elementary, a school in the Hurst-Euless-Bedford school district;
- Teaching at the Austin Cerebral Palsy Center;
- Teaching at Langford Elementary, a Title I school, which is a school serving a low-income neighborhood;
- Teaching at Patton Elementary, an elite school;
- Teaching special education;
- Attending workshops and reading books with an emphasis on children;
- Completing graduate school at the University of Texas in Austin;
- Teaching pre-service teachers at St. Edward's University;

- Presenting workshops and consultations to teachers in Texas and in Jamaica;
- Designing a new model that St. Edward's University adopted for preparing pre-service teachers;
- Developing original curricula for courses taught to students preparing to become teachers;
- Except for *Dignity in Death*, writing the books listed below for classes I taught at St. Edward's University and for consultations with teachers in the field:
  - *Dignity in Death: Accepting, Assisting, and Preparing for the End of Life*
  - *Slaying the Dragons: 21st Century Literacy*
  - *Managing Cooperative Classrooms*
  - *Teaching Responsible Behaviors*
  - *YES! I Can Teach Literacy*
  - *Making a Difference for Children with Differences*
  - *Diversified Teaching: An Anthology of Teaching Strategies*
  - *Dyslexia Analysis*;
- Parenting my own children and taking care of grandchildren;
- Participating in the lives of my great grandchildren; and
- Committing to health, education, safety, and justice for all children everywhere.

By sharing ideas, I hope to interact with you as you parent your precious children. If an idea works for you, use it. If something seems out of your comfort zone, leave it by the side of the road. In the end, after all the courses and books, I realize that I must remain true to myself and my values, which are based on love. The same will be true for you.

I hope this book will benefit all types of parents: heterosexual, homosexual, transgender, single, adoptive, foster, grandparents, and friends or relatives who take over the awesome task of raising children. I embrace all spiritual beliefs and national alliances. Parents all around planet Earth who love their children want to achieve success. Even those living in dire poverty and punishing lack can succeed if given a chance and a bit of support.

Throughout the book, I use the female pronoun. This does not indicate a gender preference on my part.

Part I

Parenting from Birth Forward

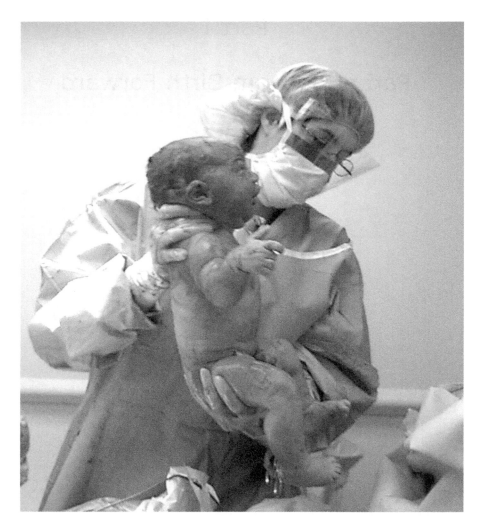

Catherine's delivery

Chapter 1
Early Learning as Opposed to Early Spoiling

An imaginary letter from Daisy, who is much too young to write anything. . .

> *Dear Mommy and Daddy,*
> *Don't get me wrong. I can tell that you two are going*
> *to be the best parents any girl could ask for. As we grow*
> *together, please keep in mind that in addition to you, I*
> *also have grandparents with loads of experience, along with*
> *aunts and uncles who promise to love me. I even have*
> *great-grandparents, who have lived so long that surely, they*
> *have learned something. I know they also want to share*
> *with you guys. Just ask, and you will receive.*

News flash for new parents: You will never spoil your newborn baby by loving her too much. You will not spoil her by responding to her needs or calming her fears. Later—much later—you can protect her from spoiling by allowing her to experience the realities of life. All behaviors have consequences. In the beginning, though, you can relax as you freely give all you have with no danger of over-indulging.

As a baby begins to interact with her world, she will encounter consequences that occur logically. While nursing, baby bites and Mom pulls her breast away. "Ouch!" instinctively comes out of the mother's mouth. Knowing the baby is too young to conceive thoughts about hurting others, Mom gently adds, "I know you didn't mean to hurt me." Mom does not need to scold as she protects herself. Acting instinctively, Mom returns the breast.

This experience initiates the beginning of teaching a baby which actions will not be tolerated. In a short time, the quick removal, followed by an opportunity to start over, becomes meaningful. The baby's understanding about behaviors and consequences has started.

Even though you want to get off to a good start, reality will influence every choice. For example, following birth, fatigue sets in. Sleep deprivation clouds thinking. An aching back or sore nipples can affect your patience. Although your new role will demand more than you imagine you have to offer, here is more good news: you will discover a strength that allows you to meet all challenges. Nature programs you for this task. In fact, your baby's survival depends on nature's programming.

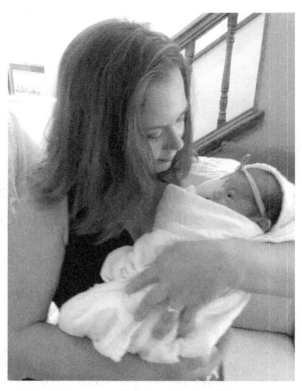

Grandma holding baby Daisy

After living snugly inside a womb for many months, your new baby will undoubtedly feel frightened by her unfamiliar new environment. She will cry, which is her only means of communicating distress. Use this opportunity to comfort as a bonding experience. Hold her snugly, swaddle her tightly, talk to her, sing to her, and provide as much skin-to-skin contact as possible. When your infant cries, she'll have a good reason. Your job will be to discover her reason and make the correction. Her diaper may not feel right, she might be hungry, or she may simply need your arms around her tiny body.

The more love, time, and safety you can provide, the stronger the foundation will be for later lessons in life. Whether day or night, use these moments to communicate love to your baby by holding her close to you, looking at her, talking to her, and meeting her needs with quiet patience. Yes, the time will come for guiding her through the trenches of consequences. Initially, though, your parenting job will be to keep her comfortable and safe. Love, in its purest form, will likely overflow as you begin the most important task of your life.

Giving birth or adopting a new baby places you squarely on holy ground. Showing love through skin-to-skin touch, gentle talk, smiles, and responses to her needs will be your greatest gift to your baby.

Story: Good News for New Parents

Shortly after my son David's first baby came home from the hospital, David called with a question. "Mom, we're totally exhausted. We need a good night's sleep. The guys at work tell me that getting up through the night with our new baby, Lane, will spoil him. They think we should let him cry himself back to sleep."

I replied, "Of course you are tired. Sleep deprivation and new babies go hand in hand. This will pass as Lane gets a little older. In the meantime, he needs your touch, your gentle voices—and some milk. He is doing exactly what he needs to do as a tiny baby."

David: "But aren't we encouraging bad habits? We don't want him to grow up thinking that every time he cries, we'll come running. My friends at work think he will be a spoiled brat—a crybaby."

Mom: "There are many loving ways to parent a new baby. Please allow me to share some of my personal thoughts with you. Your baby wakes up at night because he needs something. He is so small that his tummy can't take in enough milk to last more than a few hours. He's hungry. He needs to eat. He could even feel frightened. Life, as we know it, feels strange to him. He needs to be held, talked to, and comforted. Providing care and comfort at this time will pay off later. You are not creating a spoiled brat."

Pride of parenthood sometimes becomes an obstacle to admitting frustrations and fears that are totally normal, making it difficult for many new parents to ask for help. In addition, beginners sometimes fall prey to a myth that good parents come with natural instincts. In some cases, fear of being criticized halts a willingness to seek information from others. No one wants to feel inadequate. Although life with a new infant is one of the most demanding jobs anyone can face, in most cases parents soon feel successful. Many of those who gain confidence do so by getting help from people and ideas, such as in the following examples.

Caring Family and Friends

A knowledgeable and loving relative, friend, or grandparent may be available to help when a parent needs a break. Keep in mind that most grandparents yearn to be involved with their family and with a new baby.

If anyone you ask declines, you can graciously accept their response with the assurance that genuine reasons restrict their ability to assist you. Never feel like you are imposing. Those who cannot or do not want to help will be honest with you.

Books can provide ideas to try. Dads who participate in the experience are worth their weight in gold. Even if a dad only feels willing to change the diaper and bring a baby to a waiting mom, his help will be more important than a new father can realize. Today's dads usually seek involvement on many levels.

A book I recommend, which focuses on the benefits dads bring to birthing and supporting new moms, is *The Birth Guy's Go-To Guide for New Dads* by Brian Salmon and Kirsten Brunner.

Childcare: Help Parents Need

There will be times when you need a reliable and caring person to keep your baby. Knowing your baby is being cared for lovingly will provide time to rest, a chance to be together with your partner, or an opportunity to take care of business. Before hiring someone to keep your baby or young child, check out the individual carefully. Knowing a potential sitter from a day care center, your church or school, or getting feedback from a relative will help you feel more comfortable than hiring a stranger. You will also feel better if you get a suggestion from someone you trust and know well. Ask a potential sitter to supply references from other babysitting jobs. Before hiring a sitter for a longer amount of time, some parents assess their child's reaction after a sitter stays for an hour or two. When considering someone to stay with your baby, you want a person who enjoys babies and young children, has a sense of humor, shows patience, and demonstrates responsibility.

Discomfort arises if you do not feel confident that you are hiring the right person. Lack of information can leave a parent feeling insecure and nervous. If you feel uneasy, chances are that your baby will pick up on your concerns.

Below, read about a time when I, as a young mom in a new city, did not know anyone well enough to ask for childcare suggestions. Notice that when intuition sends a message, it is usually a good idea to listen.

Story: Leaving a Baby with Childcare

When we first moved to Austin, our baby, Joy, was less than a year old. In our former location, I had occasionally hired a teenage sitter from our church. The baby's five-year-old brother also provided his own familiar face and comfort when we were away from the house. When a meeting came up at our new church in Austin, I did not know anyone to ask for help. Knowing children were not welcome at the meeting, I looked in the yellow pages and found a childcare location near our house.

I drove with the baby to the address. As I carried Joy through the front door, I was told to take her to a back bedroom. Walking through the living area, I noticed a space full of toddlers wandering around listlessly. A television blared in the background. Few toys were evident, and the adults were paying scant attention to the children.

I delivered Joy to a baby bed in a room with three other babies in cribs. Her tiny trusting face looked up at me as I handed a bottle to her and suggested that she take a nap. Walking back through the living room did not feel comfortable. By the time I reached my car, I was crying. I turned off the ignition, walked back through the house, picked up my baby girl, and drove away. Joy attended the meeting with me. Although others in the group were not happy, I did not care.

Knowing you have left your child with someone you trust, believing your directions are clear, and feeling certain that everything needed for good care has been prepared will make leaving easier for you. When you feel comfortable, your baby will tend to mirror your calm and trusting feelings. Without this cushion of comfort, you and the baby may both end up in tears.

During the time when a child is too young to explain her discomforts, careful vetting of caretakers will be critical. Listen and respond to your instincts. When a voice in my head issues a warning, I pay attention. Often, instinct kicks in by creating a tight feeling in my stomach. I also find it helpful to compare my thoughts and feelings with the insights of someone I trust. For example, recently my daughter shared a story with me. Before she even had time to ask what I thought, I said, "This seems like a red flag, warning you to consider this situation in a new way." My daughter confirmed that she had experienced the same reaction.

Moms and Dads Bring Different Strengths

Dr. Joannie Debrito, PhD, suggests that most dads parent in different ways than the average mom, and thus provide different but equally important values.[1] Ideally, children will experience the love and the different strengths of each parent. Debrito suggests that feminine empathy, which can come from both men and women, can be balanced with the energy of male practicality. There are males who demonstrate enormous gentleness. Likewise, many females exhibit great toughness. While one parent may express less sensitivity, he or she often engages in better problem solving. The skills often exhibited by dads make a difference from birth until your baby reaches adulthood.

Bonding with Dad must be considered as important as bonding with Mom

As parents become acquainted with their baby, they learn to distinguish various needs. Parents who pay attention will know when their new little being needs something. Precisely what she needs and wants may be a total mystery, but new parents can't miss the baby's communication of "I want _____ now." Sure enough, new parents endure sleep deprivation, bewilderment, fierce protectiveness, and a heightened sense of hope that they will parent this precious little person with love. And yes—most manage to do this awesome task beautifully.

---

1   Debrito, Dads Parent Differently Than Moms.

Marygrace Taylor: Swaddle a Baby

"Swaddling sounds too simple. It can't possibly be helpful," many parents say. Today, parents would be wise to weigh the advantages and disadvantages of a practice used by Indigenous American parents. Marygrace Taylor, a swaddling expert, asks parents to consider the fact that for nine months, their new infant has been snugly confined within a small space.[2] Warm, safe, and well-fed before birth, the baby felt totally secure until being rudely thrust into the world.

Taylor believes swaddling helps make this transition more comfortable in the following ways:

- Being swaddled feels safe, like being in the womb.
- New babies frequently flail (throw their arms around spasmodically). When flailing, babies often wake themselves. Sometimes they scratch their little faces. Without any understanding of what is happening, tiny babies are often frightened by their jerking arm movements.
- Initially, a baby's body does not regulate temperature correctly. Swaddling helps keep the baby warm.

Reasons to Be Cautious About Swaddling

As beneficial as swaddling can be, you do not want to keep a baby constantly swaddled. Use common sense and caution.

To avoid creating hip dysplasia, swaddle hips and legs loosely. Be sure the baby's legs stay bent and flared out. (See an explanation of hip dysplasia on the following pages.)

Maintain a cool room temperature. An overheated baby may suffer from SIDS (sudden infant death syndrome). If a baby's cheeks get flushed and her hair feels damp, she has gotten too hot.

The mistake most parents make is not swaddling the baby's arms snugly enough. Too much space in the burrito-style covering invites arm movements, which startle and alarm infants.

---

2   Taylor, How to Swaddle a Baby.

Once baby begins to turn over, her swaddling blanket becomes a potential danger for smothering. As soon as you notice a baby struggling to roll over, stop swaddling.

For maximum benefits, follow the steps for swaddling suggested by Taylor below:

1. Spread a light baby blanket out on a flat surface. Fold the top corner about six inches toward the middle.
2. Place the baby's head above the folded corner.
3. Bring the bottom corner up to cover the baby's body.
4. Straighten the right arm and pull the right side of the blanket over her arm and body before tucking the blanket under the left side of her body.
5. Repeat with the left arm.

Make sure you can insert two or three fingers between the blanket and the baby's chest. In addition, allow the legs to bend and to flair out as they naturally do when a baby lies on her back.

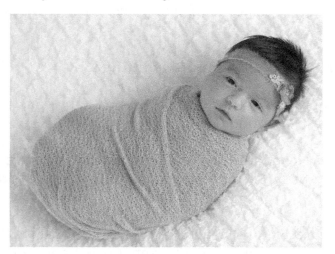

Swaddling prevents tiny babies from startling themselves

Parents can also buy Velcro or even zippered swaddles. The American Academy of Pediatrics assures parents that, done correctly, swaddling keeps a baby safe and comfortable.[3] Many parents transition a baby from swaddling to a wearable sleep sack.

Between birth and six months, some babies feel more comfortable wearing a sleep sack during naps or while sleeping at night. Light weight on the baby's chest feels like a parent's hand. Zippers help with diaper changes. In addition, sacks have snaps that can adjust the fit. Various sizes allow space for a baby's growth.

---

3   Kennedy, Unwrapping the Controversy.

Mayo Clinic on Hip Dysplasia

Mayo Clinic writes, "Hip dysplasia is the medical term for a hip socket that doesn't fully cover the ball portion of the thighbone."[4] The condition often occurs with babies born in the breech position, or those swaddled too tightly. A breech birth occurs when a baby leaves the womb bottom first, feet first, or bottom and feet first instead of headfirst.

Dr. Karp: An Expert on White Noise

After listening to a mother's blood flowing through her body for many months, a baby feels more comfortable listening to "white noise" than silence. Dr. Karp, a baby specialist, recommends a volume of 65 to 70 decibels. Just as swaddling is not used continuously, Dr. Karp also warns parents never to use white noise constantly.[5]

When a baby cries, parents can help her turn on a calming reflex by letting her listen to a rough, rumbly whoosh noise that's as loud as her crying. You can provide this sound simply by putting your mouth close to your baby's ear and making a strong "shh."

If you're using a smartphone to create white noise, reduce microwave radiation by putting the device on "airplane mode" and placing it several feet from your baby.

Other ideas Dr. Karp suggests[6] for white noises are listed below:

- Use a hair dryer with a fast and vigorous noise to comfort a fussy baby, a moderate noise to calm her, and a low noise for sleep.
- Rain sounds can be soothing.
- Automatic timers are often included in white noise machines.

A white noise machine produces a calming noise. Possibilities include sounds from nature, such as a waterfall. Pink noise has a signal with the frequency of each octave. The name comes from an appearance of visible pink light.

---

4   Mayo Clinic Staff, Hip Dysplasia.
5   Karp, White Noise.
6   Karp, White Noise.

White noise machines can be purchased on the internet from *Make Me Charm* and *Happiest Baby*. A machine called the Dohm Uno Natural Sound Machine can be found on the internet at YOGASLEEP. This device projects a soothing sound of wind, which can be adjusted for volume. Other types of white noise machines include the following:

- One white noise machine comes with 12 nightlights, 24 non-looping soothing sounds, touch control, headphone jack, timer, and memory function.
- A LectroFan generates white noise, pink noise, red noise, and fan sounds. It includes 10 fan sounds and 10 kinds of noise.
- Some clock radios include a white noise function.

SIDS: Sudden Infant Death Syndrome

It's hard to imagine a situation more painful than bringing a seemingly healthy infant home from the hospital and suddenly losing the baby to SIDS—sudden infant death syndrome. To make matters even worse, infant deaths, sometimes called crib deaths, often require a police investigation due to the many unanswered questions about this phenomenon. The brutality of being questioned and even suspected of causing the death of one's infant must be excruciating for the family, as well as for the officers who come to the house.

Causes of SIDS include the following:

- Unidentified brain defects
- Low birth weight
- Premature birth
- A respiratory infection

Doctors have identified several external issues related to sudden infant deaths. Today's wisdom recommends that a baby younger than one year should always sleep on her back. In many cases, the part of the brain that controls breathing during sleep has not developed thoroughly. In addition, parents are advised to avoid placing babies on soft, fluffy surfaces, which can block tiny nostrils and airways. Crib liners, used to protect a baby's small head, are now considered a breathing hazard. Fortunately, it is possible to purchase a breathable mesh liner for a baby's crib. Overheating can also become a hazard for SIDS.

In many cases, the cause of death remains unknown. For example, male infants are more vulnerable than female infants. The interval between the second and fourth months of life must be considered a time of concern. In addition, family histories may bring risks. Babies living in environments with second-hand smoke have a higher risk of SIDS. Even mothers can introduce risks. For example, being younger than 20 years of age, smoking cigarettes, using drugs or alcohol, and failing to get good prenatal care all present significant risks. Baby monitors, so commonly used, can be blamed because of frequent failures to alert parents of dangers.

Parents are encouraged to use a firm mattress without adding blankets, pillows, or stuffed toys. To avoid overheating a baby, parents are encouraged to swaddle infants or use sleep sacks that can eliminate the need for blankets. Covering a baby's head is considered dangerous. On the positive side, breast-feeding for at least six months lowers the risk of SIDS. Also, sucking on pacifiers without straps reduces risks. Another important consideration is that many physicians believe immunizations can help prevent sudden infant deaths.

Finally, although parents are encouraged to sleep in the same room as their infants, doctors do not recommend letting a small baby sleep in the same bed with parents. Although tempting, suffocation from close body contact remains a danger until the baby is strong enough to move away from a parent's body. Those parents who want to co-sleep may be interested in a Baby Bedside Bassinet, which has a side next to the bed that can be opened so a parent can easily touch a sleeping infant during the night.

Losing a baby to SIDS is terribly traumatic and may require therapy to heal. Mayo Clinic claims getting emotional help will be critical.[7]

A Crib That Responds to Baby

A special crib created by Dr. Karp comes with a sleep sack installed. The sleep sack is designed to keep a newborn baby on her back, which is the position currently preferred by doctors. The sack also swaddles and keeps a baby covered. While sleeping in this special crib, a baby hears sounds and feels movements like those in the womb. One type of crib recognizes when a baby wakes and begins rocking. Other less expensive versions exist and can be found at various locations.

———————

7   Siegle, The Art of Kindness.

A Baby Bedside Bassinet

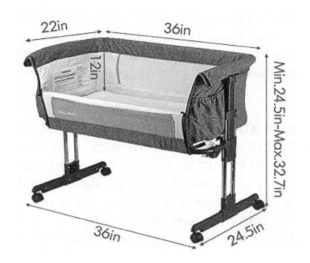

A bassinet with one side that drops down allows a mom or dad to touch the new baby without putting the infant in bed with them. During the time when a newborn lacks the strength to move out of the crib, parents can safely and easily achieve physical closeness. This crib can be purchased from many stores, but this picture is from Amazon.

Co-sleeping proponents advise parents to put a new baby in bed with them. The physical contact provided by co-sleeping feels advantageous to many parents. Others fear a baby will get too close and smother against a parent's body. Parents who want to co-sleep with infants but have lingering fears may find that this adjustable crib allows the desired closeness without the danger of smothering.

Five Ways to Soothe a Newborn

Dr. Karp suggests five ways to soothe a new baby.[8] Dr. Karp, founder and CEO of Happiest Baby, is an American pediatrician and an Assistant Professor of Pediatrics at the Keck School of Medicine at the University of Southern CA. Below, I paraphrase his suggestions.

Dr. Karp recommends swaddling only during fussy times or for sleep. No baby should be swaddled all the time.

A strong proponent of swaddling, Dr. Karp instructs parents to firmly confine a baby's arms at her sides. Like other experts, he cautions against swaddling a baby's hips and legs too tightly in the blanket. Additional concerns include allowing a baby to get too hot, covering the baby's head, and allowing the blanket to become unraveled, all of which can be dangerous.

---

8   Karp, 5 S's.

New mothers and dads learn that a baby needs to sleep on her back. Dr. Karp agrees but adds that putting a baby on her back does not work well when the baby feels cranky. During a fussy time, he suggests putting a baby over your shoulder, or holding a baby on her side or stomach. Due to worries about choking, doctors do not recommend leaving a baby alone on her side or stomach.

"Shushing," which imitates the sound of a pregnant mom's blood flowing through her body, can be comforting to a new baby. Dr. Karp also recommends white noise for soothing.

Dr. Karp recommends calming a fussy baby by supporting her head and neck while moving her rapidly back and forth. He recommends keeping the movements about an inch in width.

Pacifiers Help Some Babies

Most babies suck their thumbs, even in the uterus. No wonder they seem to enjoy pacifiers. Sucking lowers heart rate and calms babies. Even babies who nurse frequently can't do so often enough to satisfy all their sucking needs. Dr. Karp believes a baby cannot spend too much time sucking during the first few months. A baby will usually give up the pacifier sometime between six and twelve months.

Wren's pacifier fell from his mouth as he slept

All-Natural Mothering warns of the following:[9]

- Never use a pacifier to delay feeding.
- Wait until breastfeeding has been established before introducing a pacifier.

Using a pacifier may reduce the risk of SIDS (sudden infant death syndrome).

Some doctors fear pacifiers contribute to ear infections, teeth issues, and even future speech problems.

<u>Weaning from a Pacifier</u>
Make an incision on the pacifier tip. A baby will soon lose interest if the suction power is reduced or lost. Even a straw in a spill-proof cup of water can be offered. Once a baby is old enough to give up her pacifier, you can suggest giving it to another, younger baby. This may seem like a grown-up action to the baby.

Additional Ways to Soothe a Baby

Swinging, rocking, bouncing, and swaying can all soothe a baby. One mother said, "When my infant has a long fussy period, I often take him into a darkened room, turn on white noise, swaddle him tightly, and bounce him on a yoga ball." Teething toys may also provide soothing. Look for toys made from natural materials such as silicone instead of plastic. Teething toys that can be frozen may bring relief to swollen gums. Security blankets and night lights often comfort a baby.

To Nurse or Not to Nurse

Our granddaughter-in-law, Margie, knew from the beginning of her first pregnancy that she planned to nurse her baby. She did so gracefully and with the comfort nature intended. I was happy for her and for the baby.

Research on nursing cites the following benefits:

- Breastfeeding calms a baby and helps alleviate any stress a baby may feel.
- Nursing releases a hormone called cholecystokinin, which acts as a sleeping aid.

---

9   Arulraj, 11 Pacifier Alternatives.

- Breast milk contains amino acids and nucleotides, which help initiate circadian rhythms (sleep rhythms).
- Skin-to-skin contact comforts both a baby and a mother.

If a baby is sucking but not getting milk, a mother can use breast compression to stimulate the flow. Compression can also be used during pumping to empty milk ducts. To compress, a mother uses her hand to circle a breast with a thumb on one side and fingers on the other side. The mother will compress (squeeze) her breast. Before offering her second breast to the baby, she will continue squeezing until her baby stops drinking.

There are times when breastfeeding does not work well for either baby or mom. When my second baby arrived, I planned to nurse her as I had her older brother. At the time, I was extremely thin, and my breast milk lacked enough fat content to help my baby thrive. Lacking adequate calories, my baby daughter woke every two hours around the clock. During her first check-up, the doctor noted that she had not gained the appropriate weight. He suggested that I supplement breast feedings with formula. I felt a sense of failure as well as disappointment. Eventually, I accepted the fact that my body's failure to produce adequate fat did not indicate an inability to be a loving mother. Self-acceptance goes a long way toward healing a new mother's negative feelings.

Consider the following challenges:

- Baby has trouble latching on to a nipple
- Baby feels upset if the milk does not flow quickly enough
- Baby goes to sleep before filling her little tummy
- Baby nurses well, but fails to gain weight
- Mom has painful nipples
- Mom's milk ducts become blocked
- Baby resists nursing
- Older, adopted babies may have a hard time breastfeeding

There are babies who nurse with enthusiasm. They are gusty nursers who usually help sustain more breast milk than they need. Other babies may have trouble staying awake long enough to get their tummies full. When this happens, a mom will probably need to pump milk to maintain an adequate flow. Never attempt to let a baby get extra hungry so she will nurse more satisfactorily. Usually, if a baby doesn't nurse, there is a reason. This is the time to invite input from a lactation consultant.

Healthline lists some foods that provide nutrition for both mom and baby.[10] Most will taste delicious to a new mother. A few suggestions for a nursing diet include the following:

- Fish/seafood, meat, and poultry
- Fruits and vegetables
- Nuts and seeds
- Healthy fats from avocados, olive oil, coconut, eggs, and full-fat yogurt
- Starches with fiber such as potatoes, butternut squash, sweet potatoes, beans, lentils, oats, quinoa, and buckwheat
- Tofu, dark chocolate, kimchi, and sauerkraut

Nursing moms are not limited to these foods, but this list provides a healthy start. *Healthline* warns against fast foods and sugar, which may give your baby a yeast infection.[11]

Story: Wondering Whether to Nurse or Not

Consider the following conversation between a nervous mom and a supportive dad.

> Mom: "All the literature encourages nursing. I feel terrible that breastfeeding isn't working well for our baby. She nurses, seems to be full, and then starts crying in a couple of hours."
>
> Dad: "You feel tired. As our baby gets bigger, she'll begin to drink more milk at a feeding. Give it some time."
>
> Mom: "That's the problem. Our baby isn't gaining weight. She's not getting bigger. She doesn't seem to be thriving or getting stronger. That really frightens me."
>
> Dad: "Although the research indicates giving breast milk to a newborn offers nutritional values over formula, the benefits become meaningless if a baby is not thriving. Regardless of the decision, you're doing your best. Please don't beat yourself up for something you may not be able to change. Talk to your doctor about pumping. That might be an option."

---

10   Bjarnadottir, Breastfeeding Diet 101.
11   Bjarnadottir, Breastfeeding Diet 101.

The conversation above shows a couple questioning the values of nursing. If you wonder about the benefits of nursing, please realize that fatigue, sore nipples, and the fact that nursing cannot be a shared task often create doubts about whether nursing meets enough needs to be worth the sacrifices. Feelings of doubt are normal and deserve careful consideration.

Lactation Specialists Can Help

Lactation specialists will assist with nursing in several ways.

- A specialist can explain and demonstrate new ways to hold the baby when nursing.
- Specialists can also help with latching issues by physically demonstrating, explaining, and sharing videos.
- If nursing becomes painful for the mother, a consultant may recommend creams to reduce irritation.
- If the baby does not gain weight, the lactation specialist may suggest supplementing breast milk with formula.
- When a mom needs a piece of equipment such as a breast pump, the lactation consultant can recommend brands.
- Finally, a consultant can teach mothers how to store breast milk.

Before leaving the hospital, a new mother often requests referrals to lactation consultants. The International Lactation Consultant Association provides a source of information. Many mothers also claim wonderful benefits from working with La Leche. Remember to ask the following questions:

- Does the consultant live near our home?
- Can the consultant speak our language?
- Will the consultant listen to my concerns?

Wearing Your Baby in a Sling

Mothers from other countries and Indigenous Americans have worn babies in slings for centuries. In Mexico and Guatemala, wraparound slings are still used to carry infants. Until the 1950s, Indigenous American mothers wound cloth around babies and cradle boards, which they strapped to their backs. In 19th-century Europe, the poor and uneducated carried their babies and kept them close, while more elite parents maintained a distance from their babies for fear of spoiling them. Ironically, babies kept in close physical contact with parents generally have more stable heart rates and breathe more regularly. Today, parents in the United States are enjoying the benefits of wearing their babies.

A much-cited study published in the journal *Pediatrics* found that baby-wearing for three hours a day reduced infant crying significantly—43 percent overall and 51 percent at night. A more profound reason to wear a baby, though, might be the bond that it promotes between caregiver and child.[12]

Having a baby close to you improves her health. The skin-to-skin contact strengthens a baby's heartbeat, temperature, and breathing.

Wearing a baby reduces crying

Breastfeeding can occur while a mother wears her baby.

Wearing a baby strengthens bonding. Closeness and skin-to-skin contact promote a level of bonding that will continue into your child's teen years.

Wearing a baby frees a parent's hands to wash dishes, hug an older sibling, work, or organize.

Safety Concerns

Like all activities involving infants and babies, safety must be a priority. Consider the suggestions below:

- Always check to be certain airways are clear. Ways to achieve a clear airway include supporting a baby's back and neck and keeping her upright and close to your body.
- Another way to protect a baby's airway is to make sure you can place two fingers under her chin. You do not want her chin to collapse onto her chest.

---

12   Roberts, *Less Crying*.

- To support her back, keep her close enough that there are no gaps between her body and yours. However, wrap her loosely enough that you can slide your hand into the carrier.
- Make certain you can easily look down and see her face. When you do this, check her breathing, and pay attention to her mood.
- Protect your own back and neck by placing the carrier correctly.

The Importance of Tummy Time

Although doctors warn parents to never allow an infant or young baby to sleep on her tummy, providing tummy time while she is awake and when you can watch her has its benefits. In fact, if you monitor carefully, tummy time can begin as soon as you get home from the hospital. The activity strengthens baby's neck, back, and stomach, while helping to develop head control. Building strength in her neck, head, shoulders, and arms will become critically important when she begins crawling.

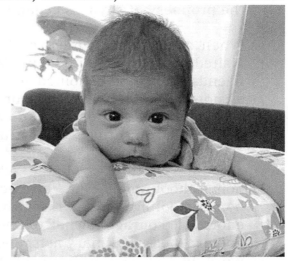

Begin tummy time by placing baby's shoulders across the top of a pillow

Even newborn infants can be placed tummy-down across your lap or chest for one to two minutes. As an alternative, you can put a pillow on the floor and place a baby across the pillow with her shoulders on top. To help create interest, place a few age-appropriate toys within reach of your baby. You can also increase interest if you get on your stomach and face her while copying her expressions and sounds. As your baby grows, gradually increase tummy time. Many parents use tummy time after baths or diaper changes.

However, never insist that a baby remain on her tummy long enough for her to get tired and fussy. In addition, it is never safe to leave a baby unwatched when she is on her tummy. Premature babies, those with reflux (a problem with spitting up milk), and babies with disabilities or illnesses should usually avoid or greatly reduce tummy time.

Words Become Buried Messages

Long before language develops, the words parents and grandparents say enter a baby's brain. Later, after baby attaches meaning to the sounds we call words, connections are made. The language of parents and grandparents may influence the baby's future development and self-esteem. Thus, I believe we need to be careful with what we say and the tones and volumes we use. As months and years pass, the importance of those words becomes even greater.

Story: Shyness

Many years ago, a loving couple gave birth to a beautiful baby girl who became our first granddaughter. Being shy himself, the dad frequently explained to friends and family, "She is shy." Although the child would probably have been shy regardless of words heard, the prophesy of shyness began to manifest.

When our granddaughter reached prekindergarten age, she and I visited a park near our home. While we were playing, one of her friends from school joined us. As I listened and observed, I felt astonished to realize that our granddaughter took the lead by suggesting what they would do and how they would play together. Bold and adventurous, she was anything but shy.

Yet the label stuck. Middle school felt tortuous to her. "Please homeschool me," she begged. With both parents working, homeschooling could not even be considered. In high school it took enormous courage for her to try out for band. She did well in band and excelled in culinary arts. She graduated with honors and, while working, took classes toward her college education. I have watched this shy little girl transform into a young woman with great courage. I have no doubt that her successes will continue to grow, and she will enjoy a happy and fulfilling life. Will she always be quiet and reserved? Probably so. She has grown into an exceptional listener.

Until you absolutely know the age when words take on importance in a baby's brain, use caution about what you say to and about her. Speaking positively with loving words of support will never harm a baby and may help a small life blossom into greater fullness than you could ever have imagined. Speaking negatively about a baby may have an equally powerful unwanted impact. I think this is a risk you do not want to take.

Chapter 2
Language and Learning: Call Me Crazy, Start Talking

When I began writing this book, Wren had not arrived yet. In his early months, he obviously had opinions about things, such as nursing, but usually kept his ideas to himself. Before too long, he became more interested in listening and replying. At nine months, he expressed strong opinions and offered advice.

Below, you will find my imaginary words from Wren.

> Hi Mom and Dad,
> I can tell that you two are trying to have conversations with me. I'm doing my best to teach you. Heck! Just listen carefully. I'll start to jabber more slowly. Maybe that will help. The most important fact of all is that I know the truth about this thing called life. Since I only arrived a short time ago, I am still in touch with the wisdom of saints and sages. You want to know what's important? Just ask me and then listen thoughtfully. I've got it.

Long before a baby can comprehend oral communication, a parent's words, intonation, volume, facial expressions, and body language have a more profound impact than most of us realize. How easy it is to believe that a baby is too young to understand. I worry that negative images and words, which will never be recalled, enter a baby's brain to later influence emotional and cognitive development.

Not only do I believe that messages may get tucked away in the baby's mysterious mental storage system, but I fear that if we wait until we believe comprehension has developed, we may lose powerful learning opportunities. Since we can't truly know when our words take on meaning for a child, I encourage parents, grandparents, and childcare attendants to build a foundation for language by starting early.

When should you initiate conversations with a baby? Begin talking, reading, or singing while your baby develops in the womb. Read, talk, play music, and reassure with gentle touches through Mommy's skin. Once the baby arrives, continue talking. "Oh goodness, you need a fresh diaper. Let's get you all fixed up and you will feel much better." When baby cooperates, say, "Thank you for helping me change your diaper."

At other times: "You are letting me know you do not want to lie still for a diaper change. Thanks for telling me. I'll do my best to hurry. Can you help?"

I know—it sounds crazy to begin talking to a baby even before birth. Do it anyway. Are you wasting your time? Definitely not. You will never hurt your baby by talking lovingly and positively. In addition, when you alternate her babble and your talk, you model the importance of listening.

For example, when you say, "It's time to eat," stress the word "eat" while offering food. Combining a specific word with a concrete object or action will increase learning. By the time our great-granddaughter Daisy was six months old, her mom and dad had begun introducing one new chopped, mashed, or pureed homemade food at a time. Combining words with specific foods helped Daisy make an oral language connection. By the time the baby could sit safely in her highchair, she was feeding herself with her hands.

Initial Language Acquisition

Acquisition of language, like the ability to walk, happens naturally. Although modeling and imitating are involved, no concrete lessons are taught about where to place one's tongue or how to relate a foot to the floor. Reading and writing, on the other hand, must be taught. Even so, a baby who has been talked to and even read to has a much easier experience learning to read than one who has a deficit of language experiences.

Regardless of the native language, children acquire the ability to understand and to speak in similar stages. Natalie Angier, a reporter and researcher for the *New Your Times*, claims that deaf babies babble with their hands.[13] This indicates that children know more about language than they can express. Babies are great little imitators.

A 1977 study in Nicaragua was done on a group of deaf children. Nathan Bierma claims that the children, who were living in jungle huts, isolated from others except their families, developed few, if any, communication skills.[14] The window for acquiring language remains open until around age seven. After that, the opportunity slowly closes, leaving children with almost no way to communicate with others.

Children go through a predictable process from babbling to literacy

In a desire to teach sign language to these deaf children from jungle huts, the Nicaraguan government brought those with almost no communication skills together and began sign instruction. The children showed little interest; however, they developed their own system of hand movements. In the process, the deaf children also developed their own syntax or language organization. It seems that humans are wired with a desire and an ability to communicate with others. In many cases, twins even create their own languages.

Noam Chomsky, who introduced the concept of universal grammar, is considered the father of linguistics. His basic theory claims that "all languages contain similar structures and rules (a universal grammar), and children everywhere acquire language the same way, and without much effort.[15] This theory seems to indicate that we're born with the basic tools of communication already present in our brains.

---

13   Angier, Deaf Babies.

14   Bierma, Nicaraguan Deaf Children.

15   Stanborough, Born This Way.

Stages of Language Acquisition

Stages	Approximate Age	Characteristics
Pre-talking	Birth to 6 months	Cooing vowel-like sounds initiate language. The infant turns her head to seek the speaker, smiles, and even chuckles.
Babbling	6–8 months	Babies produce consonant-vowel combinations such as ma-ma-ma, da-da-da, or ba-ba-ba.
Holophrastic	9–18 months	Holophrastic, or one-word, utterances are used. For example, "go" may mean "I want to go." "More" usually implies "I want more."
Two-Word	18–24 months	Examples include "Daisy go" or "Dog run." These are mini sentences. The child shows syntactic (grammar) and semantic (word meaning) development by using two words.
Telegraphic	24–30 months	Examples include "Mommy go store" or "Where Daddy go?" The child begins to communicate by using more than two words. Her expressions now closely resemble sentences.
Multiword	30+ months	Many new words are added every day. The child seems to understand what is said to her.
Semantic Development	Semantics is the basic understanding of the meaning of words, phrases, and sentences.	
Syntax Development	Language rules begin to be used without explanation or instruction.	
Pragmatic Development	Language is used as a practical social tool, to tell, to promise, or to ask.	

Although the chart above suggests average ages in months at which expressive (spoken) language development takes place, some children begin speaking earlier or later than others. Regular checkups by a doctor will help determine whether individual differences are to be respected or investigated more closely.

Importance of Dignifying Early

When teaching children with disabilities, it seems especially important to make certain their mistakes are treated with respect and understanding. This dignifies a child's learning mistakes. It turns out that all humans of all ages need to be accepted and made to feel they are worthy learners. Making any individual feel foolish discourages the risk-taking behavior that is built into learning. There is an art and skill to dignifying mistakes, which will be described later. Even infants will feel either scolded or appreciated based on facial expressions, voice tone, body language, and words used by adults. The importance of these methods of communication cannot be emphasized too strongly. Consider the story below.

Story: Dignify an Infant

Usually, the need to dignify wrong answers arises after a child becomes able to reason. The basic message indicates, "All of us make mistakes. It isn't a big deal. I love you enough to guide you to a new behavior without making you feel bad."

> Listening to our grandson talk to his two-day-old baby, I learned an important lesson. Dignifying should begin at birth and last for a lifetime.
>
> Our grandson Lane and his wife were barely home from the hospital with their new infant. Before guests arrived at their condo, Lane had cleaned up and put on a fresh shirt. As the new mom handed the tiny baby to Lane, I watched the baby do what new babies frequently do—spit up on her dad's clean shirt. Without thinking, I said, "Oh goodness, Daisy just spit up milk on you."
>
> Our grandson looked at her tiny face and said, "It's okay, Daisy. You didn't do anything wrong. Daddy can get another fresh shirt."
>
> I felt stunned as I realized what he had accomplished with a two-day-old infant. Without comprehending any of Daddy's words, that tiny infant clearly gained a feeling of acceptance. If Lane and Margie continue along this path, the baby will eventually associate her feelings with the actual words.

Lane could have complained. He could have felt angry. Margie might have muttered about how tired she was with a newborn baby and all the dirty clothes. Instead, they dignified their baby. What a terrific start.

Love Outweighs Words: Story from M*A*S*H

Without grasping the words, a baby will respond to facial expressions, voice tone, and, above all, the feeling that someone cares about her.

In one of the old M*A*S*H episodes, a truckload of young orphans seeking safety arrived at the army medical hospital.[16] After the kids got cleaned up and checked for diseases or injuries, two of the children asked for a story from doctors B.J. and Hawkeye. B.J.'s story turned out to be utterly charming, with various voice changes. At one point, one of the officers told the kids, "You know you don't understand this." Although the children may not have understood the words, they loved B.J.'s voice, his animation, and his attention.

This demonstrates the importance of communicating with voice variations, excitement, facial expressions, and loving intentions. Although the orphans in the M*A*S*H narrative did not understand the English words when B.J. spoke to them, they felt comforted by the unspoken feeling that Hawkeye and B.J. cared about them.

Language Goes Both Ways: She Has Something to Say

Once a baby begins to experiment by producing various sounds, encourage her efforts by replying to her babbles. Listen for different beginning consonant sounds. If you hear something that remotely matches a word, repeat what the baby uttered. If possible, point to the object as you repeat what you heard. For example, one of the first sounds will often be /d/. The excitement and potential meaning parents attach to a /d/ sound will eventually help her make a connection to "Dad."

When our great-granddaughter Daisy comes to play in the back yard, or when we connect through FaceTime, I always hope she will have things to tell me. When Daisy talks, I stay quiet, look at her, and listen.

When she finishes, I reply, "Daisy, thank you for telling me about that. What else?"

---

16   Greenbaum and Fritzell, "M*A*S*H.

If I am lucky, she has more to tell me. Again, I stay quiet, look at her, and listen to what she has to say. I encourage you to locate a wonderful video showing a grandma and a baby having a very enjoyable conversation about snow. The video is called *Baby's Conversation with Grandma*. You can find it on YouTube.[17]

Communicating About Those Poopy Diapers

When changing a diaper, you want your baby to know that pooping is a positive activity. In fact, a healthy poop is a reason to celebrate! "You did a poop! Good for you." Look for a book called *Everybody Poops* by Justine Avery.[18] Avery's easy-to-read book provides clear examples, such as:

EVERY . . .   *BODY* . . .   POOPS
It's true!
You poop . . .
And I poop.
EVERYBODY
POOP-POOPS!
Mothers poop.
And Fathers poop.

I encourage you to eliminate the term "dirty diaper." Although we often hear the words "dirty diaper," we know that our bodies must eliminate urine and feces to stay healthy. Any association with being dirty or disgusting inserts a negative idea where a positive one will be more useful. An alternative might be, "Your diaper (or undie) feels wet (or full). Let's get a fresh one." New diapers can be described as fresh, empty, dry, or more comfortable. Avoid making a face, acting disgusted, or pinching your nose.

A baby will most definitely feel more comfortable with a dry or empty diaper. If you wait until diaper rash appears, you've waited too long. Associate comfort with diaper changes. "You will feel so much better with a dry diaper. Let's do this. Will you help?"

When the time comes to potty train, a toddler who has experience wearing dry clothes will be more likely to develop a connection between dryness and comfort.

---

17   Coldquads, Baby's Conversation with Grandmother.
18   Avery, *Everybody Poops!*.

Teaching What "No" Means by Keeping it Positive

Ironically, the best way to teach what the word "no" means is to explain and demonstrate the behavior you want to see and hear. When we focus on a behavior we do not want our child to exhibit, that is generally the behavior we get. Instead, communicate by showing the child what to do.

Instead of Saying. . .	Demonstrate as You Say. . .
"Don't hit your baby brother."	Model a soft touch as you say, "Touch your baby brother gently."
"Don't leave this mess in your room."	Demonstrate what you want her to do as you say, "Put your toys in the toy basket."
"Quit tearing your new book."	Show your child how to hold a book correctly as you say, "Hold your new book carefully and turn the pages slowly like this."
"Do not yell in the house."	"Use a soft inside voice, please." Model as you say this to her.
"Do not eat with filthy hands."	"Let's wash our hands together before we start eating."
"Don't make me send you to the calm place."	"You and I can go to the calm place together until you feel better."
"You are driving me crazy."	"I think too much is going on. Please sit with me so we can take three deep breaths together."

Conscious Discipline, a well-known program, also encourages parents and grandparents to use the word "stop" in place of "no" when danger is involved.[19] Stop means to cease moving. To demonstrate, hold your child while moving as you say, "We walk, we walk, we walk—now we stop!" Instantly stop moving. We teach children by demonstrating movement and then stopping. Any time you feel upset, remember to say inwardly, "I may be focusing on what I do NOT want. I must change my thoughts (and mental pictures) to the behavior I want."

---

19   Bailey, Handling Temper Tantrums.

If danger is involved, say. . .	"Stop!" Then immediately tell the child what you want her to do.
You notice that your toddler is headed for a busy road. Say . . .	"Wait! Hold my hand when crossing the street."
A baby begins to pull the cat's tail. Say . . .	"Stop! If you pull the cat's tail, he might scratch you. Touch the cat gently like this." Demonstrate.
A baby begins to climb the stairs at Grandma's house. You say . . .	"Please stop and wait for me. I will walk with you up the stairs."
A toddler reaches for scissors. You say . . .	"Stop. These big scissors can be dangerous. I'll get some safe scissors you can use."

Granddaddy holds his first grandson

Chapter 3
Safeguard Your Home

Long before Wren, our great-grandson, can talk in a language his parents understand, he, like his sister Daisy, has important messages he wants to share.

Hi Friends and Family,
Now that we have moved to a new house, I have become
much more interested in exploring. Our new house has
more space, stairs going up and down, floor surfaces that
change daily, and walls that are white one day but suddenly
become purple or green the next. Weird, but interesting!
I think my parents are clever to make these changes. As
they work on our new house, my mommy, daddy, and big
sister all want to make sure I can explore and learn without
getting myself into a heap of trouble. If Mom and Dad
didn't pick up tools each night, I would have a lot more
fun experimenting with things called hammers and nails. I
guess I'm glad my folks are being so careful to make sure
I'm safe. Thanks, Mom and Dad.

When your baby begins crawling, everything she sees becomes an invitation to explore. As you baby-proof your home, first remove your treasured decorations. You will be able to return these items soon enough. Next, locate all dangers. To be certain you find everything, get on her level and crawl around. Usually, parents and grandparents put gates at the top and bottom

Cover electrical outlets and sharp corners
Protect babies from toilets and items in cabinets.

of staircases, temporary locks on cabinet doors, covers over sharp furniture corners, and inserts into electrical outlets.

There will be times when choices cannot be offered. She cannot play with sharp objects, stick something into an electric socket, or play in a dangerous area. A crawling baby or toddler has enough mobility to get hurt but lacks worldly experience to know about danger.

Use the Following Ideas to Prevent Shocks

Electric shocks can be deadly to a baby. The following ideas can help parents and grandparents consider all safeguards.

- Switch off appliances such as chargers when they are not in use.
- Cover electrical outlets or block sockets with heavy furniture.
- After baths, make sure a crawling or toddling baby is completely dry.
- Keep liquids away from electrical items such as television sets, gaming consoles, and computers.
- At night, turn off all electrical appliances to avoid fires.

What to Do if a Baby Sticks Her Fingers into an Electric Outlet

Before my husband and I started making changes to safeguard our home, I shared an article about a baby who inserted a tiny finger into an electric socket. If a child gets shocked, remember the following information.

- If the child cannot separate from the electric source, do not touch the baby until the current has been shut off. Instead, break the connection by using a non-conducing item such as a piece of wood or plastic to move the baby.
- Avoid contact with any water.
- If the child is not breathing or only has shallow breath, begin CPR.
- Drive to the closest emergency room or call 9-1-1.

Dangers of Poisons, Sharp Objects, and Furniture Corners

Household cleaners and insect repellants fall under the same category as electric sockets. With my own babies, our grandchildren, and again with great-grandchildren, part of safeguarding the house included purchasing baby-proof door latches that prevented tiny hands from getting into dangerous areas. Unless cabinets and drawers can be secured, you will rest easier if you move all dangerous items to higher levels.

Corners on furniture can be softened by placing caps over sharp edges. For a small amount of money and a little time and effort, most dangers can be reduced or eliminated. It is easy to think a toddler will not run into a furniture corner. The risk is not worth the possibility of puncturing an eye or a cheek.

Story: Eating Sand, Paint, Chalk, and Markers

In our back yard, under the shade of a gazebo, we had a child's table that held sections for mixing water and sand. When hot weather arrived, I encouraged Daisy to experience the changes that occurred from dry to moist to saturated sand. Daisy's mom said, "Daisy, if you eat the sand, we will stop playing with it."

Quick as a wink, Daisy put a pinch of sand in her mouth. With a look of empathy, Margie responded by sliding the table out of reach while saying, "You ate the sand. Now, we can't play with it today. We will try again tomorrow."

I admired the succinct way the young mom communicated. At the beginning of the activity, Mom stated a limitation by clearly indicating Daisy was not to eat the sand.

The first time Daisy slipped a taste into her mouth, Margie gently shoved the pan of sand out of reach. Without complaining or attempting to make Daisy feel wrong or bad, the mom simply stated that playing with sand had ended. No lecture, no slapped hand, no angry scowl was needed. Communication was short and simple. Daisy's mom also provided hope by saying, "We will try again tomorrow."

More recently, Daisy found a sack filled with polished rocks the size of nickels. Quickly, her mom drew a series of circles the size of the rocks. Mom first demonstrated and then suggested that Daisy place each rock in one of the circles. This worked well until I watched Daisy pop a shiny rock into her mouth. Immediately we put the rocks back in the sack and tucked them into a corner on a high closet shelf. We will bring the rocks out again in a few weeks or months.

Babies and toddlers tend to put everything into their mouths. A curious baby believes that chalk, crayons, clay, Play-Doh, sand, small rocks, pet food, and dead bugs all deserve to be tasted as part of the discovery experiment, which nature designed so the baby can learn everything possible about each item. Ends of markers can be sucked dry in a matter of seconds. Parents and grandparents must regularly assess the potential danger of items babies put in their mouths. Small objects such as buttons or rocks can be choking hazards.

Some children go beyond tasting experiments and eat items and substances that are not edible. Doctors may identify the condition as pica, which could possibly indicate anemia, a condition characterized by weakness and fatigue caused by a lack of healthy red blood cells. If your child seems obsessed with tasting almost everything she touches, especially chalk and ice, a visit to your pediatrician might be a good idea.

Parents and grandparents, eager to provide new learning experiences, frequently try various items and assess whether the child is mature enough to play with them or not. Putting objects away is not forever. Within a short time, the toddler will be able to look, listen, and touch without popping every item into her small mouth.

As you consider what will be safe, and which behaviors have the potential to hurt a baby or make her sick, you must make decisions. Will eating paint be messy but harmless? (It depends on the ingredients in the paint.) Is it okay if a toddler continually eats tiny bites of Play-Doh? Probably not. Put the Play-Doh away until her interest in tasting ends. Can she play on the stairs, or will danger outweigh the fun? A gate in front of stairs can curb her ability to climb until she gains more motor control. Even then, an adult should climb with her to keep her safe. When possible, make decisions ahead of time and take steps to eliminate conflicts.

Replace "Be Careful" with "Take Care of Yourself"

Saying "be careful" suggests a hint of fear. Stopping an adventurous spirit with fear seems less productive than providing a foundation for the day when your child will be able to make choices to keep herself safe. When that time of growing independence begins (around age three or four), you want her to know she can make wise choices. In a sense, you are forming the foundation for personal responsibility.

The words "take care of yourself" have a distinct sub-message. You are doing more than warning your baby that something is not safe. You are also planting the idea that you have faith in her ability to eventually make her own safe decisions. "Take care of yourself" prepares her for the time when you will not always be by her side to protect her. Consider what this concept can mean when she goes to school, becomes a teenager, and matures into a young adult.

Limit the Word "No" and Give Power to the Word

For dangerous items you cannot remove or cover, be firm but not angry. These remaining dangers clearly become no-no's. Getting angry will not help babies or young children understand and may cause unintended consequences such as inhibition or fearfulness around you. In fact, a constant dose of "no" ultimately creates resistance to the word. When overused, the word becomes almost meaningless. Use the word "no" only when needed to emphasize importance. Never shout, slap, hit, or spank at any age. The child's lack of ability to understand your rationale will only confuse her and cause emotional damage.

I have heard parents issue an almost constant stream of "no."

"No, do not touch that."

"No, stop moving so much."

"No! No! You are being so messy."

You can automatically reduce your use of "no" by eliminating as many dangers as possible. On the other hand, make a habit of saying "yes" as often as possible. Notice the look of pleasure you usually get when you respond with a hearty "yes" and a big smile. Establish an environment that makes "yes" easier and "no" rarely necessary. When the answer clearly must be "no," use it with firmness and determination.

Be Congruent: When No Really Means No

Danger clearly requires a firm and convincing "no." You also want to teach her the word "danger." Saying, "No—danger" will begin to have meaning if you remain consistent and congruent. Being congruent means your facial expression shows concern, your voice is firm (but not loud), and your body language indicates that you are there to protect her. Every method of conveying information must send the same message. If you smile or laugh as you firmly say "no," your baby will pay attention to your actions and ignore your words. Avoid pairing danger with playfulness. Being congruent means being totally convincing by matching every part of your body with your words.

Chapter 4
Developing Emotional Resilience

A major part of parenting is guiding a baby and toddler to enjoy laughter as well as to learn and grow from sad events, fears, and negative feelings. Your job will be to support all her feelings as you remind her that you will always love her.

A Baby's Behavior Is Neither Good nor Bad

Instead of telling an infant, "Bad baby for falling asleep before your tummy got full. Now I'll have to feed you again in two hours," say, "Thank you for doing your best to stay awake long enough to fill your tummy with milk." You can also help her stay awake by jiggling her foot, touching her face, and continuing to talk to her. As she begins toddling, you will continue to support healthy growth each time you replace words such as "good" or "bad" with descriptions of actions.

When thanking a toddler for picking up toys, change, "You are a good girl" to "Thank you for helping me pick up toys. You are a helper." Instead of "You are being a good girl when you share your cracker," say, "It feels good to share. Thank you for offering a bite to me."

An "-er" form of the action is more powerful than an "-ing" word. Other phrases to encourage baby's positive self-image include:

- You are a happy eater.
- You are a thinker.
- Wow! What a worker you are!
- You are a learner.
- You are a talker.

Set a Limit to Food Throwing Without Upsetting Dinner

Imagine for a moment how rewarding it must feel to emerge from being a totally helpless infant into a baby with enough control to pick up an object, move it to the edge of a high-chair tray, and release it over the side. Pure power in action! No wonder a baby usually does this with a look of satisfaction.

However, food on the floor does not make a baby's mom or dad happy. Throwing food is not a habit any parent hopes to perpetuate. The question becomes how to encourage the new skills of grasping and releasing while also establishing behaviors that will not increase the workload of new parents.

Begin by replacing "You are being a bad girl when you throw food on the floor" with "If you are finished eating, please leave the food on your tray. Food does not belong on the floor." If a baby continues to throw food over the edge of the tray, remove the tray or dish as you say, "I can tell you are finished."

Since no parent wants a baby to feel hungry, return the food if she clearly wants to continue eating. Food on the floor again? Repeat: "It looks like you are finished eating." You are not losing if you need to repeat this process. Each statement and action will help connect meaning with your words. The more succinct and consistent you can be with what you say, the more you help her connect the sounds with understanding.

*Toys for teething
are safe to throw*

In addition, provide one or two small toys that are appropriate for throwing, such as rubber balls or soft objects that will not hurt parents or damage the floor. Teething instruments can also satisfy a baby's need to grasp and release, as well as reduce your frustration. A variety of teething toys are available.

If you provide a few balls or toys, you can say, "These toys are for throwing. Food stays on your plate (or the tray)." Again, remain succinct and consistent. Unless you recall that it is your job to connect meaning to words, you may be tempted to decide your baby is deliberately disobeying. Remember that language is new to her. Repetition and patience will eventually come together in ways that work for you and for your baby.

Story: Support a Baby's Disappointments

One morning, Daisy, at 16 months, noticed a large and colorful dead insect on the sidewalk in front of the apartment where she lived with her parents. Although Daisy initially felt frightened, her mom's gentle explanations quickly erased her fears.

"Look, Daisy. See his pretty colors? He won't hurt you. You will be safe if you want to get close enough to look at him." After accepting her mom's assurances, Daisy made "friends" with the colorful insect. Each morning and evening, Daisy greeted and chatted with her friend. When leaving, Daisy waved goodbye. Spotting that colorful insect always made Daisy smile.

Colorful insects are fun

As often happens in life, the situation changed. While Daisy attended day care, the complex cleaned the sidewalks and steps surrounding the apartments. In the process, the insect, now dead for several days, washed away. That evening, Daisy's parents quietly watched as she searched in vain for her friend. They wordlessly shared Daisy's sadness and obvious confusion.

Loving parents always suffer a little when witnessing their child's sadness from a loss. Knowing that disappointments inevitably happen will not remove a parental tug to make everything right.

Although it's often uncomfortable, noticing when others feel sad becomes a parent's strength. Often, being quietly present provides more comfort than the most carefully crafted explanation. The disappearance of a colorful insect will not be Daisy's last or greatest loss. Hopefully, the quiet support of her parents eased her bewilderment. With the incident tucked away in her budding psyche, Daisy possibly began building her personal foundation for dealing with life on its own terms.

Life doesn't permanently feel good. Parents will not always be able to prevent disappointments. In the larger scheme of life, helping diminish fears and being present during disappointments become much more important than avoiding sad moments. The silent but loving presence of her parents communicated, "We love you, and we can see that you feel confused and disappointed. We will stay with you, Daisy, for as long as you want to keep looking."

Lessons Daisy learned from losing her insect friend *possibly* included "My parents care," or "I'm not alone," or maybe "Life goes on." Fairly profound insights for a one-year-old. Ways her parents helped included:

- Initially, Daisy's mom reassured her that she was safe to explore the insect.
- When returning home, Daisy was allowed to discover for herself that her insect friend was gone.
- Her parents remained quietly present. They did not attempt to explain a concept that would have been beyond Daisy's ability to understand.
- Their love provided constant support without interference.

What to Do When a Baby Feels Upset and Angry

As your crawling baby or toddler heads toward the open fireplace, you firmly say, "No! Hot!" As she continues her determined exploration of this interesting item, you repeat your warning. You also move your body to block her from getting to the open fire. Your body, face, and tone of voice must all communicate the same message of danger. Even though her determination seems so cute, avoid smiling or rewarding cuteness when danger is involved. As you read earlier, congruent behavior includes your face, body language, words, and an unbending effort to maintain safety. When she realizes you really mean no, she may communicate her feelings of disappointment and even anger.

Although you may be tempted to say something like, "Don't cry, this isn't a big deal," please resist. A wiser plan will be to realize that not getting to play with that fascinating flame feels enormous to her. What do *you* do when you are terribly disappointed? Maybe you sometimes cry, or at least complain. By accepting her emotions, you encourage expression of her legitimate feelings. Therapists tell us that stifling emotions doesn't work well.

As long as tears remain her only means of expressing herself, your message will be, "It is okay to feel angry. Crying is one way for you to tell me how you are feeling." Following her tears, redirect her by saying, "You feel upset. Let's take a little break by taking a short walk."

Through all the future years you hope to share with your child, you want her to feel safe to tell and show you her deepest fears, her most profound dreams, and her terribly painful disappointments. If you are there for her from the beginning, you will build a lifelong foundation to support honest communication. It begins early and must be cultivated with devotion.

As she gains a little maturity, you can also encourage her to use the following methods to express anger or upset. Always accept her genuine expressions, whether negative or positive. Many adults need sessions with therapists because, as children, they spent years covering up their feelings. Being aware of the damages caused by denying feelings increases the importance of teaching healthy methods for releasing and expressing deep emotions. Below are a few positive ways a child can express herself.

Once your child ceases to eat paint, chalk, markers, and crayons, you can invite her to create a picture showing how her anger looks. Please note that while she is a baby, her drawings will not look like anything except marks on paper. Please do not ask her to tell you what she drew. She is simply expressing feelings and will lack the words to tell you about them.

My daughter, who tended to be dramatic at a young age, did an angry dance to demonstrate her feelings. I watched without asking for or providing verbal messages. The same child sometimes went to the bass end of the piano to create a sound that represented her negative feelings.

Help a Baby Separate from Mom and Dad

Does your baby or young child resist, cry, or cling when she knows you are about to leave? Of course, she feels hesitant to see you go. Attachments to Mom and Dad are healthy and even necessary in a child's emotional development. In fact, she may not have realized yet that she and Mommy are two separate beings. She may believe *Mama and I are one.* As her parent, you have fed her, comforted her, cared for her when she did not feel well, and laughed with her when she was feeling playful. In short, your baby would not have survived without you (or someone else to fill the parenting job). No wonder being left behind often brings a baby to tears.

Why not wait until the baby is preoccupied before quietly sneaking out? Wouldn't this help everyone? Imagine stealthily sliding into your car without an incident. You might even feel like congratulating yourself. Yes, I realize that leaving quietly feels like a win. At least it feels positive until you remember that you are in this for the long haul. If you think the teen years are far, far in your future, think again. Turn your back for a moment and you will find yourself staring into the face of a teenager. Therefore, a major goal as you go about the awesome job of raising your child is to build a foundation of trust.

Even before your baby has the vocabulary to understand or use actual words, sneaking away may plant a seed of doubt. Baby may wonder, *If I take my eyes off Mommy, will she disappear?* During all those growing and developing years, trust will make an amazing difference in influencing how well she will listen, respect, and follow your guidance. Consider, just for a moment, the following alternative to quietly slipping away.

Story: When Leaving Her Becomes Difficult

Mommy gets her baby's attention and says, "Daisy, Daddy and I are going on a date. Your Aunt Jess will stay with you while we are gone."

Daisy begins to cling and complain.

Mommy continues by saying, "Thank you for telling me how you feel. We will be back soon. Whether we are here with you or away, we will always be loving you."

More complaining and clinging. Tears are now streaming down Daisy's little cheeks. Desperately, her small hands clutch Mommy's shirt to prevent her from walking away.

Mommy calmly continues, "We love you. We believe you will have fun with Aunt Jess. She has some games ready to play with you. You can help her fix dinner for you." Mommy ends by reassuring Daisy, "We love you and will see you soon."

And then, with nothing more to say or do except calmly walk out the door with a reassuring smile and a wave, Mommy and Daddy leave for their date.

Once they completed their brief goodbyes, Aunt Jess redirects Daisy by starting dinner preparation together or going outside.

Prepare for Separations

Living through a pandemic, which forced many families to remain home together, intensified the anxiety of separations for parents as well as children. Although sometimes painful, remember that it is healthy for a child to attach to her parents. This is nature's plan. Children who fail to bond with parents will probably face attachment issues later in life. Bonding feels great, but also creates anxiety when you and your child must be apart. This is normal. Life will be filled with unavoidable separations. Consider the ideas below.

Plan #1:
If separating becomes a major issue, begin with very short outings. For example, leave your baby with someone you trust as you take a walk around the block, just for the quiet pleasure of getting out of the house and being in nature. Gradually, extend short absences into increasingly longer ones. Build trust by stating the facts and following through. Establishing a foundation of trust will be critical now and even more so in the future.

Avoid leaving your child with a sitter if your child is tired, hungry, or already agitated. If possible, leave after her nap, when she is rested.

Plan #2:
Pretend to go somewhere before the time comes when you really must leave. Role play saying goodbye, hugging, and affirming, "I love you, you are safe, and I will be back soon." Get in your car but do not drive away.

Make the pretend sessions fun. At the same time, let the child know you are preparing for next Saturday, when you will leave for a short time.

Additional Ideas:
If a sitter or relative will be staying with your child, be sure they spend some time with her before the actual event. During this get-acquainted time, do your best to remain in the background, and if your child will allow it, ask the sitter to take the lead. It will be worth paying a sitter to help prepare your child.

You may want to have a new toy for the sitter to show your child immediately after you leave. An alternative is to advise the sitter to get a favorite toy and be ready to distract your child after are gone.

Especially in the beginning, return early or at least on time.

Having confidence in the person who will stay with your child will help you, which in turn will help your baby.

If you are keeping an anxious child for someone else, be prepared to distract the child with something fun such as a toy, song, or new book to read. Often, taking the child outdoors provides the best distraction. Make certain the area is safe as well as inviting.

Leave Without Drama or Delay

I have noticed that frequently a child behaves quite dramatically if a parent lingers. Once Mom or Dad leaves, the child almost always calms down and begins to have fun. In fact, a childcare worker once told our son-in-law that if he did not leave his baby daughter and go to work, no one else would be able to develop the baby's confidence by taking care of her. In his efforts to help, the dad was delaying the baby's ability to trust someone new. Once this loving dad understood, he began to quickly say goodbye and go to work. The baby soon began to adjust.

One of our daughters left her younger son with my husband and me for a few hours. The child cried and complained and did everything possible to delay his mom's departure. Even before his mom reached the end of the driveway, her son was ready to have fun. The drama was over. Following his mother's agonizing exit, the young boy immediately changed his body language, facial expressions, and words. During her time away, we engaged in several interesting projects and had a wonderful and happy evening.

One key is to always know and trust the individual who will be caring for your baby or child. You will also increase your own comfort level when you know you have left food, bottles, and anything else your child might need during your absence. Exchanging contact information will also be important for your peace of mind and for the safety of your child. Even when you totally trust your sitter, a baby monitor will help you develop confidence if, from time to time, you check in to take a look. On the other hand, if things are not progressing well, the baby monitor will prompt you to return quickly. By the way, the good news is that your own comfort level will often have an influence on your child's attitude.

Prepare for a Separation at Daycare

Leaving a baby or toddler at a day care facility can be as frightening for parents as for the child. Even after you've read all the brochures and checked out the facility and managers, you realize your child will be in the care of individuals you may never have met. An even more frightening aspect of the situation is that babies and most toddlers have very limited expressive language and will not know how to inform you if things are not quite right. Below are suggestions to help relieve your own and your child's anxieties.

If your child will be starting a new day care or school, make several visits before you leave her.

When the time comes, tell your child the truth. "I will be leaving you at school. I love you and know you are safe."

When you say goodbye, stay calm. Smile. You can do it! Give her a hug as you say, "I love you and will be back this afternoon." Leave quickly. The longer you draw out the goodbyes, the harder leaving will be for everyone. Even if your child cries, clings, or screams, remain as calm and composed as possible. (This is especially hard when you also want to cry, cling, and scream, but you must be the strong one!)

Usually, the discomfort of separating from parents passes quickly. In the meantime, do what you can to reassure your child and calm yourself. Each afternoon, when you pick her up after school, ask questions about her day.

Sample questions might include, "What did you like the most today, singing with friends or listening during story time?" Each day, ask about different activities. For example, the next day you might inquire, "Did you have more fun playing outside or playing at indoor learning centers?"

Other suggestions could include, "Did you play with friends today?" or "Did anything at school make you laugh?"

As she gets older, expand your after-school conversations to include questions that require more elaborate answers. Consider the sample questions below:

- "Tell me about the happiest part of your day at school."
- "What was the hardest thing you did at school today?"
- "Tell me what is fun about math. What is a challenge for you?"
- "What did you read today? Did you like what you read? Did you gain any new ideas?"
- "Did you or anyone else show kindness today? If so, can you tell me about it?"

What if Real Concerns Exist?

While wanting to be positive, always remain vigilant to your child's moods, sleeping patterns, and attitudes about returning to school. While she is young, you need to monitor diaper rash, which probably means that your child is not being changed often enough. Subtle signs from your child along with your own intuition may convince you that a new childcare arrangement must be found. Trust yourself if you come to this conclusion. After all, you signed on as your child's lifelong advocate.

If anxiety continues into preschool or the elementary grades, consider talking to your child's doctor about a condition called Separation Anxiety Disorder. Signs for concern include:

- Panic resulting in nausea or vomiting
- Nightmares
- Inability to sleep alone
- Worry about being lost

Chapter 5
Learning from Diverse Parenting Traditions

Wren, who only knows how to babble, shares his thoughts on diversity.

> *Hi World,*
> *Yay for diversity! I am all about diverse backgrounds and influences. My sister Daisy and I are happy to claim that we are results of different cultures coming together to share the best of each. My mom's family comes from Mexico. Daisy and I have great-grandparents who speak Nahuatl, a language from the Aztecs. About 1.7 million people speak varieties of Nahuatl. I'm glad that my mom brings her colorful customs and beliefs into our home.*
> *My dad's background traces back to Europe. Dad's ancestors include artisans, farmers, writers, teachers, and ministers. My sister and I know we are blessed by the beliefs and values that come from various parts of the world. I, myself, intend to represent the best of diversity by sharing the truth, which is, "We are all one human family."*

Parenting practices around the world offer many good ideas. Instead of seeking a perfect, one-size-fits-all solution, we will be much wiser to consider what aspects we might include alongside current practices in the United States. There was a time when I believed the best solution to racial injustice would be to intermarry until distinctions were lost. Today, I recognize the external and inner beauty found in each racial and ethnic group. No longer do I champion the melting pot theory. Today, I celebrate each unique individual within each group. By respecting and honoring our diverse physical, religious, cultural, and social characteristics, we will find the freedom to rejoice in our differences. Consider the terms below:

Term	Definition or Explanation
BIPOC	This term is pronounced as a two-syllable word (buy poc) rather than by initials. The letters stand for: B = Black I = Indigenous POC= People of color BIPOC came into use after the death of George Floyd.
POC	People of color include Asian, Latinx, Black, Pacific Islander, and Middle Eastern. In the future, more names will probably be added to the term. Each group has its own culture.
Indigenous people	Americans Indians or Indigenous peoples were here before Europeans arrived. Today, they are the descendants of the original people of North America. If referring to an issue that affects Indigenous Americans, use the name of the tribe or nation if possible.
Black	Older terminology addressed Black people as African Americans. Today, Black is used more often. If uncertain, ask an individual for a preference.
Spanish or Mexican	A new term is Latinx. Many prefer to be called Hispanic (if the person speaks Spanish) or Latino for a male and Latina for a female.

Differences in Race, Ethnicity, and Culture

Race generally refers to physical and biological characteristics. Examples may include hair texture or skin color. Often individuals check more than one race on a form. Ethnicity is a broader term based on culture and place of origin. Ways to define ethnicity include tribal, religious, linguistic, or cultural origins. Culture is defined as a way of life and includes manners, dress, language, religion, rituals, cuisine, social habits, art, and music. Culture also includes patterns of behaviors and interactions learned through socialization.

Inuit Parents Teach Control of Anger

Definitions: The terms Eskimo/Eskimos have grown in disfavor in recent years. The terms Inuk (a singular person) and Inuit (plural) have replaced the words Eskimo/Eskimos for Indigenous people living in Canada, the Arctic coastal regions of North America, Greenland, and northeast Siberia.

Inuit parents have practiced traditional parenting skills for hundreds, maybe thousands, of years. Their golden rule? Never yell at a child. If asked about the rule, Inuit parents may shrug and ask, "Why yell? You only make the child more upset."

Inuit people raise their children without yelling

Parents claim that when a child exhibits a tantrum, the child has a reason. They believe that nothing can be gained by trying to teach while the child remains upset. On the other hand, if you wait until your child feels calm, you will be able to share teaching ideas.

Inuit parents frequently use storytelling and drama to emphasize teaching concepts. Parents also use humor to ease an angry or stressful situation. I must admit that the stories seem frightening. For example, when teaching a young child about the dangers of falling in the sea, parents may claim that a monster lives in the ocean. If the child gets too close to the edge, the monster will pull the child down into the depths of the water. Yikes!

Other monsters may include a yelling monster or a sharing monster. Parents in the United States who have used the Inuit's concept of monsters insist that the tales work. I suspect that since children enjoy good stories, especially those with a hint of danger and a dash of humor, the stories can be put to good use. Certainly, I agree that powerful tales provide powerful lessons.

Oral stories are passed from one generation to the next. The National Geographic Society claims "Storytelling is universal to the human experience. We know that all cultures have told stories."[20]

20   National Geographic Society Resource Library. Storytelling.

Jean Briggs, a world-renowned anthropologist who studied the nature of anger, was 34 years old when she moved above the Arctic Circle for 17 months.[21] During that time, Briggs lived without roads, heat, or grocery stores. She endured temperatures that dropped to –40 degrees Fahrenheit. Fortunately, an Inuit family adopted her. During the winter, Briggs and the family lived in igloos. Summers found them in tents.

Briggs soon realized that the Inuit had mastered control of anger. The people considered even mild irritation an example of weakness. If someone felt offended, the one doing the offending often said, "Too bad that you feel that way."

She asked, "How do you teach your children?" Briggs watched a two-year-old boy hit his mom. The mom, following Inuit ways, responded, "Oow. That hurts!" No scolding took place. When Briggs questioned the woman, the mom replied, "When they're little, it doesn't help to raise your voice. It will just make your own heart rate go up."

Later, a mom might say, "Hit me." The child wonders, "What should I do?" If the child hits, Mom does not scold or yell but dramatizes being hurt. The mother playfully asks, "Don't you like me? Are you a baby?" Parents also act out dramas using stuffed toy animals, dolls, or puppets.

Michaeleen Doucleff, a correspondent for NPR's Science Desk, claims that to teach children to be strong emotionally and avoid "taking everything so seriously, parents must repeat the dramas from time to time."[22] Dramas give the child a chance to practice being in control. While feeling angry, this can be hard to do, but practice will help develop calmness. Inuit's traditions assure parents that practice rewires the brain. During the time when children lack a developed prefrontal cortex, Inuit parents believe it is their job to help shape their children's brains.

<u>What Can We Learn from Inuit Parents?</u>
Inuit parents have learned to control anger. What an amazing concept. They never yell at their children because they realize that yelling only upsets the child more. If a child throws a tantrum, the Inuit parents know there is a reason that makes sense to the child. The tantrum should never be taken personally. Parents teach through storytelling and dramatizations. I realize

---

21   Gushue, Eminent Anthropologist.
22   Doucleff and Greenhalgh, How Inuit Parents Teach.

the value of a good story and the power of drama. We in the United States (and elsewhere) can learn to control our anger and to make better use of stories to teach our children.

African Children Learn from a Community

JC Niala, a teacher and author who was born and raised in Kenya, returned from the UK when her daughter was born. Niala states, "It takes a village to raise a child," along with the claim, "and a community to keep the parents sane."[23] She returned to Kenya because she wanted her daughter to be raised in a community environment. The philosophy extends beyond family and close friends to include acquaintances and even strangers. In Kenya, if someone a parent does not know notices a child in danger, that stranger is expected to intervene without parental permission. In addition, Kenyan homes welcome guests. When interviewing a potential nanny for her daughter, the author asked the woman what she would do if the child needed to be corrected for an unacceptable behavior. The woman replied, "I would reason with her, we would work things out, but I would not be angry with her because children do not respond to anger."

Later, while hearing her child cry, the author overhead the nanny softly saying, "Cry, but don't forget to save some of your tears for when you might need them later." The crying soon ceased. Having a nanny, as well as help from others in the village, reduces stress for a working mom. The author believes that the image of a super-mom who manages work, the home, meals, and care of the children has become a harmful image for modern mothers.

She is convinced that when outsiders help care for children, everyone wins. Asking for and accepting help requires some humility. She quotes a Swahili saying: "A single hand cannot nurse a child."

A mother and son enjoy a walk with friends

Kim Siegal and her husband are also parents in Kenya, where they are currently raising two sons. She and her husband traded a great medical system in the U.S. for a fear of diseases in

---

23   Niala, African Parenting.

Africa.[24] When they moved to Africa to work, they also traded the support of grandparents for help from strangers. After paying a third of their U.S. income for a nanny, plus rent and groceries, the couple had little money left. In Africa, they pay their nanny a good salary that is a fraction of their incomes. With no washing machine or dish washer, they need help, along with care for the two children.

In Kenya, Kim was able to give up her super-mom image. She learned to allow the village to help her parent. When her toddler fell, a stranger would pick the baby up and dust him off. Along with all the assistance comes advice, which she admits is sometimes irritating. Another mom taught her to laugh at her child's tantrums. Others say, "Let the kids play. They are having fun. You can't control children."

What Can We Learn from African Parenting?
An emphasis on the importance of being part of a community would be a welcome addition to family life in the United States. Support from others might remove the stress most American moms feel when attempting to fill super-mom roles. Experiencing discrepancies in family incomes in Africa has the potential to promote compassion for others who have much less. Most children in the United States would benefit from this understanding.

Chinese Parents Have High Standards

Professor Amy Chua claims that impressive Chinese successes are due to parenting traditions rather than innate intelligence. She states, "Chinese mothers are superior because they demand absolute perfection and won't refrain from berating, threatening and even starving their kids until they're satisfied."[25]

Another professor, Yong Zhao, states that Chinese students "score higher on the SAT and ACT, especially in math. On public school report cards . . . they perform much better than other minority groups."[26] In Zhao's work, he stresses the importance of globalization and technology in education.

Two slightly different Chinese parenting beliefs can be considered:

---

24   Siegal, Why I Love.
25   Chua, Amy Chua.
26   Zhao and Qiu, How Good Are the Asians?.

Authoritarian child rearing emphasizes high standards reinforced with shaming, threats, and punishments. However, even with an emphasis on punishment, bonding between parents and children usually occurs.

Authoritative parenting emphasizes high standards but also stresses warmth and reasoning. Many Western parents embrace an authoritative parenting style.

Authoritative Chinese parents support high standards with love and support. Parents replace punishment with encouragement. With guidance and support matched with high expectations, authoritative parenting is often called democratic parenting. Effort is emphasized. Parents remain committed to protecting their children by preparing them for the future.

Authoritative parents engage in positive behaviors by:

- Offering fair and consistent limits for behavior
- Accepting children's opinions
- Encouraging children
- Providing warmth and nurturing
- Supporting a child's independence
- Listening to children
- Setting limits along with consequences

Authoritative parents tend to enjoy success with children because they use rules that clearly communicate what is expected of everyone in the family. Parents demonstrate stability and manage their own emotions. These parents also allow their children to be as independent as possible within the boundaries of safety. Self-esteem and confidence are fostered by inviting children to help make decisions through parent-child discussions.

Authoritative parents combine high expectations with love and support

An emphasis on effort can be identified in Chinese and Western parents who raise their children to experience success as well as happiness. Effort, it turns out, contributes more than either intelligence or talent to emotional, physical, and academic achievements.

<u>What Can We Learn from Chinese Parents?</u>
The modern Chinese emphasis on authoritative parenting is a practice parents around the world can adopt with success. All children will benefit from loving support matched with high standards. Perhaps the most important concept revolves around the importance of effort over raw talent, genetics, or intelligence.

The emphasis on effort is an important concept U.S. parents can adopt. A child's success must always be measured against her individual abilities and strengths. In addition to the emphasis on effort, rules that clearly communicate expectations for each family member offer an idea American parents can copy.

German Parenting Practices Include Independence

In 1934, during the Nazi era, a German physician named Johanna Haarer recommended that parents should not allow babies to form attachments.[27]

German children in traditional clothes

Modern psychotherapists fear Haarer may have led parents to engage in practices that will create attachment difficulties for many generations.[28] For example, Haarer encouraged mothers to ignore their children's emotional needs by showing little or no affection. In addition, she directed mothers to feed, bathe, and dry babies, and then leave them alone.[29]

Sara Zaske claims that since the 1930s and 1940s, German parents have changed their parenting practices.[30] Many modern German parents prefer to talk to children about misbehaviors rather than use physical punishment. Most Germans do not believe in corporal punishment.

---

27   Haarer, The German Mother.
28   Kratzner, Harsh Nazi Parenting.
29   Haarer, The German Mother.
30   Zaske, Achtung.

<u>What Can We Learn from German Parents?</u>
U.S. parents can benefit from adopting German parents' promotion of independence and responsibility in children. Rejection of helicopter parenting and an emphasis on outdoor play, regardless of weather conditions, are healthy parenting strategies that families in the United States can copy. In addition, extending children's years of play by delaying instruction in academics is a concept American educators and parents should seriously consider. (However, if play mostly consists of screen time, then it is not play at all. Play that genuinely benefits children relies on physical movement and opportunities to be creative and imaginative.)

Indigenous Peoples' Parenting

Traditionally, Indigenous peoples/Indigenous Americans considered both blood relatives and non-blood-related individuals as family. Extended family was traditionally included in the tribal community and the nation of Indigenous Americans. No one was to ever feel alone, without family. Today, some tribes remain patriarchal, and others are matriarchal.

In many cases, women continue to assume cultural roles for child-rearing and domestic responsibilities. Women in the west and southwest have less status than those who live in the east and south. Although the roles of women are changing, they remain rooted in tribal traditions. Many Indigenous Americans believe women are the ones who maintain old traditions. An emphasis on caring for family members provides more support than in European-American families.

When seeking employment outside the tribe, males often have a harder time than females. Although it is not impossible to find employment, it is a challenge for Indigenous American males to gain white-collar jobs. Many men take on tribal responsibilities as medicine men, spiritual guides, and leaders in the tribe.

Although usually excluded from our American history books, the forced placement of Indigenous American children into boarding schools or adoptive homes became a tragic reality. Between 1860 and the 1960s, hundreds of thousands of Indigenous American children were placed in church-run and federal boarding schools. By 1900, there were 20,000 children in Indigenous American boarding schools. By 1925, the number had tripled.

The removal of children from their parents and extended families was done by the Bureau of Indian Affairs agents and later by missionaries acting as government agents. The purpose was to destroy native languages and traditions and to replace tribal teachings with European-American ideas. Children caught speaking their native languages were punished by being denied their traditional clothing, hair styles, belongings, and behaviors learned in their families and communities. Many were tortured and sexually abused.

Not only did this practice severely damage the children and break up families, but more than 500 tribes in the United States were tragically disrupted. Children tended to feel isolated from lack of interaction with parents and tribal members. In addition, when children returned to their parents, they no longer knew how to fit in or function in the tribe. Often the children were rejected for having adopted the language, customs, and values of white people. Parents did not know how to handle their children. It was especially challenging when children returned speaking and understanding only English, a language their parents did not know.

Indigenous American parents and their children have suffered terrible loss and grief, resulting in high incidences of mental health issues and alcoholism. Children who grew up in boarding schools also failed to learn tribal parenting ideas. Once they had their own children, they lacked the ability to care for and raise them.

<u>What Can We Learn from Indigenous American Parents?</u>
We have much to learn from the traditional ideas of Indigenous Peoples, which claimed that extended families included a combination of blood and non-blood relatives. The concept of tribe was also included within the understanding of family. If all children in the United States experienced this broader attitude, perhaps they would survive losses such as divorce or the death of a family member with less pain and greater peace and acceptance.

In addition, our schools must teach the history of Indigenous Americans truthfully. Omitting historical facts is not only unethical, it denies our children an opportunity to reflect and grow cognitively, socially, and spiritually. Education lacking humanitarian values is no education at all.

An Indigenous American mother teaches her daughter to weave

Toddlers and Chores in the Yucatán

A totally different concept regarding parents, toddlers, and chores comes from a Maya village near Valladolid, Yucatán. Dr. Suzanne Gaskins clarified her desire to understand the development of children. Her research focused on play and work. As part of Gaskins' research, she learned about chores from two young Yucatán sisters as she visited with then. Both girls took great pride in the work they accomplished each day. The secret may be that parents invite toddlers to participate in helping. In fact, as they mature, "Many times the children ask to do work around the house," Gaskins says.[31]

In Guadalajara, Mexico, children help with laundry, cooking, and washing dishes. No gold stars or rewards are earned. Mexican families call this *acomedido*, which suggests that the children are not only doing what they are told to do, they help voluntarily. The biggest surprise is that mothers teach toddlers to help. "Toddlers are very eager to be helpful," says David Lancy, an anthropologist at Utah State University.[32]

---

31   Gaskins, A Village to Raise a Child.
32   Doucleff, How to Get Your Kids.

At first, the toddlers make messes that add more work for their moms. In fact, the help a toddler gives in the beginning slows the work down. One mom reported, "When my toddler was doing the dishes at the beginning, the water was all over the place, but I allowed my son to do the dishes because that's how he learned." The mom also explained the steps below, which she and the other moms use.

Initially, moms allow the toddlers to learn by observing.

Toddlers are then given a small task. The job must be helpful. It can't be a fake chore. Moms and toddlers always work together.

Children are encouraged but never forced to do the chores.

By growing up doing chores together, a pleasant association develops. A positive attitude leads to additional volunteering as children become more capable.

What Can We Learn from Parents in Mexico?
If American mothers could understand that toddlers want to help, they could find ways to teach children by working together. The real benefit would come later in terms of a positive work attitude and ethic. Being part of the family promotes intrinsic feelings of pleasure. "This is the way families work to help one another," claims Dr. Murray Bowen, a family systems theory specialist.[33] He continues by saying that individuals are interconnected within families and cannot be understood in isolation.

South American sisters carry laundry on top of their wash boards

---

33   GenoPro, Family Systems Theory.

Part II

Parenting with Kindness

Chapter 6
Model Being Kind

Below, you will find an imaginary letter from Daisy, who is still much too young to write anything at all.

Dear Mommy and Daddy,
Let's clear this up from the very beginning. I am not
spoiled. How silly! Most of the time, when I cry, it will be
because I really need something. Later, if I get a bit bossy,
it will be because I think you are not listening to what I
am telling you. If, by chance, I demonstrate some selfish
(spoiled) behavior in the future, I know I can count on you
to set some firm but loving limits. Together, we will figure
it out. Trust me. I'm on to this growing thing and am
doing it quite well.

Toddlers Can Consider Others

I encourage parents and grandparents to begin introducing the concept of others long before a child reaches age three. Your own personal examples of kindness provide your child with the most effective way to learn. By patiently explaining, you begin to emphasize the importance of others as separate beings. The foundation for a concept of others can begin even during the important "me" stage of emotional development.

Story: A Toddler at a Birthday Party

Imagine taking your two-year-old to her friend's birthday party. As you and your toddler walk in, she peers with big, brown, worried eyes from behind your legs. One thumb is firmly planted in your toddler's mouth. Her other hand clings to your skirt. You worry about how this party will go for her.

Suddenly, seeing the pile of gifts, your toddler's face lights up. She points to the gifts as she releases your skirt and hurries toward the brightly wrapped presents. You realize with panic that she has no way to understand that the party and all the gifts are for her friend. This two-year-old toddler exists in her age-appropriate me-world.

You step forward and get on her eye level to explain, "This party is for Ellen's birthday. These are Ellen's gifts. In a short time, we will have a birthday party just for you."

Immediately, her eyes drop and her lower lip trembles as she quietly continues to slowly edge toward the gifts. Even though you realize she will not be capable of grasping the idea that everything she sees belongs to Ellen, you just planted the idea of others. You may want to add, "I know this feels sad for you. Do you want to tell me or show me how you feel?"

As Mom recalls buying a little gift for Ellen, she scolds herself: *I should have bought a lot of gifts for my own child to open. She could have enjoyed them before the party or maybe she could have opened her gifts at the same time as Ellen. That would have made her happy.* Although the thought seems loving, this idea is way over the top. Imagine all the parties in this child's future. Is Mom going to buy multiple presents for her child every time she attends a birthday party?

As Mom wonders how she can redirect her toddler, she notices children playing in the yard. Pointing out the window, she suggests, "Look, sweetheart. Some of the children are playing outside. Let's check out the fun." Mom successfully redirects her daughter away from the gifts to the children playing in the yard.

Loving Is Not Spoiling

Loving your child for the rest of her life will not spoil her. Unless you never allow her to entertain herself, you will not spoil her by playing with her and being involved in her life. New and exciting experiences never spoil. In fact, new learning experiences create neural connections between brain cells using dendrites. Learning a new skill helps the brain as well as the body develop.

Within reason, even too many toys will not spoil a child unless she later decides she can't be happy without a specific toy or experience. Whether or not a child ultimately falls into the category of being spoiled depends on her attitudes toward others and her feelings about herself. Basic kindness holds the key. How can you teach your child to be kind to other people and to herself? Primarily, she learns by watching you and copying your behavior.

Explanation of Dendrites

Author Christa Sterling states that when we are learning new information, neural (nerve cell) connections form.[34] Sterling claims this change has been referred to as the "plasticity" of the brain. Dendrites, tree-like projections at the end of neurons, communicate with other dendrites. While learning, an electrochemical charge (axon) goes to the cell body. Boredom usually indicates a lack of stimulation caused by an absence of learning. Skills that require repetition and practice, such as mastering a musical instrument or acquiring the expertise needed to participate in sports, will rewire the brain while also making the new skill easier.

The job of dendrites is to:

- Gather information from other dendrites
- Process new information
- Transfer information to different dendrites
- Send information to the soma (cell body) of the neuron

Learning any new skill will create neural connections

---

34   Sterling, Keeping Your Mind.

Like branches of a tree, dendrites extend into smaller projections. Some neurons have dendritic spikes, which act like small receptors. The figure below depicts what a dendrite looks like in a neuron.

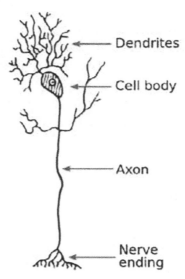

Brain Science Makes Claims About Kindness

"Be kind whenever possible. It is always possible." ~The Dalai Lama

We have all heard, "It is better to give than to receive." I was surprised to learn that this statement is backed up by scientific research. Scientists now believe that being kind to others promotes good health, reduces stress, and creates feelings of happiness. It turns out that small, gentle acts make a greater difference for the sender than for the one who receives the kindness.

Kindness Supported by Mayo Clinic

The Mayo Clinic Health System states that kindness changes the brain by releasing dopamine and serotonin, the neurotransmitters that lead to feeling satisfied and happy.[35] Expressing kindness also leads to a healthier brain with better blood circulation. In addition, endorphins, which are natural painkillers, also get released when we perform small acts of kindness. Not only are these chemicals released when we show kindness to others, they also change the brain when we are kind to ourselves.

---

35   Siegle, The Art of Kindness.

Practicing gratitude throughout the day also creates a cycle of genuine appreciation for self and others. It is possible to share acts of kindness on a website called "Acts of Random Kindness."

Story: An Act of Kindness at Age Three

For our son's third Christmas, we invited a young military officer and my husband's parents. The tree lights glowed. Gifts, some wrapped in colorful Christmas paper and others left unwrapped by Santa, had been stacked around the base of the tree. Three-year-old David walked in wearing blue pajamas while rubbing sleepy eyes. In the background, his grandparents smiled with excitement.

"David, do you want to see what Santa left for you?"

David: "In a minute."

As we watched in bewilderment, David walked into the kitchen. Soon we heard the rummaging of small kitchen objects being moved around. The rustle of a small sack caused raised eyebrows and wondering looks.

Through the door, our three-year-old proudly returned, blue eyes sparkling, his small face shining with a big smile. In his hands he carried a small paper bag. Ceremoniously, he delivered his gift to me. Didn't he want to check his own gifts? No, he did not.

I opened the bag and peered in at kitchen items I kept in a special drawer for David. Often, he sat inside the drawer and played while I cooked or cleaned up the kitchen. He and I considered the items in the drawer as his. Realizing what David had put in the bag, I carefully removed each object: a small metal pot with a lid, short spoons, a cookie cutter, measuring cups and spoons, and a sink stopper. Only after I examined and exclaimed about each gift would David turn to his own presents.

I realized that our three-year-old son had chosen to put someone else above his own Christmas excitement. As it turned out, failure to think about others would never be a problem for our son.

Get One and Give One

John S. Williams, a revisionist and editor for WriteByNight, believes parents can encourage empathy by encouraging children to give one toy away for each new toy gained. This accomplishes several worthy goals.

- Clutter is reduced, making space for each toy.
- Children are asked to be aware of their own abundance.
- Empathy for less-fortunate children increases compassion.
- Space for possessions can be maintained with awareness and planning.

*Giving to others
expands happiness for givers*

Story: Teach Courtesy

While enjoying lunch, two-year-old Daisy began playing with fall decorations on our kitchen table. Her mom, Margie, initiated the following conversation.

Mom: "Daisy, when we are at someone else's house and you want to examine something, it is courteous to ask for permission. You could ask, 'Grandma, may I touch this?'"

Daisy, copying Margie's exact words, asked, "Grandma, may I touch this berry?"

"Yes, Daisy. You may. Thank you for asking."

Daisy continued from berries to leaves to twigs, asking for permission to touch each item.

Each time the toddler asked, I said yes and thanked her for her courtesy.

The simplicity of sharing and modeling the exact words reaped such a small, pleasant success. At times, we adults seem so foolish to assume a toddler or young child will know (or should know) what courteous behavior is. This short and caring lesson was a thousand times more effective than fussing would have been.

Involvement with Charities

When children are old enough to participate, parents or grandparents can involve them in charities. Possible examples include Meals on Wheels, CROP (Christian Rural Overseas Program), Heifer International, purchasing school supplies for children living in poverty, and selecting names of children to receive holiday gifts.

Children who give to others have a chance to gain two concepts. The first concept is awareness of how much they have. When our kids complain or become fixated on gifts they want to receive, they benefit from listening to their parents' and grandparents' expressions of gratitude. Most of us have all we need and much of what we want. Appreciation and gratitude raise happiness levels.

The second concept is empathy, which revolves around the unfortunate truth that many children, even in this wealthy nation, lack much of what they need and almost all of what they want. Awareness of this economic reality opens the possibility of compassion for others.

Individuals who consistently receive everything they want without exerting any effort often expect to get what they want without contributing any grit or grind. This attitude also relates to the concept of chores and work. People who fail to appreciate the world of work miss the genuine satisfaction that accompanies a job well done. Expecting something for nothing does not bring fulfillment.

Respecting oneself becomes a steppingstone that leads to respect for others. As children learn to take care of themselves, self-care expands into kindness to others.

Expect Your Child to Show Respect

A child's refusal to comply with your requests may feel disrespectful. Her tone may also impact you negatively. If your child, age three or older, talks to you rudely, her behavior provides a chance to reinforce courtesy by saying:

"When you talk to me in that tone of voice, I feel disrespected. Are you willing to respect me?"

When asked to give respect, most people, most of the time, will do so. If your child, or anyone else, refuses to show respect, this is a time for you to respond by saying: "Thank you for your honesty. That's helpful information. I'm not willing for anyone to be disrespectful to me. Perhaps we can have this conversation again later."

Establish Beneficial Boundaries

Boundaries establish a bottom line for each family member's behavior. Sample issues include respecting one another by speaking kindly and honoring reasonable requests. Although a boundary is not a rigid wall, it provides a shield, which can be relaxed when not needed or expressed strongly when lack of respect is evident. When parents and children agree on a boundary, they establish what is expected as well as what is not acceptable. With babies and toddlers, boundaries usually revolve around safety. Thus, if you tell your toddler to avoid the fireplace, you need to tell her why it is unsafe. Realizing that many boundaries must include flexibility, a few considerations about family boundaries can be read below:

Time:
Even before children are mature enough to totally understand, it is important to pay attention to personal needs. Each individual needs time alone, time with a trusted partner, and time with children and the entire family. In addition, consider how much your child benefits from being with you and how long she can entertain herself.

Money:
Each member of the family has material needs. There are situations when one member of the family has greater requirements than others. These are often the times when individual needs become more important than the boundaries established by a budget.

90

Space:

Some individuals yearn to cuddle and be close much of the time. Others need a personal space around their bodies.

In addition to physical preferences, each member of the family needs a safe place to put belongings.

Health:

Having healthy habits can make an enormous difference in how effectively each member of the family interacts.

Eating a healthy portion of fresh fruits and vegetables, getting adequate proteins, and limiting consumption of sugar impact physical and emotional health.

Technology:

Technology has provided many benefits to our lives.

At the same time, over-reliance on devices has reduced time to be in nature and to actively move.

Courtesy:

Each member of a family treats others with basic courtesy. Everyone gets angry at times. However, when anger escalates into rude or even cruel statements or actions, end the situation immediately if children can hear. Everything you say and do amounts to modeling for children and will return to either bring happiness or haunt you in the future. Angry feelings can be delayed, and emotional safety can be maintained for young eyes and ears.

Kindness then spreads to extended family and to society at large.

It is not acceptable to treat others rudely. Model this expectation by noticing times when you, as a parent, feel you have been talked to in unacceptable ways. Gently share this information. Model the treatment you want and expect from others.

If you do not articulate and maintain appropriate limits, babies and children will not feel safe. As part of the learning process, children of all ages will often push back against your boundaries. Unless you have made a mistake when stating an expectation, you will be wise to sustain what you claimed was important. Establishing and maintaining expectations help children learn to be responsible. In time, boundaries become daily habits.

Failure to consistently follow through on a boundary sends a message that your child cannot count on you. (Let's face it, some evenings you may feel too exhausted to mess with brushing your child's teeth. In the spirit of being gentle on yourself, you may decide that neither the teeth nor the habit will suffer permanent damage if, most of the time, the job gets done.)

Instead of setting more boundaries than you or your child can remember, make certain the few you have are important.

After a child understands the meaning of written agreements, you may want to develop and sign contracts that guide behaviors and expectations.

Avoid using adjectives such as "good" or "bad."

Make certain that when enforcing boundaries, you and your partner demonstrate respect for one another. For example, never indulge in "Don't tell your daddy. . ."

Everyone gets upset at times. A healthy discussion can be beneficial and can promote honesty to children.

Use natural consequences as often as possible. If natural consequences do not feel safe or appropriate, use consequences that are logical and make sense.

Keep in mind that if a child forgets a rule (a boundary agreement) such as always speaking courteously, a consequence can replace a punishment. For example, a logical consequence to using inappropriate language might be to think of two acceptable ways to send the same message.

Modeling behaviors will always be your most powerful way to teach your child. If she hears you talk to others with respect, she will tend to copy your words and tone. After she watches you show kindness to animals, smile at people, maintain good hygiene, and keep your agreements, she will probably take the same actions. Be the parent your child will be proud to introduce as her mom or dad.

Boundaries will reflect your values as parents. Here are a few additional examples:

- Everyone in the family has a right to seek good health and physical safety.
- The emotional needs of each person will be respected.
- All family members help keep our home clean, neat, and comfortable.
- Having fun is an important boundary issue.
- Educational gains will be supported.
- Everyone deserves to be given eye contact, a courteous voice, and respect.
- Spiritual goals will be respected.

Baby sister's emotional wiring is increasing

Chapter 7
Social and Emotional Growth Versus Entitlement

Personal conflicts between children, like wars between nations, happen when people do not have empathy for others. Lack of emotional growth, which is required to promote empathy, will destroy an individual, a family, a classroom, a nation, and even the world. On the other hand, the willingness to care about one another promotes a healthy emotional foundation.

What Is Social and Emotional Growth?

At birth, an infant has 100 trillion neurons waiting to be wired. Thus, until life experiences complete the process, the brain remains unfinished. Mirror neurons form during the first years of life and cause babies to grin back at smiling faces. Often a crying baby triggers other babies to cry due to their mirror neurons. The more mirror neurons a baby has, the stronger her ability will be to show empathy as she matures.

The baby girl in this picture is developing mirror neurons as she expresses her happy feelings about her two older brothers. The awareness the three siblings have about one another will hopefully provide a foundation for later kindness and avoidance of conflicts.

Brain research informs us that all emotional wiring takes place during the first few years of life. Each time a positive emotional experience is repeated, the connections become stronger. Since healthy emotional wiring depends on social interactions, social and emotional wiring differ from cognitive and physical wiring.

Social and emotional skills nurtured during the beginning months of an infant's life can make a difference in a baby's self-esteem, satisfaction, and ability to live peacefully with family and society. Without assuming the pain of others, children can be taught to listen, share, and be kind. Seeing value in others becomes a choice that we hope to model and develop in children. In fact, a happy and productive life depends on developing and maintaining emotional health.

During the first year of life, an infant requires touch, caring voices, and even someone who will listen to her sounds. Approximate ages for social and emotional strengths and skills are listed below.

Although social and emotional development begin at birth, a baby will start to express her feelings with facial expressions at approximately three months. She will also begin to copy the faces her parents make.

- By five months, a baby will differentiate parents from others and will prefer interacting with parents.
- At seven months, a baby will respond to her name, a pleasant voice inflection, and seeing herself in a mirror.
- By twelve months a baby may show shyness as well as preferences for favorite toys. She will be able to repeat some sounds.
- At age two, she will imitate the actions and behaviors of others. She will also begin to recognize that she is a separate person.
- By age three, she will be able to play simple games, take turns, and understand the meanings of words such as "yours" and "mine."

Television and other screen devices do not build connections and can upset brain development. Television viewing, a passive activity that fails to encourage movement or interaction with people, may delay or even prevent the healthy wiring needed for emotional and social reactions. The American Medical Association recommends avoiding screen time before age two.

Teaching social and emotional skills to children encourages them to realize that others have feelings, wants, and needs. As awareness of others progresses, hopefully children will demonstrate kindness along with a desire to solve conflicts. Healthy emotional growth allows children to postpone gratification.

Concepts in the chart below will be developed more thoroughly by ages four and five. The chart separates emotional strengths from social skills. Although related, the two are slightly different.

Emotional Strengths	Social Skills
The child knows the difference between feelings and actions.	She can respond to others if they need help.
The child has enough control to talk about her feelings.	She learns to cooperate with others. She also gains impulse control.
She gains enough self-awareness to recognize when she needs food or rest.	She begins to ask others if they are hungry or thirsty.
She becomes socially aware of others.	The child can empathize with children from different backgrounds and will take actions that support others.
She gains information about ways to treat other people.	She treats others with cooperation, respect, and kindness.

To gain social and emotional skills, a child must experience opportunities with peers. As she develops friendships, her relationships with her parents and teachers improve and she becomes more comfortable expressing her own feelings and needs. Early childhood practices that promote social skills include:

- Listening to stories
- Talking about characters in stories
- Hearing about book characters with different points of view
- Living in encouraging environments
- Learning to give compliments
- Using words such as "please" and "thank you"
- Discussing and acting out feelings
- Playing emotional matching games

Not Thinking About Others Leads to Entitlement

A child who does not eventually learn to think about others becomes an individual whose life has been marred—thus, spoiled. Spoiled children, who simply can't think beyond their own wants, do not make fun playmates. Later in life, these children do not make good teammates or life partners. The ability to consider others remains important. A spoiled teenager or adult who cannot recognize the value of others will never feel truly happy.

An adult who has been spoiled as a baby, child, or teen appears to lack satisfaction or enjoyment. At least two characteristics can be noted. First, children who grow up without thinking of others will have a hard time keeping close friends. In addition, a "me" world does not promote happiness as children grow older.

The transition from a "me" world to the concept of "us" is not easy for children. Initially they will vacillate between showing patience and kindness to others and wanting to immediately get their own wants and needs met. Parents, grandparents, and teachers can make certain each child's needs get met. Games that involve taking turns support a healthy transition. By age five or six, the social awareness of most children will be well enough developed to understand that we live in a world that involves all of us. Many times, when making this transition, children will resist as they alter their boundaries and learn to be part of a group. Although somewhat painful, this important life lesson makes a difference between a life with purpose and one of total self-absorption.

Story: Entitlement Is Not Love

Child: "Give it to me now! I want it now!"

Parent: "You have already had too many cookies. This is one of your brother's cookies."

During continued arguments with her parent, the child's face is red, she is perspiring, her hands are clenched into fists and her feet are stomping as she screams, "I hate you. My brother is so lazy he doesn't deserve any cookies. Give me one of his cookies right now or I'm going to hit you."

Parent: "Well. . . maybe your brother won't mind too much if you eat one of his cookies. But only one. Do you understand?"

Child: "I don't care whether my stupid brother cares or not. I deserve the cookie because I want it. If you don't give me that cookie right this minute, you will be sorry."

Of course, you see where this is going. By the end of this argument, the parent gives every single one of the brother's cookies to his sister.

The old term "spoiled" has been replaced by "entitled." An entitled child expects everything in life to be handed to her without putting out effort. Convinced that she should get whatever she wants, she assumes others exist to serve her every desire. I would consider this a spoiled life—basically a ruined life.

An entitled or spoiled child demonstrates the following unpleasant behaviors:

- Cannot handle the word "no"
- Does not hide disgust for unwanted gifts
- Refuses to follow rules
- Has frequent temper tantrums at age three and older
- Does not offer to help others
- Cannot play well with peers
- Will not do chores
- Usually does not say "please" or "thank you"
- Begins talking by saying, "I need/want. . ."
- Cannot share well
- Talks to adults as she does with peers
- Fails to show empathy
- Does not compromise
- Fails to be a good sport
- Says the wrong things at the wrong times
- Does not care if others feel inconvenienced
- Lashes out if she does not get what she wants
- Has poor self-esteem
- Demands to be treated in special ways
- Bullies others
- Manipulates others
- Always wants more

When your child insists on getting what she wants, experts advise you to avoid falling for the following examples of an entitled child's reasoning.

- I should get it because I want it.
- Everyone else has one.
- I broke my old one.
- I want a new, better one.

There is a great difference between meeting your child's basic needs for food, shelter, clothing, and fun (yes, fun is a basic need) and giving her everything she wants. Ideas to consider can be read below.

- Avoid excess, even for toddlers. Excess might look like a great-grandmother buying four dolls when one would be enough.
- When your child gets old enough for a more sophisticated toy such as a cell phone, stick with one that works but does not have all the bells and whistles.
- Avoid rescuing your child or preventing natural or logical consequences. Expect your child to learn lessons from the consequences of her behaviors.
- Provide chores.
- Arrange opportunities for her to help others.
- Model being a good citizen by following rules and helping others.

Consider Excess

When is enough, *really* enough? Are having experiences more important than gaining material possessions? In his book *The Year Without a Purchase*, Dannemiller claimed, "Our whole reason for starting this challenge was to focus on what we believed to be important in our lives."[36] Dannemiller continued by saying that involvement with their children provided powerful life events and memories. He stated that money spent connecting family members will matter more than mountains of broken plastic toys, which often kill sea animals and plants.

"There is nothing inherently wrong with material gifts. They become a problem only when we give them far more meaning than they deserve."[37] The hope is to guide children to realize that they already have enough toys and

---

36   Dannemiller, *The Year*, 67.
37   Dannemiller, *The Year*, 161.

electronics. "The truth is, the value of experience is far greater than the value of any tangible gift."[38] Dannemiller claims that unconditional acceptance and love are the only things children really need. The author provides eight ways to "own what you have."[39]

Create a family rule to fix things that are broken rather than toss them and buy new ones. A commitment to repair creates an emphasis on taking care of things we have. YouTube has tutorials for fixing many items.

Eliminate or reduce TV commercials. Television commercials persuasively create false beliefs that we need something being sold. Netflix or Digital Video Recordings (DVRs) eliminate commercials.

When children see an advertisement that seems too appealing to resist, have a conversation to help them investigate the truth. The same can be said about catalog companies. Reduce exposure to the world of stuff.

Coupons, which claim to save money, lead to increased spending. Consider the fact that without a coupon, parents and grandparents might not consider the purchase in the first place. Companies that offer coupons do not do so out of generosity.

Each day for a month, help children list five reasons to be grateful.

"Get One, Give One" is a promise that for each new toy or item gained, one must be given away. Decrease hoarding by considering who might need the item more than you do.

Rather than buying something because it is on sale, hold the item and ask, "Do I really love this?" Dannemiller says, "If the answer is no, don't buy it. Just because something is a good deal doesn't mean it's a good idea."[40]

---

38   Dannemiller, *The Year*, 126.
39   Dannemiller, *The Year*, 244.
40   Dannemiller, *The Year*, 244.

Give Experiences as Gifts

Additional ideas include providing experiences rather than purchasing material objects. Depending on the ages and interests of your children, replace giving things with giving experiences such as:

- Cooking classes
- Museum day passes
- Waterpark passes
- Archery classes
- Dance or theater classes
- Factory tours
- Visits to a farm
- Horseback riding lessons
- Concert tickets
- A day at a trampoline park
- Pottery classes
- Guitar lessons
- A helicopter flight
- A wilderness survival campout
- Hiking
- Tickets to a sporting event
- A video-making class
- Rope climbing
- Swimming classes
- Ice skating or roller skating
- Yoga classes
- Creative writing classes
- Watching an appropriate movie together and talking about the experience

Sacred Conversations Over Dinner

Make the dinner hour a sacred opportunity to eat together and share as a family. Even though nutrition will always be important, your conversations and shared ideas offer even more value to a growing child or teen. Use the opportunity to ask open-ended questions. Place questions in a jar. Each evening, one individual will pick an idea to discuss. Some sample questions are listed on the next page.

- What do you think about . . .?
- Why did this happen?
- What can you (or we) do about this?
- What is the best thing about school? What is the worst thing about school? What can you do to make the situation better?
- If you see someone being bullied, what can you say or do? How can you get help?
- If you could talk to your principal, what might you suggest as an idea to improve the school?
- Why did you draw that picture? Why did you write that story?
- What makes someone a good friend? What can you do to become a better friend?
- If you could visit another planet, which one would it be and why?
- If you owned a restaurant, what would you serve?
- If you could be invisible for a day, what would you do?
- What is the worst name for a cat you ever heard?
- If you could own anything in the world, what would it be?
- Which cartoon character would you choose to be?
- If you could time travel, would you go back in time or forward? Describe what you would do.
- If you had a secret hideout, where would it be? What would you do there? Would you want to be alone, or would you prefer to take others with you?
- If a popular friend wants you to participate in a dangerous action, what will you say? What will you do?
- If you had a parrot, what would you teach it to say?
- What did you do today that caused you to think hard?

The importance of maintaining a relaxed and pleasant atmosphere during shared meals cannot be overstated. Keep in mind that your purpose is to show support for one another. Meals are not the time for drills or lectures, which will defeat your purpose. Recent surveys also demonstrate that eating at least five family meals with meaningful conversations each week reduces child and teen use of tobacco, marijuana, and illegal drugs.

Dannemiller writes, "We're all searching for something we've never lost. It's the love of God buried deep inside our souls. We've somehow missed it."[41] We have become disconnected from ourselves. The voice in our heads will remind us that we already have enough. The voice can also whisper to parents and children alike: I love you. You have enough. You are enough.

---

41   Dannemiller, *The Year*, 238.

Additional Ways to Serve

In addition to meaningful conversations at family meals, encourage children to participate in the following ways.

- Help write a family mission statement.
- Share your personal goals and invite children to write their own goals.
- Work in a local food bank.
- Plant and care for a garden together.
- Sponsor a child living in poverty in a third-world country through organizations such as:
    - Compassion International: http://www.compassion.com
    - World Vision: http://www.worldvision.org
    - Heifer International: www.heifer.org

Have dinner with someone living in poverty. Look the person in the eye. Focus on being present and asking the individual to teach you.

Give small gifts or donations to individuals who seem forced by circumstances to work on holidays.

Ask children to hide one-dollar bills where clerks will find them. Tell your children that this is one way to "pay it forward."

Story: Connect Deserving and Earning

Excess and entitlement are deeply connected. One way to avoid raising a child who feels entitled is to demonstrate the connection between a strong work ethic and fair earnings.

For example, a dad asked his fifth-grade daughter to wash and wax his car. In return, he agreed to pay a co-determined amount. The next day the daughter ventured out to clean her dad's car.

In a short time, she said, "Dad, I've finished cleaning your car. I didn't get the waxing done because Sara called and invited me to go to a movie with her. Since I did such a good job cleaning, I hope you will pay the agreed amount."

Dad: "Let's go look at the car. I really wanted the wax job done today."

104

After examining his car, Dad felt disappointed. Although his car had been cleaned fairly well, some areas had been left untouched. Not waxing the car felt like a breach of the agreement.

Dad stated, "I do not feel good about some spots you missed when washing. In addition, waxing the car was a big part of our agreement. I can either pay you a little less than half the amount we agreed on, or I can let you work on the car again tomorrow and get the job done right. You decide."

This dad provided honest and straightforward feedback to his daughter. Had he paid her well for work done poorly, she would have concluded that simply showing up is enough to earn full pay.

The Goose with Golden Eggs Is Too Excessive

An article by Julie Baumgardner begins with a story from *Willy Wonka and the Chocolate Factory*.[42] In the story, a small girl tells her dad that she wants the goose that lays golden eggs. Dad asks Willy, "How much for the goose?"

Although parents and grandparents may have wonderful intentions, giving in to excessive cravings will not help children grow into satisfied adults with better lives. A wise parent may say, "You may have a goose. The special goose that lays golden eggs will be much too expensive. I'm not willing to spend that much money."

---

42   Baumgardner, How to Avoid Raising.

Notice the confident smile on this happy baby's face

Chapter 8
How to Dignify Children's Mistakes

Dignifying means providing honest feedback without hurting or embarrassing. Feedback, which is a helpful learning tool, can be delivered in a way that humiliates and discourages, or it can be couched in understanding. Strong emotions tend to cement learning concepts. Parents and grandparents can elicit powerful feelings by validating or by hurting. Usually, the concept of dignifying arises after a child begins to reason. However, I've learned an important lesson: Dignifying should begin at birth and last for a lifetime.

You may wonder why it is important to dignify mistakes. For most individuals, feelings of shame damage self-esteem. Telling someone of any age "You are wrong" makes her feel ashamed. The goal will be to provide feedback in ways that teach, while protecting and dignifying self-worth. Begin by remembering that babies, toddlers, young children, teens, and adults all make mistakes. Embarrassment quickly attaches feelings of being foolish.

The beautiful, self-assured baby girl in the picture has consistently been treated with dignity and love by her parents and her grandparents. Knowing her grandparents, I feel certain that she will have the tools she needs to meet life with success.

Examples of Dignifying

Many years ago, an educator named Dr. Madeline Hunter suggested the following ways to provide feedback without promoting shame.[43]

- "Close! Think about it." (Then offer a clue.)
- "I can see why you thought that. The correct answer is . . ."
- "You almost got the puzzle piece in the right place. Try again."
- "You are on the right track."
- "You are close. I know you can do this!" When success comes, add, "I knew you would succeed."
- "I understand your thinking."
- "It takes courage to do something new."
- "I did not ask that question clearly."
- "You really do know how. Would you like for me to help you get started?"
- "Interesting thinking. I had not considered your idea. Thanks."
- In some situations, simply say, "Thank you."
- After dignifying, clarify the child's misunderstanding.

A smile encourages. Almost from the beginning, most infants and babies respond to a smiling face and a cheerful "Yes!" Likewise, a frown and angry "No" will not feel loving or encouraging to an infant, baby, young child, or teen. In fact, sensitivity to your facial expressions and your tone of voice continues into the adult years.

Story: Dignify an Infant

Earlier in this book, I shared a story about our grandson, Lane, dignifying his two-day-old infant when the baby spit up milk on Lane's fresh shirt. I felt touched by his actions and words.

> Our grandson held the infant so they were eye to eye. As he looked at her tiny face, he said, "It's okay, Daisy. You didn't do anything wrong. Daddy can get another fresh shirt." Even without understanding her dad's words, the baby felt safe. Eventually, words will take on meaning. In the meantime, the baby's parents can make certain they do not reject her or make her feel foolish. From birth forward, parents can instill feelings of safety by assuring infants of total acceptance.

---

43   Hunter, *Enhancing Teaching.*

Avoid Saying "It's Easy!"

Adults frequently, and mistakenly, say, "This is easy." We forget that a skill we spent years developing was challenging when our fingers were clumsy, and the steps were unclear. The suggestion that a skill will be easy to master is intended to encourage confidence. Unfortunately, if the task becomes difficult for a child, the words will imply *What's wrong with you? You must be stupid.* Instead, accept a child's fear of a new task by saying, "This is challenging. Many children struggle to master this. If you don't succeed at first, please ask questions." Examples below range from learning to walk to mastering letter sounds.

- Seeing your toddler fall down, you say, "Walking is hard. I know you will learn to do it soon. Try again."
- "Feeding yourself isn't easy. You are starting to succeed and will soon be able to do this."
- "It's okay that your new panties are wet. You are learning a new skill. Everyone finds this difficult at first."
- "Reading is a grown-up skill. You are making good progress."
- "Math is a challenge for many people. Would you like some help? I won't do the work for you, but maybe I can answer some of your questions."
- "Riding your bike without training wheels is scary. Would you like me to run along beside you at first? I know you will get that feeling of balance soon."

Story: A Lesson from Baseball

Coach: "Hitting the ball is easy. All you do is keep your eye on the ball. If you keep looking right at the ball, your bat will automatically connect."

Child wonders: *What does keeping your eye on the ball mean? At what point do I stop trying to see the ball?*

After the child once again swings and misses the ball, the coach yells, "Dang it! Why won't you do what I tell you?"

The child thinks: *I feel so hopeless. I just can't do sports and I'm going to stop trying.*

A situation may seem easy to an adult, but that does not mean it will be easy for the child who is in the process of learning. After being told that the task is easy, does lack of success indicate that the child is inadequate? Instead of saying a task or answer is easy, strongly declare the following: "This is tricky. Many people have trouble mastering this."

For children to grow emotionally and cognitively, they must receive feedback. Parents and grandparents, who are usually baby's first teachers, can provide guidance along with a solid foundation of self-esteem by truthfully acknowledging that mastering new skills can feel challenging.

Chapter 9
Redirect Toward Desired Behavior

Any time you distract a baby and focus her attention on something different, you have redirected her behavior. For example, you can say, "You can paint on paper instead of painting the walls. I'll get some paper for your artwork." There will be times when you simply want her to pay attention to you, look at a picture, or play with a toy. For example, sometimes when Daisy and I interact on FaceTime, I go to the piano and play a few notes. When Daisy looks up, I ask, "Daisy, would you like to get your little guitar or your harmonica and help me make some music?"

The chords on the piano redirect her attention so she can focus on a new activity. After hearing the piano, her little face turns to look at the camera, and usually she toddles off to find her own musical instruments. Even more important, if we see her heading toward danger, we can redirect her attention to a safer area.

Sample Ways to Redirect

Laughter can often help a child break out of a negative emotional place.

"Let's take a break. You and I can walk for a few minutes until you feel calm again."

Saying, "I have a good idea. Let's _____!" This statement may redirect her away from a negative feeling to interest in your new thought. Think fast!

Music or rhythmic sounds redirect some babies and children.

A game of Hide and Seek will often shift her interest to you.

Asking, "Where is your _____ (a favorite toy)?" may catch her attention.

Moving outside will often redirect a negative mood.

If a baby feels thirsty or hungry, meeting this need will help her refocus attention.

Story: Redirect Behavior

One afternoon Daisy, her parents, and I were playing in our back yard. As soon as Daisy saw the swimming pool, her big brown eyes lit up and her toddling pace picked up speed. With a broad, determined smile and her curly piggy tails bobbing, she knew exactly where she was going. Although her parents were fast enough to catch her, I also rattled a bucket filled with a variety of items to get her attention.

"Daisy, let's throw these things in the water."

After I demonstrated with a small rock, she reached in the bucket and withdrew a little piece of wood. "Do you think the wood will float on top of the water or will it sink to the bottom?" I asked. (At this point, I simply wanted to divert her attention away from jumping or falling into the pool. Later, she and I will explore things that sink or float many times.)

When Daisy begins building toward a tantrum, we want to redirect her feelings before she loses control. Acting quickly has a better chance of redirecting than waiting until later.

You redirect behavior any time you shift a child's attention from what you do not want her to do to a safer place or more desirable behavior. By switching attention, you can usually alter the feelings and change the behavior.

Diet and Behaviors are Connected

Establishing and maintaining focus become important life skills for school and for work. An article written for hyperactive children recommends a change of diet to help improve focus. The article claims, "Diet and behavior go hand in hand."[44] The following foods are recommended.

- Walnuts (Omega 3)
- Crab cakes (zinc) for children who are not sensitive to crustaceans
- Bananas (magnesium)
- Spinach (iron)
- Citrus fruits (vitamin C)
- Peanut butter (protein) for children who do not have allergies to peanuts

When you know your baby is thirsty or hungry, you will first meet her basic needs. However, if it is not time for a bottle or meal, resist using food as either a reward or a punishment to change her behavior. Especially avoid using sugar to gain attention or alter her feelings. You will be tempted to give your baby a bite of candy to get her to stop crying. Although something sweet will redirect attention, using food to change behavior may lead to later eating disorders.

---

44   Brain Balance Achievement Centers. Nutrition for ADHD.

Chapter 10
When and How to Start Toilet Training

Knowing when and how to begin potty training can be tricky. Watch for the following behaviors.

- Your child may pull at her wet or poop-filled diaper or pull-up.
- She may begin to hide when she needs to eliminate.
- She may also be interested in noticing and even copying how other family members use the toilet.
- When your child begins waking up dry after a nap, immediately put her on her little potty. Waking up dry indicates a physical readiness.
- If she tells you she needs to go or lets you know she has just finished, she is communicating that it is time to begin the teaching process.

Before starting toilet training, have the essentials ready, including pull-ups or training pants and a potty chair or child-size toilet-seat reducer that goes on top of a regular seat. Having a small potty chair or a chair with steps may build more confidence than letting her little legs dangle in mid-air. If possible, let the child help choose her potty chair or seat. If a potty seat isn't working, try a different type. Tools to consider include:

- Padded potty seats
- Potty seats with handles for extra security
- Flip-up seats that stay on the toilet (thus only requiring you to flip the seat down)
- Seats with built-in steps

- Either pull-ups or training pants
- Flushable wipes
- Soap of different colors, or foam, which may seem more interesting
- Books to maintain attention
- Paper, spirals, or books with blank pages so she can draw pictures

Experts claim that the type of seat does not matter if the child shows an interest. While shopping for potty seats with your child, consider examining big-girl or big-boy underwear for later use. For some children, purchasing big-boy or big-girl underwear becomes a motivating factor. There may be an element of prestige when changing into more grown-up panties.

When your toddler is ready to learn the basics of using the toilet, you can say, "I need to potty. You want to go with me?" If she accompanies you, use the opportunity to describe each of the steps involved. If your child has a separate small potty, you can invite your toddler to join you in every step of the process. You may want to play "Can you do what I do?"

Invite your child to sit on her small potty. Even if she does not have any concrete success, you will be suggesting an interesting new idea in the growing-up process. To encourage her to sit, keep a collection of new books in a bathroom cabinet. Pull one out at a time. Prepare to play simple games, blow bubbles, sing songs, or work easy puzzles. This may even be a time to encourage her to watch a video on an iPad.

If you teach a boy to stand at the toilet, you can throw some small, water-soluble items into the toilet bowl and invite the little guy to hit one of the objects. One grandson learned to pull his pants down and "water" bushes in the yard. His worried mother wondered why he never wet himself outside but wasn't as successful in the house. Thankfully, with time the idea crossed over and his success was celebrated by his parents and grandparents.

Personality Types and Potty Training

Knowing your child's personality may be helpful when potty training. The various personality types to consider include cautious, eager to please, free-spirited, high energy, and shy. Of course, children often surprise parents and grandparents. As soon as you announce, "My child is shy," she may become free-spirited or high energy. No one, at any age, remains the same. Expect layers of overlap between types, as well as sudden changes.

Below, you will find slight communication variations to use for each of the types.

The Cautious Child

Cautious children notice everything. Usually, this type of child wants to stay clean and will often tell you when a diaper is wet or full of poop. Shopping for potty training supplies will probably be interesting to this child. Suggestions for teaching a cautious child include:

- Allow your child to accompany you to the bathroom and explore the room.
- Give your child a step-by-step tour of how to use the toilet. Explain all the equipment and examine supplies you purchased for this occasion. Later, ask the child what she learned.
- Help your child celebrate her new information and small successes with fist bumps or high fives.
- This type of child loves to learn, and your consistency will soon lead to success.

Eager-to-Please Child

Children who seek to please the adults in their lives are eager to learn any big-boy or big-girl skills. Ideas to help communicate with this child include:

- Show enthusiasm and eagerness about your child's toilet training.
- Go to the bathroom together as often as possible.
- Maintain a positive and encouraging attitude toward her efforts.
- Emphasize that pull-ups or training pants are intended to teach her how to be a big girl.
- If you decide to use rewards, this type of child may respond well to some small token.

Free Spirited Child

Children with free spirits want to play and explore. Curiosity and exploration may seem much more interesting than using the potty. She may not be willing to sit and wait for any length of time. Although she may be excited at first, you may need to wait for the moments when she is ready to use the potty. You can assist her with potty-training by using some of the ideas below:

- Make going to the potty a fun social activity. You can encourage close relatives to participate. Taking stuffed animals or dolls to the potty may engage her interest.

- When she tries, you may want to say, "This is exciting. Let's all cheer for her." Cheering and clapping may engage her spirited desire for fun.
- Keep a few favorite books near the potty. Read to her or encourage her to entertain herself by looking at pictures.
- Purchase a small notebook and some markers or crayons so she can scribble while she waits.
- Play games while you wait with her.
- Relax and have fun with this spirited little one.
- Remind her to flush and to wash her hands with a variety of interesting soaps. She will be in such a rush to play that she may forget.
- Remind her that wearing pull-ups or training pants will give her greater freedom than diapers.

High-Energy Child

A high-energy child is usually not interested in stopping to use the potty. Adventure is the name of her game. Training panties wet? Not a problem. Filled with poop? She will not be bothered. Usually, she will be too busy to even notice. Below are some ideas for teaching the high-energy child:

- Skip all the details that may interest other personality types. She is busy and does not have enough patience to listen.
- Begin with a new or favorite game that can be used during potty time.
- Emphasize speedy changes with pull-ups or training pants over diapers.
- Help her be aware of her own body. Ask, "How does your body feel when you need to potty?" You will need to help her articulate the right words.
- Make certain she gets a lot of play time, so when potty time comes, she can relax and take the time to sit.
- Watching a high-energy video on a small iPad may entice her to stop playing for a few minutes.

The Shy Child

If your child has a shy and reserved personality, she will probably feel content to leave things as they are. In fact, she may resist potty training. The suggestions listed below may help overcome her resistance.

- Your child may need extra time to gradually accept the concept of potty training.
- When explaining potty training to her, keep the conversation casual. Allow her to see family members demonstrating good bathroom habits.

- Encourage her to accept the idea of becoming a big girl. Remind her of the benefits of learning new, big-girl skills.
- Never force her to do anything related to potty training. If you get too pushy, she will regress into deeper shyness and resistance.
- Always be consistent with what you say and do. Develop a routine and stick with it.

Teach Your Child to Understand Her Body

Generally, when you notice your child wiggling, crouching, hiding, or crossing her legs, you will recognize a teachable moment. The trick is to get her to read her own body well enough to recognize the signals. One parent frequently asked, "Do you need to potty?" She also pointed out to her child that she was wiggling. "When you wiggle, do you think that means you need to go?" Ask frequently.

When a child needs to have a bowel movement, she often passes gas. Once again, a parent can use this as a teachable moment. Model by saying, "I feel full, and I just passed gas. I think I need to go potty."

Always praise your child for trying. Every attempt moves your child in the right direction. Celebrate successes with her. You can also set a timer for every 30 minutes to help your child get into a habit.

Please remember that if your child's body is not ready, your reminders, modeling, and encouragement will not help with potty training. If you have a caregiver, teach him or her to say and do exactly what you are saying and doing. Everyone involved needs to use encouragement and statements such as, "You peed in the potty. You can feel proud of yourself."

Story: Potty Training is Not a Time for Disgust

Lane: "Grandma, do you like my poo-poo?" asked three-year-old Lane as he walked into the kitchen.

"Lane, I love every part of you."

Lane: "Do you love my poo-poo enough to help me clean it?"

"Of course, I do," I replied as I turned off the burner and headed to the bathroom holding his small hand.

On the way, I noticed brown streaks on our new white carpet in the master bedroom. Wordlessly I thought, *Oh well, what the heck.*

Fortunately, both Lane and the carpet cleaned easily and were none the worse. That memory of a small child's trust and innocence remains. No association with disgust can ever be helpful when toilet training.

Nighttime Potty Training

Once your child stays dry all day, it is logical to assume she is also ready to stay dry all night. Unfortunately, it does not always happen automatically. The bladder needs time to grow larger, and small bodies need to develop a nighttime slow-down in urine production, which will happen sometime between ages two and seven. Until your child's body has developed these changes, you will need to remain patient.

Nighttime dryness relates to genetics rather than to personality traits. In addition, how deeply your child sleeps will make a difference. You can assist by establishing a dependable routine.

Create a bedtime schedule by taking your child to the potty 30 minutes before bedtime and again just before bed. Put on a nighttime pull-up. You can purchase this product for girls or for boys.

This product is designed to absorb more urine. Your routine can include a bedtime story, sweet lullaby, or a review of the day's activities as your child prepares to go to sleep.

Limit the amount of liquids taken before bedtime. Do not use a bottle or sippy cup in bed at night.

Keep a nightlight on in the bathroom. Encourage your child to go to the potty anytime she wakes up at night. Create a clear and uncluttered path from her bed to her potty.

When your child wakes up in the morning, teach her to go straight to the bathroom. Always remind her, "When you wake up, go right to the potty."

If your child wets the bed, remain positive. Patience will be important.

Finally, listen to the advice of others, but realize that each child is unique. The American Academy of Pediatrics tells us that 20% of five-year-old children, 10% of those seven years old, and 5% of those age ten may still wet the bed.[45]

If you feel nervous about your child getting through the night without soiling the sheets and mattress pad, add disposable sheet protectors. Once your child remains consistently dry through the night, you can ditch the nighttime training pants and begin using regular underwear.

When your child wakes up dry every morning for five to seven days, you can talk about ending the use of pull-ups at night and begin using undies and pajamas. You can say, "Your body isn't needing to pee as often as when you were smaller. Would you like to sleep in underwear or pajamas tonight?"

Allison Jandu, a potty-training consultant, shares ideas for toilet training in three days. Her guidelines for knowing when to start include the following ideas:[46]

- Staying dry during naps and for longer times during the day shows readiness.
- When your child asks for a dry diaper, you know the time has come.
- Hiding to have a bowel movement can be an indicator.
- Wanting to copy adults demonstrates readiness.

Verbal and nonverbal communications will provide indications of readiness. Jandu suggests the average age for potty training is around 22 to 28 months.[47] Do your best to begin potty training when life is calm and normal. Jandu recommends choosing a weekend or three-day time span when Mom or Dad can be devoted to toilet training. This will require you to give up time cooking, cleaning, or visiting with friends or family. During these three days, do the following:

- Purchase some T-shirts long enough to cover her body below the waist.
- Remove clothes from the waist down. Do not rely on a diaper or pull-up to catch pee or poop.

45   American Academy of Pediatrics, Bedwetting.
46   Jandu, Expert Tips.
47   Jandu, Expert Tips.

- Use rubber-backed bathmats to protect upholstered furniture or good rugs from accidents.
- Never make a big deal out of an accident.

If a baby wets the floor, say matter-of-factly, "You peed on the floor. No problem. We will clean it up. Pee goes into the potty. Poop also goes into your potty." A baby will learn from accidents.

Although Jandu and others recommend small incentives,[48] you may achieve equal success by cheering, clapping, thanking, and allowing a baby to pour pee or poop into the big toilet before encouraging her to push the handle to flush. The reward of feeling successful can be even more important than a sticker. Avoid using candy to reward. Below, you will find the steps to take as you begin the three-day learning experience.

1. As soon as a baby wakes up, change the soggy diaper. Ask your baby to throw the soggy diaper away as she says, "Goodbye."
2. Dress your baby in a large T-shirt without a diaper or pull-up.
3. Provide breakfast and an extra drink.
4. Visit the potty immediately. Hopefully, the extra liquids will help produce urine.
5. Stay home reading, watching cartoons, doing puzzles, and drawing.
6. Keep a sippy cup full of water for her.
7. Every 15 minutes, take your child to the potty.
8. After dinner and close to bedtime, cease liquids.
9. Take a trip to the potty 30 minutes before bedtime and one final time before tucking her in bed.
10. Repeat for two additional days.

Stay calm when accidents occur. We all learn more from our mistakes than from our successes. Once you notice success at home, try simple outings such as walks or picnics. During your outing, build in frequent potty breaks. You will also prepare a bag with the following items:

- Two changes of clothes
- Wipes
- Paper towels or absorbent towels to clean up accidents
- Hand sanitizers
- Sticky notes to place over automatic flush sensors on public toilets

---

48   Jandu, Expert Tips.

Chapter 11
Use Choices to Teach

An excited note from great-granddaughter Daisy:

Dear Mommy and Daddy,
Offering choices is the best idea yet! I feel so powerful. I think I can almost run the show. I also feel respected when you ask a question about what I want. You two are getting the hang of this parenting thing. Don't worry. I'll show you what to do.

Background Considerations

I am a strong proponent of offering choices. There are times when providing choices can smooth an upsetting situation and resolve conflicts. In addition, choices that make absolutely no difference to you can feel empowering to a young child.

At the same time, some choices deserve the wisdom that only an adult has. Parents sometimes give too much power to children who lack the experience and background to make wise decisions. Your children depend on you to keep them safe by making decisions in areas beyond their maturity, such as health and finances. As with all good ideas, balance and common sense must prevail.

Even young children will enjoy participating in conversations about a family vacation. Although children's ideas for having fun will be welcome, parents must be the ones to determine the amount of money to spend, when to take the vacation, how long to be gone, the route to take, and arrangements for lodging. Too much power too early in life becomes overwhelming and frightening.

Thus, the difference in being a dictator and a parental guide requires a delicate balance between respecting the thoughts and preferences of children even while protecting them in areas that are beyond their discernment abilities. Asking, "Do you want to ride the Ferris wheel now or go down the slide first?" will feel like a respectful and empowering choice to offer a child. Weigh this level of choice against the decision to take vacation time for two weeks or for a month. The latter decision requires more information than a child, even a teen, can access. Allow a child to make choices that are appropriate for her young brain. She will feel respected as she starts down a path that will grow in importance as she matures. Heavy duty-choices that impact the entire family's well-being belong to parents.

Terrific Twos and Positive Choices

Your baby will reach a stage often referred to as "the terrible twos." Although you may be tempted to agree with the phrase, please resist. Around age two, she will begin to grasp the concept of her separateness. Her attitude will shift to "I will do it myself." To proclaim this newfound insight, she will reject many of your ideas. (This stage will resemble a baby-size teenage rebellion. Think of this developmental stage as a preview of what will come to full bloom later.)

For example, if you ask, "Do you want some juice?" she will probably say no, even as she reaches for the glass. You can avoid the conflict if you offer choices, such as, "Do you want apple juice or orange juice?"

Avoid asking, "Do you want to sleep with a blanket?" Instead ask, "Do you want the blue blanket or the green one?"

Instead of inquiring, "Do you want to give your baby doll a binky?" try, "Does your baby doll want a binky or a bottle? What do you think?"

Continue by considering additional examples below.

- "Do you want to change your pull-up while on the bed or while standing on the floor?"
- "Which toys do you want in your bath?"
- "Shall we play inside, or would you like to go out in the yard?"

Notice that although neither choice matters to you, the opportunity to express a preference enhances your child's self-development. State the message in a positive voice by saying, "You have a choice . . ." The idea of choice will also come in handy in future years. When working with older children, you may want to alter the statement by saying, "Feel free to do _____ or _____. It's up to you. What do you choose?"

What if She Rejects Your Choices?

Sooner or later, she will reject both of your totally reasonable options. You ask, "Do you want fruit or a cracker with cheese?" She responds, "No! Cookie."

Oops! What now? Time for critical parent thinking. Ask yourself, "Is giving her a cookie really okay, or am I caving in?" There will be times when you can honestly say, "Thanks for that good idea. I'll get a cookie for you."

Usually, her new request will be an idea you do not endorse. Your judgment about what will be best for your baby will overrule your desire for peace and quiet. Below you will find a sequence to consider. Adjust as needed to fit your situation.

Offer two choices. If your child has a third idea that you like, accept it, and thank her.

If you reject her idea, firmly say, "Getting a cookie is not one of your choices. Your choices are cheese and crackers or fruit. You choose."

Stop after repeating two times. This may be a good time to redirect her to a new possibility such as taking a walk or finding a book to read together.

Clashes Between Safety and Adventure

By approximately nine months, the age when a baby often begins crawling, she will attempt to go after what she wants. Her newly developed mobility invites the potential for danger. Crawling and then toddling, which ranges from year one to year three, opens new possibilities for danger. In her efforts to communicate, she may act in ways that might appear naughty. Once our great-granddaughter began toddling well enough to move from one location to another, she sought adventure (and maybe even a little intrigue with danger). One afternoon on FaceTime, I watched the following story unfold. Daisy and her mom were playing on their patio when Daisy became intensely interested in her rocking chair.

Daisy understood that her mommy wanted her to remain seated in her small rocking chair. Daisy had little interest in sitting. Instead of sitting down in the chair, she climbed onto the seat with her feet. When she reached a standing position, she stood up straight and smiled broadly. Her brown eyes twinkled. Her entire body silently exuded, *See what I can do? Isn't this wonderful?*

Instead of saying, "Daisy, you are a bad baby for standing in your rocking chair," her mom stated that she wanted Daisy to sit in the rocker. Mommy has always taken great care to keep Daisy safe. Seeing her toddler standing proudly, Margie realized that she had an adventurous little girl on her hands. What would "bad girl" accomplish with a child whose eagerness to learn outstrips her understanding of dangers? Did her parents want to discourage her excitement about mastering new skills? I think not. And yet, her parents had to keep her safe.

Providing choices helps in situations when minimal risks are involved. I heard Margie say, "Daisy, you have a choice. You can stand in the chair when I am close enough to hold your arm. If you want to use the rocking chair all by yourself, you will need to sit down. You can choose."

A few days later, Margie noticed Daisy standing in the rocker without waiting for Margie's protection. Margie explained a logical consequence by saying, "Daisy, you decided to stand in your chair when I was not close. That means we will need to put your rocker away for a short time. We can try again later today." This consequence was logical.

Lacking adequate words (and self-understanding), Daisy nonverbally communicated, *I want adventure. I want to do this myself and feel proud of my achievement.* How else can she let her parents know she is convinced that she needs this sense of accomplishment? Toddlers get to be toddlers, communicating the best they can. Even though parents must set limits, a child's behavior should never be labeled as good or bad.

Story: A Sibling Conflict

When our first two grandsons were babies, both came to spend time with us one afternoon. Eighteen-month-old Dalton sat happily chewing on a toy. His older brother, Lane, a three-year-old, ran by and snatched the toy from his baby brother's hands. Of course, baby Dalton began to cry. I said, "We have a problem. Dalton is crying. He was playing with a toy, and you took it away from him. How can we solve this?"

Lane, playing happily with the toy, did not care one bit that his brother's face had turned red and now streamed with tears. Realizing that in addition to not caring, Lane did not have any ideas about how to repair the situation, I made some suggestions.

- You could play with a different toy.
- You could offer a new toy to Dalton.
- You could play with the toy together.

Did our toddler grandson choose any of my suggestions? No, he did not. I did not expect him to take an interest in repairing his baby brother's feelings. I quickly stated, "If you cannot solve this, I'll keep this toy for a short time." For the time being, I put the toy away.

Indicating that I was not keeping the toy reduced concerns. As a first-year teacher, I once made the mistake of saying I would keep an item forever. The first-grade child who owned the object felt terribly upset and created quite a scene. After that, I always clarified that I would not keep any item very long.

Although eventually your child will be able to think of her own ways to solve the problem, she will need your guidance for a long time. When she is older, you can ask:

- "Did you make a good choice when you took the toy from your brother?"
- "Did your choice make you feel happy?"
- "Your choices will help you feel sad or happy. It's up to you. Either way, I love you."

Brother's conflict

Use Choices That Teach

Choices empower. Do your best to offer choices that will be acceptable to both you and your child. If you suggest a choice that you know your child will reject, be aware that you did not provide any genuine choice at all. Simple choices that do not matter to you seem important to a baby or young child. Any time you can do so, provide choices that make absolutely no difference to you. Do this to empower your child. Consider the examples below for babies:

"You can choose to feed yourself or I can feed you with this spoon. You choose."

"You can play with this toy or find another one. You decide."

"Would you like to doodle while I read to you, or do you prefer to sit still and listen?" (My experiences with children indicate that doodling while listening increases understanding of the message.)

"We can play together, or you can play by yourself."

If you offer choices, you will need to accept your child's preferences. Failure to do so will feel disrespectful to her.

When your child gets a little older, choices may include options such as the ones listed below. There will be times when her aspiration is not one of the choices you can offer. For example, hitting the family dog with a truck is not a choice. However, she can choose to play with the dog gently or she can choose to play in her imaginary store. As you read the ideas below about giving choices to a school-age child, notice that an option about whether to complete homework is not offered.

- "You may do your homework now or after we eat."
- "You may want to study at your desk, or you may prefer to study at the kitchen table."
- "Would you like to have a snack while you read your book? It's up to you."
- "Some people enjoy background music without words when they study. You may choose to listen or to work quietly."

Part III

Parenting with Consequences

Rylie at soccer

Chapter 12
Connect Behaviors to Consequences

Another note from great granddaughter Daisy:

> *Dear Mommy and Daddy,*
> *I have good news. For the rest of my life, you will never*
> *have to punish me. Isn't that great? However, for me*
> *to learn all I must know, you will need to make certain I*
> *experience consequences that I can understand. If I can see*
> *a connection between my actions and the consequences,*
> *I will be more likely to learn and less likely to become*
> *resentful. Would you like to give this a try?*

Without consequences, which are sometimes called corrections, children fail to learn about physical and emotional boundaries. Boundaries are also referred to as limits or even rules. Although all humans begin life with a "me" focus, those who never move beyond this stage decide, *I am the best and I get to do what I want. The feelings and desires of others do not matter.* Once a child understands that consequences are connected to her behaviors, significant learning can happen.

Three terms used in behavior management are natural consequences, logical consequences, and punishments. Each will be described.

Natural consequences fall into place without effort on the part of adults in the child's life. For example, a child who refuses to wear gloves while playing outside in cold weather will get cold hands. It will occur naturally.

Logical consequences require thought and even some effort from parents, grandparents, or teachers. Thought is required because a consequence must have a connection to the behavior. In addition, that connection must be logical enough that it will make sense to the child.

Punishments are contrived by parents to teach through a bit of pain. Seen through the eyes of children, punishments may feel mean, unrelated, and even unfair. An example might be grounding a child for a week after the child rolled her eyes at her mother.

Early Behaviors and Consequences

While young enough that poor choices will result only in small consequences, a child has a chance to learn valuable lessons. Small children need small choices and small consequences. With maturity, the choices and consequences must adjust to real-world needs. Lessons will be learned only if parents and grandparents have the courage to allow the consequences of poor choices to take place. Granted, at any age, there are going to be consequences that are too dangerous to allow. Babies can't learn the dangers of traffic by playing in the streets. However, when behaviors create only inconvenient consequences, children benefit from having to live with a bit of discomfort. It is important to remember that even if the child enjoys the consequence, she is still learning. Your goal is to solve the problem. What the child thinks of the consequence is not important.

When children grow up without experiencing the consequences of their behaviors, they miss critical opportunities to learn. Their interpretation becomes, *I can do whatever I want. Nothing can ever happen to me.* Truthfully, everyone makes mistakes. Owning mistakes and living with logical consequences are important ways to learn.

For consequences to work, parents and grandparents must follow through consistently. The younger the child, the more immediate the consequences must be. A baby or toddler will not remember the event that created a consequence for more than a few seconds. Even older children benefit from an immediate or a short time interval between behavior and consequence.

Parenting with Consequences

Threats Versus Conversations

Avoid a statement that feels and sounds like a threat, such as harshly saying, "If you do _____, _____ will happen." This comment, made ahead of time, removes the spontaneous learning that occurs when a child realizes, *I just hit my friend and now he doesn't want to play with me.*

- If a child believes you are issuing a threat, she will feel compelled to test you.
- Young children and even older ones often forget a threat issued earlier.
- Worse yet, you may forget what you threatened to do.

Although conversations about behaviors are appropriate, threats are not. Asking questions may differentiate a conversation from a threat.

Begin a conversation by asking, "If you hit your friend, how will he feel? Do you think he will want to keep playing with you? Why not? Will you feel sad if he goes home?"

Continue by asking, "How can you avoid upsetting your friend? Are you willing to do that?"

If consequences are used quickly, calmly, and without anger, they have the power to eliminate punishments. As children mature, a parent may occasionally need to say, "I am too upset to think about this right now. Let's get together in an hour (or tomorrow) to talk again. By then, I will be thinking clearly." Hopefully, consequences that make sense to your child will also feel fair. When you use logic and fairness, it is hard for a child to feel resentful. You want your child to connect the dots between *I did _____, and _____ happened. I may or may not like it, but I understand it.*

Natural Consequences

Consequences manifest in one of two ways—natural or logical. Natural consequences simply fall into place with no effort on the part of parents or grandparents. Consider the natural consequences for babies and toddlers on the following page.

Action of the Baby or Toddler	Natural Consequence
A toddler throws her toy truck off the balcony.	The truck is broken. Her parents do not buy a new truck.
A toddler refuses to wear gloves to play outside.	Her hands get cold.
A two-year-old bites her daddy while playing.	Daddy is hurt and needs to stop playing.
A toddler hurts her friend's feelings by refusing to share.	Her friend does not want to play with her.

Notice that natural consequences do not feel pleasant, but do not endanger the child. Powerful learning can occur if the child realizes *When I do _____, _____ happens*. Parents who constantly rescue their babies, children, and teens deprive them of learning powerful concepts.

Natural consequences work even more effectively with preschool and early elementary-age children. Consider the examples of natural consequences for young children in the chart below.

Action of the Child	Natural Consequence
Jim left his game pieces all over the floor.	Jim walked on the pieces and accidently broke many. When his friend came to play the game, too many pieces were missing.
Juan decided to watch television instead of studying addition.	Juan got a C on his math quiz. He felt disappointed.
Yolanda secretly taught her parrot to say curse words.	When Yolanda's grandparents came to visit, the bird insulted them. Yolanda felt embarrassed.

Why Natural Consequences Work Well

In most cases, consequences that are either natural or logical seem easier for children to accept. Consider the reasons why the natural consequences below worked well.

Behavior	Natural Consequence	Reason This Natural Consequence Worked Well
Rosita refused to share crayons at the art center.	The other children did not want to sit near her during art class.	Rosita missed having friends at the art center. She understood why the other children felt upset and began to share. The teachers and parents remained uninvolved.
Mike yelled angrily at Jose.	After Mike yelled at his friend, Jose no longer wanted to play with Mike.	Parents did not have to get involved because the consequence came about naturally. Although Mike felt sad about Jose's decision, he understood Jose's reasons.
After being told not to do so, Mary ate half a box of candy.	Mary felt sick and could not play with her friends.	Mary's parents did not cause her illness, and the consequence unfolded naturally. After eating so much candy, Mary got a chance to connect the candy to her illness without blaming her parents.

Story: Consequence of Not Wearing a Coat

When my daughter Joy was five years old, two other mothers and I decided our young children would benefit from a day care program. If pressed to tell the truth, we would have acknowledged that our kids were fine, but we moms seriously needed a little childcare relief. Ultimately, we decided that if we wanted the job done right, we would have to do it ourselves. And so, we did. We divided the days, and each of us became a preschool teacher once a week.

On a cold, windy morning, it was Marian's turn to be the teacher of the day for all the children. Even with a cold, blustery wind, Marian decided a walk would be good for everyone. All children save one hustled into their winter coats.

Marian, noticing that Joy had not put on her coat, said, "Joy, it's cold and windy outside. Put your coat on, please."

Joy: "I don't want to wear my coat. My mommy lets me make my own choices."

And so, Joy made her choice and didn't wear her coat. After walking two blocks from Marian's house, Joy said, "Marian, I'm cold. I want us to go back to your house now."

Marian replied, "Joy, you made the choice to leave your coat at the house. The other children are having fun. I'm sorry, but you are going to have to be cold."

The power in this story is that Marian did not give in to Joy. Marian allowed Joy to experience the natural consequence of her choice to go coatless. Shivering for a short time provided an important lesson. What would Joy have learned if Marian had abruptly taken the group home? Joy might have decided, "It's all about me. I can always get what I want." In truth, it's all about learning lessons.

Logical Consequences

Both natural and logical consequences depend on the strength of the adult in charge. Can a parent or grandparent allow the child to experience the outcome of a choice or action? As loving parents and grandparents, we want to protect, give in, and make life pleasant for the children we love so much. How easy to forget that for children to learn, sometimes love looks like allowing a bit of discomfort. Of course, we never allow a consequence that puts a child in any danger.

Like natural consequences, logical consequences operate as powerful teaching mechanisms. Unlike natural consequences, logical ones do not fall easily into place. Logical outcomes require careful thought. Logical consequences, which make sense when handled correctly, versus punishments, which tend to feel mean, result in vastly different reactions in children.

Keep in mind that whether your child dislikes a consequence or happily accepts it does not make any difference. Your goal is to find a solution to a problem as you teach cause and effect. If your child recognizes that when she behaves a certain way, she experiences a logical reaction, you are succeeding. If you act on an assumption that a child can learn only from being miserable, you are establishing an adversarial situation. Once battle lines are drawn, you will not win, and neither will your child.

Consider the following examples of logical consequences for babies or toddlers that require thought and action by parents or grandparents.

Behavior of Baby or Toddler	Logical Consequence for a Baby or Toddler
While nursing, a baby bites her mom.	Mom immediately removes her breast while gently saying, "Mommies are not for biting." After a quick separation, Mom commences nursing again. However, each time the baby bites, Mom quickly removes the breast. She says, "We don't bite people. We love each other," or, "I know you did not mean to hurt me. I love you."
A toddler hurts the family dog by throwing a hard metal toy car at him.	As Mom removes the toy, she says, "I think our dog is hurt. Cars are not for throwing. I'll keep the car for a short time." Mom replaces the car with a soft ball. This consequence allows the child to continue having fun while making certain the dog is safe. After replacing the car with a ball, Mom can add, "Although we can throw balls, we don't throw at dogs or at people."
Just for fun (and to experience her new power), baby throws food on the floor.	Parents remove the plate of food while saying, "I guess this means you are all through eating." If the baby indicates that she wants to continue eating, return the plate with a reminder that food stays on the baby's plate or tray. Each time the baby throws food on the floor, the plate of food is temporarily taken away. You are not failing if you need to repeat this action many times.

Logical consequences for slightly older children might look like the examples below.

Behavior of a Young Child	Logical Consequence for a Young Child
A five-year-old child leaves the safety of the sidewalk and rides her bike across the street.	The child puts her bike away for the remainder of the day. The child is old enough that the consequence can last longer than a consequence for a baby. However, keep the time reasonable. You do not need to remove the bicycle for a week or longer. By that time, your child will probably forget the connection and simply feel angry at you.
In school, a child disrupts class.	The child moves her desk a short distance away from the group. If the child enjoys moving her desk to a quieter area, her teacher has not failed. The teacher accomplished her goal, which was to stop the child's disruption of the class. The teacher is not punishing the child. She is solving the problem. Count it a win all the way around.
A first grader steals a special pencil eraser from a classmate.	The child returns the eraser. She is encouraged (but not forced) to mend the problem she caused by inviting the child, whose eraser she took, to share some cookies. Her offer demonstrates, "I regret that I took something of yours. I hope you will allow me to share with you."
An elementary-school-age child talks disrespectfully to her parent.	The parent refuses to continue the conversation at that time but will try again later. Later can be in a few minutes or a few days, depending on the situation and the maturity of the child.

Why Logical Consequences Work Well

The chart on the next page emphasizes why even with toddlers, logical consequences work effectively.

Behavior of Baby or Toddler	Logical Consequences	Why Logical Consequences Work Well
Daisy eats Play-Doh.	Mother quietly puts the Play-Doh on a high shelf. "Play-Doh is not for eating. We can try again soon."	When parents or grandparents consistently restate the same message, the baby will eventually make a connection. It is important to establish a consequence that she will soon understand. This solution also prevents her from getting sick from eating Play-Doh.
While playing in her grandma's front yard, a toddler continued to walk toward the street.	Grandma took the toddler inside after saying, "It is too dangerous for you to go near the street. We will try playing in the front yard again soon."	Although the toddler preferred to remain in the yard, she was soon playing happily inside. The toddler did not totally understand why they went inside, but seeds about street safety were planted. Also, Grandma did not worry that the toddler felt happy inside, since the solution kept her safe. There was no need to punish her lack of understanding about the street.
Daisy's mom and dad bought a small puppy. Originally, the dog and Daisy had fun playing together. Soon, the puppy began to scratch Daisy. In return, Daisy squeezed the puppy too hard. She also began to hit the little dog.	When Daisy's parents realized that the toddler and the puppy were both getting hurt, they understood that both the baby and the dog were too young to know how to play well together. The consequence (and the solution) was that Daisy's parents found a new home for the puppy.	Neither Daisy nor the dog understood. However, both benefitted from being separated. The purpose of this consequence was to solve the problem.

Notice the reasons why the following examples for young elementary-school-age children work.

Behavior of Preschool and Early Elementary-School-Age Child	Logical Consequences	Why Logical Consequences Work Well
Mike hit Jose.	The boys' mothers talked and decided to cancel the next play date.	The mothers' decision made sense. Mike accepted that the consequence seemed logical. He understood that neither mom wanted the boys to get hurt. The mothers' concern about their boys getting hurt was solved.
Mary ate pieces of candy after being told not to do so.	Mary's parents asked her to create a list of all food eaten each day.	At the end of a week, Mary and her mom analyzed Mary's chart and came up with an eating plan that included healthy food as well as acceptable amounts of sugar. The process encouraged the value of eating healthy food.
Jim left toys all over his room.	Jim's mom and dad swept all the toys into a basket.	Jim's parents stored all the toys in a safe place. In addition, they helped Jim create an easy plan for picking up his room each evening. After Jim applied ideas from the plan (which he helped create), he earned the right to play with his toys again.

Consequences of No Consequences and No Limits for Toddlers

Unintended results occur when parents fail to use consequences or to set reasonable limits. For example, a toddler who is allowed to throw anything her hand touches will not learn the importance of protecting others. The value of considering long-term outcomes cannot be overstated. At the toddler age, you are building a foundation.

Many parents value co-sleeping with babies. Although this option totally depends on the preferences of the parents, the reality may be that in a few years the baby will have become a child who takes up too much space in her parents' bed. Convincing a child who has always slept between Mom and Dad to go to her own room may be a challenge. An expression that contains a bit of wisdom instructs, "Start what you want to continue."

A three-year-old gets away with snatching toys from her baby brother. Left unchallenged, the siblings may spend their future years struggling with issues related to basic fairness and sharing. The older sibling may decide she should always get what she wants. The younger brother may continue to feel like a victim who does not have a chance to get his wants met.

Consequences of Having No Consequences for School-Age Children

An elementary-school-age girl wanted a better watch. She had a watch that worked fine, and yet she wanted a newer and fancier one. While playing with a friend, her watch got smashed and ruined. She said her friend broke it. Did the child ruin her own watch knowing her parents would replace it with something better? Although somewhat uncertain, the girl's parents accepted the story about her friend and bought their daughter a new, fancier watch, which she soon stopped wearing. Appreciation for the watch had not been established. In fact, the new watch was taken for granted.

The same child also wanted an expensive bicycle for Christmas. Although she felt delighted when the gift arrived, within a short time she left her bike out in the rain and a few parts rusted. In response, her parents bought another one. What did the child learn? Lessons about the responsibilities that accompany ownership seemed lost.

Nothing Obvious? I Can't Think of Anything Natural or Logical to Do!

Let's be honest. There are times when a natural consequence will be dangerous or unhealthy. Sometimes the price tag for letting nature run its course will simply be unreasonable.

Other times, nothing natural or logical comes to mind. What can a parent do when this occurs? *Love and Logic*, a system for raising children, suggests that parents "press the pause button" and wait to decide.[49] Sometimes, immediate reactions made under pressure create more problems than solutions. When working with children in kindergarten and above, leaders of *Love and Logic* encourage using honest statements, like the ones listed below.[50]

"I feel too upset to decide what to do right now. I need to think about this." Add, "Try not to worry. We can talk tomorrow."

"This is so sad. I'm going to have to do something about this! But not now. . . later."

"I'm so angry about this right now that I need to calm down before I talk to you about it. I make better decisions when I'm calm."

By choosing to wait, you model an important life skill. In the heat of anger, delaying what to say or do may result in the best outcome. Also, your opportunity to influence comes when you follow through. Waiting provides time to think, discuss ideas with your partner, visit with a school counselor, or even call *Love and Logic* at 800-338-4065.

Adding the phrase, "Try not to worry about this; I'm still thinking," reinforces the importance of the issue to you and your child.

Keep in mind that you must remember to return to the issue soon. Forgetting would send a negative (and powerful) message to your child.

---

49   Fay, The Delayed.
50   Fay, The Delayed.

Chapter 13
Mistakes We Can Correct

Parents and grandparents, who sincerely want to motivate and encourage, frequently and innocently make mistakes.

Mistake #1 Don't + Verb	If words such as "don't," "stop," or "quit" plus a verb are used, you can expect to witness the behavior you do not want. "Don't run" will almost certainly solicit running.
Mistake #2 External Emphasis	Using adjectives such as "pretty," "smart," or "quick" tend to burden children negatively as much as saying a child is ugly, stupid, or slow. We tend to emphasize external qualities like good looks, athletic abilities, and intelligence instead of affirming internal qualities such as effort, hard work, persistence, and kindness.
Mistake #3 I'm Proud	Instead of encouraging a child to feel good about herself, grandparents and parents tend to take credit by saying, "I'm so proud of you."
Mistake #4 "But . . ."	An encouraging statement begins well. Then, the parent or grandparent adds the word "but." This small, three-letter word cancels the preceding message.

Mistake #5 Bribing	"If you stop _____ , I'll give you _____ ." What could be more innocent? The problem is the power the child just gained in the world of getting exactly what she wants.
Mistake #6 "Stop crying!"	When a child cries, she does so because she does not know a better, more effective way to communicate her fear, disappointment, or frustration. Better to cry to than stifle feelings for a later therapist.

Each of these six mistakes will be explored in depth.

 Mistake #1: "Don't" Plus a Verb

Without realizing it, we unintentionally trigger children of all ages to do exactly what we do not want. Most of us tend to latch our thoughts onto the verb. When parents or grandparents say the following combination of words, children generally respond in ways we do not want.

What We Tend to Say	Unwanted Result of What We Say
"Don't hit your brother."	Brother will probably get smacked.
"Don't run on wet concrete."	This is an invitation for the child to increase speed on the wet concrete.
"Don't forget your homework."	This almost guarantees your child will soon call asking you to deliver her homework.
"Don't cry."	Tears are coming. Get the tissues.

Make Positive Statements
The more positive alternative is to state what you want the child to do:

- "Please walk in the store."
- "Please keep your hands to yourself."
- "Remember to walk carefully on the wet concrete around the pool."
- "Take your sweater."
- "Please swallow your food before you talk. We will wait to hear your story."

144

Story: A Teacher Who Guaranteed Behavior She Did *Not* Want

While Chandler was still in elementary school, he noticed some older guys flipping almost-empty Coke bottles high into the air. The bottles somersaulted in mid-air and then miraculously landed upright. What a challenge.

Chandler entered class with an almost-empty bottle of Gatorade. About a fourth of the liquid was left in the bottom. Perfect! To the delight of his friends, Chandler began demonstrating his newly honed skill. The teacher entered the classroom. Feeling unamused, the teacher did not congratulate Chandler on his new mastery. Instead, she said, "Chandler, stop flipping that bottle." (Note how this statement will quickly work against the adult!)

Well of course Chandler could not—absolutely could not—make his hand stop flipping that bottle. It wasn't that Chandler didn't want to please the teacher. Emotionally, he simply couldn't control his hand.

The question to consider is why the request to stop flipping the bottle was a mistake. Trust me on this. When adults begin with words such as "stop" or "don't" and follow that directive with a verb, you can almost bet that the verb will determine the action taken by the child. If the teacher had reworded her request by saying, "Chandler, very clever. Please put the bottle on my desk until after class ends," she would probably have gotten a courteous response from Chandler.

Removing "don't" from our vocabularies takes thought and willpower. To master this communication challenge, begin practicing early. Remember that even before babies can decode spoken words, your comments will be processed by their developing brains.

Even with a baby, teach yourself to say:

- "Keep your food on the highchair tray."
- "Share your toy with your friend. You will both have more fun."
- "Take a nap so you will have energy to play."

Mistake #2: External Qualities Over Intrinsic Values

A little girl who grows up on an emotional diet of hearing how pretty she is may spend her entire life failing to grasp her intrinsic values. Life is more than a beauty contest. The quality of one's existence depends on traits such as kindness to others, courage to stand up for what is fair to all, and strength to tell the truth.

In similar fashion, a young boy whose childhood feedback is focused on his high IQ may miss out on developing inner fortitude. If he is confronted by a topic that does not come easily to him, he may not have the ability to believe in his self-value, put in the time and effort needed to gain mastery, or demonstrate the patience required for delayed gratification.

Even though we know that external qualities such as athletic skill, intelligence, and beauty will fade with years, we often fail to accentuate inner qualities that can last and even increase with time. Patience is an example of an inner value. Faith can carry an individual through the worst of situations. Love is the most important inner quality of all.

In *What Great Parents Do*, Dr. Erica Reischer shares that people who praise outer traits tend to promote less confidence rather than more.[51] As a young mother, I heaped bushels of praise on my children's looks and intelligence. Why would this not build confidence and self-esteem? As I recall my earlier years as a parent, I doubt that I emphasized my children's internal strengths enough. Internal characteristics, the ones that are important, include the following:

- Courage
- Honesty
- Kindness
- Persistence
- Empathy
- Faith
- Loyalty
- Effort

---

51   Reischer, *What Great Parents Do*.

Story: Honesty—An Intrinsic Value

When a young girl was ten years old, her dad wanted her to take square dancing lessons. Although she was not excited about square dancing, she wanted to make Dad happy. One Saturday afternoon, the child stubbornly declared that she did not want to go and was going to stay home. Later, she and her dad shared a conversation as she sat on his lap.

Daddy: "How was square dancing?"

Child: "The lesson was fun," she lied. Quietly, she decided, *There's no reason to disappoint him.*

Daddy: "Who was your partner?"

Child: ..."Oh, you know—Jim is always my partner."

Daddy: "Did you have a favorite dance routine? Can you show me the steps?"

Child: ..."I can't remember."

At this point, the young girl tilted her head to one side and began to twist her long, straight hair around a finger on her right hand. Later, she recalled that her eyes darted around the living room noticing a red lamp shade standing in front of pink flowered wallpaper. While making up facts that did not happen, she squirmed uncomfortably. As she continued to compose a meaningless and confusing explanation about the music used in class, the child slipped off her dad's lap and began doing hand stands on the brown carpet. She later recalled seeing her thin legs sticking straight up in the air.

Finally, the child blurted out the truth, "Daddy, I'm so sorry. I didn't go to the class."

Daddy: "Did you notice that the more you lied, the more uncomfortable you got? From now on, I hope you will always tell the truth. Honesty can be a challenge at times, but nothing will be as miserable as attempting to cover up the truth."

Stress Internal Qualities

One way to cultivate an internal quality is to notice a child's beginning efforts in the right direction. You might say, "I have noticed that you are becoming kinder to your little brother lately. Thank you. I think he really likes the thoughtful ways you talk to him and share your toys. Do you think he will begin to copy what you say and do?"

In addition, ask self-reflecting questions such as, "After you put so much effort into cleaning your room, how did you feel about yourself? Did you have a happy feeling when you finished? Give yourself a pat on the back." Notice that no concrete reward such as a sticker ever feels as satisfying as one's personal recognition of honest effort and worthy accomplishment.

Stating the greater truth may also be important to a child's development of intrinsic values. Recently, when a grandson faced a difficult football game, I wrote the following message to him prior to the event.

"I have been told this will be a challenging game. We humans thrive and learn from challenges. Regardless of the final score, you are always a winner when you give your finest effort. Rise to your personal best and you will walk away a champion. Whatever the score at the end, you are always a winner to me. Love, Grandma"

On the other hand, external qualities, which become less important over time, include the following:

- Good looks
- Intelligence
- Athletic ability
- Beautiful hair
- Strong muscles
- Height
- Weight
- Accumulation of wealth or, for kids, "stuff"

Dr. Reischer provides additional reasons to reduce an emphasis on external qualities, which are paraphrased in the chart on the following page.[52]

---

[52]   Reischer, *What Great Parents Do*, 118.

External Quality	Potential Problems
"You are so talented."	At some point the child may wonder, *Could Mom be mistaken about me? Maybe I do not sing as well as she thinks. Am I going to be a terrible disappointment to her?* Not only is Mom's credibility questioned, but fear of disappointing a parent may also create unintended stress.
"You are the smartest child I know."	A child who is told she's smart often feels hesitant to try new skills or accept challenges. The child may fear that if the new task demands more work than usual, parents and teachers might decide that she is not as intelligent or as gifted as they first thought. Rather than risk being a failure, she doesn't try at all. Even worse, a child who always chooses activities or classes she can master easily will not stretch her cognitive abilities. Vigorous mental workouts build stamina. Resistance to challenges sometimes becomes a barrier for children identified as gifted and talented.

When external traits get too much attention, a child may not appreciate the importance of intrinsic qualities such as acceptance of others and patience. Consider the difference between a focus on good looks and the satisfaction of helping others.

As a young child, my daughter took dance lessons. Following a recital, we told her how cute she looked and how well she danced on stage. Without realizing the impact of my words at that time, I frequently said, "Joy, you are pretty. Just look at your big eyes." Finally, I noticed that she had developed an attitude of "I'm special."

Once I understood the damage I'd created, I began to focus on Joy's internal qualities, such as her optimistic attitude and her kindness to others. The changes did not come easily for me. Frequent self-reminders eventually made me more comfortable using new phrases, such as the examples on the following page.

Instead of Saying . . .	Build Appreciation for Inner Qualities by Saying . . .
"You are so popular."	"When you take the time and effort to learn the names of other students, you help them feel at home. Thank you."
"You are smart. I know you will ace this quiz."	"You are putting effort into mastering this material by studying and spending time getting ready for the quiz. Do you notice your effort?"
"Good job!" (Although "good job" is not wrong, you can strengthen the words by naming the child's effort.)	"You put a lot of time and thought into writing thank-you notes to people who sent gifts. I appreciate the time and effort you gave."

Consider the differences between "You are so smart" and "Can you see your own progress?" Which statement has the potential to become a burden? Maybe your baby is a genius and maybe she's a wonderful, ordinary, precious little person who will learn normally. Perhaps she will have learning challenges. Suggesting a standard that may not fit her reality could become a burden. On the other hand, acknowledging effort, which can be observed and measured, feels truthful. A child can think, *I'll keep doing my best until I reach my goal.*

The words that provide the most benefit will be those directed toward effort, persistence, and hard work. Emphasizing exertion has the potential to create a powerful path toward self-acceptance and continued growth. As a parent, you know that no matter how special your child is, she will not always win first place. Despite life's disappointments, she can enjoy personal satisfaction if she knows she worked hard and gave her best. True confidence manifests from genuine improvements rather than from adjectives that may or may not be true.

Fixed Mindsets Associated with IQ and Talent
Dr. Carol Dweck, a phycologist, claims that excessive praise tends to create a fixed mindset.[53] *This is who I am whether I work hard or not.* Another conclusion might be, *I'm so smart that I don't have to work hard to master anything.*

---

53   Dweck, *Mindset.*

Some phrases that are intended to encourage can create burdens by establishing a fixed attitude. Notice the expressions below that feel excessive. An over-the-top or untrue compliment does not invite the type of growth that comes from effort and persistence.

<u>Adjectives that might become burdens and result in fixed mindsets</u>

- "You are the smartest. . . cutest. . . fastest. . ."
- "You are always so sweet."
- "You are my favorite."
- "You are a born genius."
- "This report card with As and Bs is okay. Next time, I'm sure you will get all As."
- "I told everyone that you are very smart."

<u>Growth Mindsets Associated with Effort</u>
A growth mindset emphasizes *I can continue to learn, and, with practice, can improve my skills*. Research indicates that intelligence increases with stimulation and determination to learn. Most of us learn more from a wrong answer or a mistake than from all our correct responses.

After missing the scientific name for kneecap on a test, a student remembered the word "patella," which means kneecap, the rest of her life. She reflected that there were 50 questions on the test. She could not recall a single other question or answer.

After confusing teaspoon and tablespoon on a homework assignment, a child mastered various measurements on a major test. The initial mistake became a motivation for mastering the content.

The class turtle got sick when the child responsible for its care misunderstood how much food to give it each day. After making this mistake, the child became an advocate for all creatures.

Each of the children above realized the importance of learning from mistakes. Often, mistakes prompt us to study harder, learn more, and improve ourselves.

<u>Importance of Effort</u>
Words that identify effort encourage attitudes that accompany growth mindsets.

<u>Encouraging Good Feelings About Learning</u>

- "You must feel good about your progress. You worked hard."
- "Doesn't it feel good to form healthy habits?"
- "Let's give a silent cheer for your effort!"
- "You must have listened carefully. Listening requires effort."
- "Congratulations on giving this your best!"
- "You stayed with this until you noticed your own gains."

As parents and grandparents, we want to model the concept of continual lifelong learning. Ask your grandchild to teach a new skill to you. The shared activity will fulfill needs for the child as well as improve your personal relationship.

 Mistake #3: "I'm Proud of You"

A baby's emerging mobility and growing vocabulary automatically promote pride and pleasure in parents and grandparents. Truthfully, you have a right to feel fantastic, since you probably had some input in the baby's success. The question is whether you can share your own pride with a bit of humility. After all, regardless of how much you helped and encouraged, the baby ultimately did the hard work. In truth, the pride rightfully belongs to the child.

Although statements such as "I'm so proud of you" sound good, if used too often, these words may detract from a child's self-acceptance and pleasure. What other words might work better? The suggestions below come from *Parent Effectiveness Training* by Dr. Thomas Gordon.[54]

The words "I'm so proud of you" alter ownership. Even if you also worked hard to support your child's progress, the success belongs to her. Say, "I hope you feel good about your hard work and persistence." Put the honor where it belongs—with the child. Instead of proclaiming your own pride in your child's achievement, consider saying, "Yay for you! Be happy about your hard work. Let's clap for you."

There will be times when "I'm so proud of you" slips out. No problem. You can add, "I want you to feel good about your work and improvements. You never gave up. You tried again and again until you got it. Let's celebrate together by giving a cheer for you."

---

54   Gordon, *Parent Effectiveness Training*.

Most parents hope their children will become self-confident individuals with feelings of self-worth. Parents and grandparents contribute to this outcome by encouraging babies, children, and teens to recognize their own authentic improvement and hard work. Empty praise for unfinished or less-than-successful tasks will not build confidence. Children always know the difference between empty phrases and genuine recognition of achievement. If the child did not work hard, failed to persist, or did not show courtesy to another person, do not make false claims. Lack of truth will not feel good to anyone. Children benefit more when they own their authentic successes.

- "Each step you take gets you closer to your goals."
- "You are making headway," can be a good phrase to use when you notice a child is working hard but has not yet achieved her goal.
- "Good for you for continuing to work hard!"
- "You do not give up quickly."
- "Give yourself a pat on the back!"

 Mistake #4: "But"—the Awesome Downer

Unfortunately, humans tend to forget sincere compliments and remember a small criticism. Although the word "but" has its place in grammar, the word often cancels any preceding positive statement. Imagine the following:

Let's Celebrate	Ruined with the Word "But"
We watched Daisy take her first steps after weeks of crawling. We said, "Daisy, you just took your first steps! Let's clap for you." Her little face beamed with pleasure.	How would she have felt if we had frowned and added, "But you fell down. Bummer!"
"You must have studied to make these good grades."	Fine so far. How will the child feel if we add, "But, next time, raise that B to an A in math."
A coach says, "You ran very fast. I timed you. This is the fastest you have ever run. Keep up the hard work."	If Coach adds, "But your baton handoff looked clumsy," the remark will certainly decrease the initial pleasure. Save the review of baton passing for a new lesson. Whatever encouragement was initially offered got lost in the "but" statement.

Mistake #5: Problems with Bribes

Many parents bribe a young child to convince her to stop crying or misbehaving. During a child's birthday party, a young mother's child began wailing. Not wanting guests to have to listen to her crying child, the mom quickly took out a piece of candy and unwrapped it for her daughter. Sure enough, the tears ended. Success! Maybe—and maybe not. Although a small piece of candy will almost always end the upset, a parent might consider, *What am I teaching?* The lesson being learned by the child might be, *Behaving badly is an easy way to get what I want. Candy makes me feel so much better.*

Sugar, the stuff of deal-making with parents, thus becomes a terrific avenue of escape from real emotions. In truth, we hope our young children will have the stamina and courage to feel their feelings and to express them in healthy ways. Bribing kids out of tears with food, a new toy, or a treat encourages a lifetime of seeking release from pain through unhealthy methods. Isn't this what drugs and alcohol do? Numb uncomfortable thoughts and emotions?

<u>Alternatives to Bribes</u>
We hope our children will develop the courage to face real life as it is, to feel and express emotions, and to make healthy choices. The foundation of strength and acceptance of life begins early. Consider the examples below.

Incident	Bribe	Alternative Action
When my son was two years old, his grandparents came to his party and gave him a shiny swing set. During the party, when his little friends wanted to swing, he was not willing to share his new gift. My memories of this party include a howling, angry little guy.	I could have said, "If you stop crying, I'll give you an extra piece of cake."	Hopefully I said, "I can tell that you really like your new gift from Grandma and Grandpa. I understand that you don't want the other children to use your new swing. It's okay to feel that way. Thanks for telling me. However, your friends came to your party. Until they leave, I expect you to share." (Hopefully, I also redirected him to another activity.)

Incident	Bribe	Alternative Action
After damaging her inner ear, our baby daughter needed painful shots to prevent spinal meningitis. For good reason, she cried angry, upset tears each time she had to get the shot.	A bribe could have been, "Here, open this gift I brought for you. This shot is not going to hurt much at all." (A lie is never okay.)	To the child who knows the shot will be painful, I might have said, "I know this shot feels terrible. You can show me how much the shot hurts by squeezing my hand. You must get this shot to help you get healthy." Establish a foundation of truthfulness. If you know the shot will hurt, either tell the truth or say nothing.
As a toddler, Catherine, our first granddaughter, cried copious tears when her parents changed day care facilities. She clung to her dad and refused to remove her cap and jacket.	Daddy might have stayed until nap time and quietly crept out. In this case, Catherine would have probably felt tricked. Dad might have also lost his job for being late to work each day.	Finally, the caregiver suggested that the dad should leave for work more quickly so the new adults in Catherine's life could begin to gain her trust. The following day, when Catherine cried at the new day care center, her dad said, "Catherine, thanks for letting me know how you feel. I know the teachers will take good care of you until I get back. I love you."

When upsets happen to children, you want to communicate, "I love you. I'm willing for you to show me how you feel."

Mistake #6: Saying "Stop Being So Noisy with Your Feelings"

There are times when parents and grandparents simply want peace and quiet. That's understandable. However, yelling at a child to stop all the crying and complaining may not be worth gaining a moment of quiet. When a child has a reason to be sad, acknowledge the sadness. Encourage the child to express herself. When tears come, provide a bit of understanding. There are times for adults to be quiet and listen as children or teens express fear or sadness.

Story: Stop Your Loud Crying

One afternoon at a graveside service, an eight-year-old child began crying loudly as her mother's coffin was being lowered into the ground. The child's fear and loss felt inconsolable. Her cries were mournful, and haunting for all to hear.

Suddenly, an aunt turned and demanded that the child immediately stop being so noisy. Abruptly, quiet reigned—not a single word, not another tear. The memory of her aunt's command lasted for the rest of her life.

Perhaps crying, even screaming, were appropriate expressions of grief for a child whose life had been torn apart; yet, as a result of her aunt's behavior, she learned the following:

- Do not be a bother to others
- Stay quiet
- Take care of everyone else
- What you feel is not important

Children frequently feel as though their lives will end even over small disappointments. Although you may realize that a child is being too dramatic for a situation, please remember that she lacks your adult perspective. Your job is to provide avenues of release and to seek paths for genuine healing. Make self-expression opportunities such as drawing, writing, talking, walking, and acting out available.

Crying, when appropriate, may be a first step toward inner healing. Therapy may also be needed to start a life-long search for security and happiness.

Stifling grief, even if the loss seems small, possibly buries what may later need to be retrieved and healed.

In addition to encouraging your child to cry and tell you how upset she is, you can add depth to the experience by asking her to show her feelings in creative ways. Stay close, remain protective, and make certain your child knows that she will be totally safe while expressing herself. You want her to know you will remain patient and accepting. Provide the following types of options.

• Mashing Play-Doh (tactile expression)
• Drawing a picture to visually depict how she feels (visual expression)
• Telling you what she fears (auditory expression)
• Recording her angry thoughts and words (auditory expression)
• Dancing out the anger (kinesthetic expression)
• Writing or dictating a letter based on feelings (tactile expression)

Adult reactions to a child's crying can range from mild annoyance to misery. Although in many situations a child's fears or grief can be terribly painful for you, please do your best to encourage her to express her feelings by saying, "Cry as much and for as long as you need. You can tell me what you want to say. You are safe. As awful as this is, you can do this, and I am here to help you."

Playing with Granddaddy and the cat

Chapter 14
Emphasizing the Importance of Chores and Work

An enthusiastic letter from nine-month-old Wren can be read below.

> Dear Mom and Dad,
> Here are a few things I think you need to know. I am a
> swell little kid. Do you realize that I am a hard worker?
> Have you noticed that I do not stop when I head across
> the room to get something I want? That shows you that
> I am persistent, which will lead to great success as I get
> older.

Children, even toddlers between the ages of two and three, want to be part of the family unit. Often babies show a desire to participate with family members by trying to help.

Story: Encourage a Baby to Be a Helper

While on FaceTime with 18-month-old Daisy, I watched as she repeatedly removed towels from the front-loading dryer and threw them into a basket.

"Daisy, thank you for being a helper. You are a worker." Out of the laundry room Daisy proudly strode with a big smile, eyes shining, and brown curls bouncing as she pulled the basket behind her. After each tour of the living area, she returned to the laundry room and began throwing the same towels back into the dryer.

"What a worker you are. You like to help your mommy, don't you?" I should have also said, "Thank you, Mommy, for allowing Daisy to parade back and forth with your clean towels."

At all ages, satisfaction accompanies responsibility. Even babies and young children who believe they contribute in some way feel more satisfied. Perhaps all humans have a basic instinct to connect to others in meaningful ways. It appears that along with a human desire to connect comes a yearning to be useful. Helping also provides a step toward mastery of skills.

Acknowledge the importance of your own work as well as the age-appropriate chores your child does. By instilling appreciation for chores, you encourage her to become a lifelong learner. For example, caring for a pet can become an important chore.

Importance of Simple Chores

Most children enjoy helping parents. When your child is between the ages of two and three, begin working together. Assign a small part to your child. Keep her task simple so she will be successful. Always make certain your instructions are clear and easy.

1. Demonstrate what you want her to do.

2. Begin by doing the task together.

3. Explain carefully as she does her part of the chore.

4. Provide feedback about mistakes (by dignifying, of course). For example, you might need to say, "I can see why you did that. I did not explain the job well enough."

5. Name all the things she does well.

6. Always thank her for her help.

7. If she complains, be empathetic as you say, "Sometimes I don't want to wash the dishes. I wash them anyway. Then I feel good about a neat, clean kitchen."

As your child grows older and adds new chores, you may want to say, "It helps when someone works with me. Would you like for me to work with you as you do your chores?" While working together, make sure you do not take over and finish the task without your child's participation. Your goal is to plant the idea that it feels good to:

- Do chores
- Work together
- Allow others to help
- Complete a job

At the end, you can comment, "Wasn't it fun to work together? Doesn't it feel good that your room looks neat and pretty? You are a good worker." Begin while your child is still young. If you wait until she's a teenager, you may have an uphill struggle. There are several ways to connect chores and pleasures.

- One of the easiest ways to help liven up chores is to add music. Music invites moving, even dancing, as chores are being done.
- Do chores together to gain cooperation and partnership.
- On some occasions, go for speed by using a timer. Other times, set a goal for quality by photographing the area before and after work.
- Occasionally, hide treats or pennies for children to find as they do chores. If you always hide treats, the hidden items become bribes. Let the treats remain unexpected surprises.
- Integrate exercises such as bending and stretching while doing chores.
- Invite children to help with parents' chores.
- Listen to audio books while working.
- Collect trash and throw it into a trash can across the room. Vary the distance depending on the age of the child.

When to Help a Child, When to Encourage

There will always be the question of when to help and when to allow a child to struggle. When a child tackles a task that you absolutely know will be too hard for her to achieve, ask, "Would you like a little help getting started?" If you decide to see how far the child can go without interference, use words to encourage. "Yesterday, when you set the table, you got the plates in the right spots. Would you like to add water glasses also? I believe you can do this."

By watching and listening to your child, you will know when to encourage and when to help. If she indicates frustration, say, "Would you like some help? Maybe if you put the glasses above the plates, they will be easier for the family to use. Try and see what happens." When completing a chore such as taking dirty dishes from the table to the kitchen sink, you might say, "Let's do this chore together. When I carry the dishes from the table to the sink, I often place them in this basket, which makes it easier to carry them safely. Would you like to try a basket?"

On the other hand, if you decide that your child is too tired to achieve success, say, "You are close to getting this done. Tomorrow, you can try again. I know you will learn how to do this soon." Between the ages of two and three, your toddler may defiantly insist that she will do it herself. Accept her rejection of your offer to help by adding, "If you change your mind, let me know. I'm happy to give you a small bit of help."

Whether you help or not, once she succeeds, say, "I knew you could do it! Let's have a fist bump for you!"

Research About Effort

Carol Dweck writes, "Students who were praised for being smart tended to take fewer risks, were easily frustrated with challenges, and even considered cheating to make themselves look better. Those who were praised for working hard, however, persevered during challenges and were more likely to reflect on improvements they could make in the future."[55]

More recently, researchers are concluding that the dynamics of intelligence can be altered, even increased. Talents and athletic abilities can be improved with effort, hard work, and practice. Researchers believe in a growth mindset. Dweck notes her own perseverance through learning challenges. As a result of her personal study, Dweck began asking children to keep track of their effort in doing homework, participating in class discussions, and having conversations with parents. A message she consistently gives to children and teens states, "You alone are in control of your destiny. Your hard work will pay off."[56]

---

55   Dweck, *Mindset.*
56   Dweck, *Mindset.*

Story: My Missed Chance to Comment on Effort

One of my greatest pleasures occurs when our grandson and his wife bring their toddler to play in our back yard. When Daisy was almost two, my husband constructed a small swing set with an attached slide in our back yard.

With no prompting, the toddler began climbing the steps of the slide. Out of my mouth came, "Good job, Daisy."

Oops! Instantly, I realized that I needed to repair my comment by naming her actions and recognizing her effort. Quickly, I added, "Daisy you can feel great that you climbed the steps by yourself. You worked hard."

As Daisy gets older, comments might change to:

"You have been studying your math. Even though you wanted to send text messages to your friends, you continued to study. Don't you feel good about your study efforts?"

"Even though you felt a little hesitant, you greeted the new girl at school. Being friendly to new people takes courage. When you face fears and then take the right action, your courage grows."

"Learning to throw balls takes time and effort. You can feel happy about your progress."

"If you allow fear to stop you from doing what you believe is the best action, your fear increases. Give your best effort and your confidence and courage will grow with you."

"Say a hearty, 'Yes!' to life. Then, step up and take the right action."

Daisy felt good about her success

163

The Satisfaction of Quality Effort

Not only does work exist as part of life, but the quality of effort makes a significant difference in building self-respect. Children who learn to get by with the least amount of effort often become adults who continue the same practice. Whether a philosophy is to insist on engaging in work one loves, or working to buy what is wanted, any job done with one's best effort will be appreciated by self and others.

Aidan's face shows his pride and fun

When Aidan gives his best effort, satisfaction can be experienced beyond winning awards or earning top grades. Self-satisfaction becomes the most valuable reward of all.

With these thoughts in mind, I want to suggest to children that they will usually find work and satisfaction comingled in the same experience. Often the issue involves no more than a change of attitude from annoyance to acceptance. Even two-year-old Daisy hears me say, "Daisy and I like to work, and we like to play. We feel happy when we work hard and play hard."

Even before Daisy started walking, I used several of the following phrases to plant ideas about working with effort.

- "Look at you! I see that you are working so hard to feed yourself. Even though getting food in your mouth is hard to do, you practice at every meal."
- "It feels good to learn, doesn't it?"
- "When you stand without holding on, your courage grows."
- "Keep trying. You will soon get this."
- "You will learn from your mistakes."
- "Let's clap for learning new things!"

During my teen years, I learned the hard way that feeling good about myself depended on the amount of commitment I gave to a task. Knowing I did my best felt much better than having to admit that I had been careless or indifferent.

A poem by Devon Brough may fit this consideration of working hard.[57]

Marriage is hard. Divorce is hard.
    Choose your hard.

Obesity is hard. Being fit is hard.
    Choose your hard.

Being in debt is hard. Being financially disciplined is hard.
    Choose your hard.

Communication is hard. Not communicating is hard.
    Choose your hard.

Life will never be easy. It will always be hard.
    But we can choose our hard.
        Choose wisely.

Consequences of Negative Work Attitudes

I know adults who never learned to associate positive feelings with working hard. Placing a value on the satisfaction of work makes the difference between enjoying a task and simply making money. Many individuals who find pleasure in work have continued their employment long after reaching retirement age. One man in his 70s manages his own business during the week and preaches to a small congregation on Sundays. All of us who find pleasure in working do so because we value the work itself. I'm not rejecting the pleasure and importance of making money. Why not appreciate both the task and the money earned?

Attitudes about work form early in life. Parents and grandparents will either model pleasure or irritation about the tasks they do. Who knows the importance of the words we say in front of young ears? Witnessing parents and grandparents who enjoy solving work challenges will have an even greater impact on children. A baby, young child, or teen will record the facial expressions, body language, and statements of parents and grandparents when they engage in work.

---

57   Brough, *Get OVA It.*

Perhaps the key to forming a lifelong appreciation of work begins with instilling fun into a child's chores. Instead of a strict, "You *must* finish your chores," integrate pleasure and cooperation. Small changes such as listening to music, talking to one another, dancing, and working together provide a foundation of satisfaction and success for the world of work.

Make certain that pleasure is not presented as a bribe but as a logical outcome. You hope to plant the idea that work, a natural part of life, can be viewed with pleasant expectations instead of with resentment and dread. A bribe might sound like, "If you finish your chores, you will be allowed to watch a television show." Anticipation might be stated as, "Let's work together to get these dishes done so we will have time to watch a show together before your bedtime. Let's do this!" Attitude makes the difference. An emphasis on pleasure motivates. Bribes feel controlling and create resentment.

Unfinished chores can become their own form of logical consequence when parents gently point out how yucky it feels to fail to complete an agreement. If the child fails to finish a chore and still seems totally satisfied with herself, a parent might add, "Most of us believe that not reaching a goal feels sad."

You may want to add a logical consequence by saying, "Since I will now have to complete your chore, as well as my own, I will not have the time or energy for a movie or bedtime story." Avoid lengthy complaints, lectures, warnings, or punishments. Let disappointments as well as satisfactions come naturally from consequences that fit the situation.

Chapter 15
The Power of "I'm Not Willing for You to . . ."

Consider an imaginary scene with your fifth-grade child. You walk into your home and hear the sound system bursting your house at the seams. You get your child's attention and say, "I'm not willing for the sound to be this loud. I know you want to hear your music at this volume. How can we solve this so we both get our needs and wants met?" You just established an important communication experience.

Unresourceful Statements

Consider the statements below, which usually do not work well with babies, children, or teens.

If you tell your child that you *won't* allow her to play music at this volume, she may think, "Oh yes, you will! I just played it at this volume, and I will do it again when you leave."

If you say, "As your parent, I *can't* let you destroy your hearing," you sound weak. Her reply may be, "You can't? Dad, I thought you could do anything!"

Parent temper tantrums frighten children and eventually destroy respect.

Constant harping becomes easy to ignore and establishes a negative climate.

Threats, such as, "If you keep playing your music at this volume, I'll take all of your devices and throw them in the trash," may win this small battle, but you run the risk of losing your child's respect since you will probably have to walk this threat back.

Shaming with statements, such as, "You do not deserve this expensive music system," teaches a child to dislike herself. Shaming does not build self-acceptance.

Say, "I love you and I know your hearing is as important to you as it is to me. I'm not willing for you to damage your hearing. Let's work together to find a volume that will be satisfying to you without being harmful."

<u>Additional Examples of "I'm not willing . . ."</u>
You begin, "I love you and want you to be healthy. I'm not willing for you to eat junk food." If you continue by saying, "I am willing for you to enjoy all the fruit you want," you maintain your strength. Your feelings and your willingness belong to you. Other helpful statements include:

"I'm not willing for you to be rude. Please rephrase that statement."

"I'm not willing for you to hurt your baby brother. Please play with him gently or play by yourself."

"I'm not willing for you to get so tired that you begin to get grumpy. Play for ten more minutes and then start your bath."

What to Do If Your Toddler Refuses to Comply

You feel threatened when your toddler stomps her foot and defiantly shouts, "No!" Let's be honest. Parenting is a daunting job. It is time for your two-to-three-year-old child to take her bath in preparation for bedtime. When you ask her to stop playing, she initially ignores you. You repeat the request, and she says "No!" Below, please explore several steps to take.

<u>Give a Warning Based on Time</u>
It is usually a good idea to give a child of any age a warning before indicating that the time for action has come. With some children, it may help to break the time into two parts. For example, "In ten minutes, you will need to stop playing and get ready for your bedtime bath. I'll let you know when you have

five minutes left." Setting a timer may help. When the second five-minute warning ends, you say, "Okay. It is time to head toward the bathroom."

At the end of the second warning, she continues to play. "I can tell that you don't want to stop playing. I'm willing to listen to how you feel. However, playtime is over for tonight."

Redirect Attention

"Let's look for some different toys for your bath. Is there something special you want? We can sing a song as we head toward the bathroom. Would you like to show me how you feel by walking with an angry stomp? Maybe you can bang a drum as I help you undress and get your bath water started."

Use Choices

*   "Would you like plain water or bubbles for your bath?"
*   "Would you like your nightlight on or off?"
*   "Will you feel better if I crawl into bed with you or do you want to be alone?"
*   "Would you prefer this book or another one?"
*   "Another stuffed animal might help you feel better. Which would you like to choose? It's up to you."
*   "Let's think of the fun we can have tomorrow when you are rested. Would you like to help make a list?" Add, "Maybe you are ready to be quiet and go to sleep. You decide."

When All Else Fails . . .

If she continues to get out of bed, gently take her back and tuck her in again. Continue to be gentle and understanding by saying, "I know you are terribly upset. It is time to go to bed." (I realize this is asking a lot of tired parents.)

Story: Slightly Older Child Refuses to Comply

Your slightly older child (approximately four years old or older) needs a shot. She enters the doctor's office fighting every inch of the way.

Maria: "I don't want a shot. Please don't make me do this. I don't even need a shot."

Mom: "I know you're frightened and don't want to get a shot because it will hurt. The good news is that it will be over quickly."

Maria: "You are being mean to me. You know this is going to hurt. Why are you being so mean?"

Mom: "Even though I understand how scared you are, this is not a time when you get to choose. You have an earache, and you need the shot to heal. I am not willing to risk a terrible illness or a possible loss of hearing."

If you decide the dangers are too great for your child to go home without the shot, you may have to help hold her down.

Mom: "I love you enough to make certain you get the medicine you need. It is okay for you to tell me and show me that you feel frightened and angry. Shots hurt and are scary."

There will be times when you do what you know is best for your child, regardless of her resistance. You comfort her by accepting her feelings.

<u>Invite Your Child to Help Find a Solution</u>
If your child is three years old or older, you may want to invite her to participate in finding a solution to a problem.

For example, you can ask, "We need to find a solution that we can both accept. How can we solve this problem?" With three- and four-year-old children, you will need to guide the answers toward solutions. When working with an older child, you can problem-solve together by saying, "I want to hear your ideas. Can you think of a way to fix this problem? What ideas do you have?" Introducing the words and the concept will form a foundation for the time when your child will, in fact, be able to think of solutions without your guidance. Teaching the concept of solving problems will help her develop one of life's most important skills.

Immediately End Whining

When a child argues, whines, or cries, replace your own frustration with the realization that your young child hopes to establish herself as an independent person. How you handle your child's arguing, whining, or crying will determine whether she learns new ways to express her needs or uses her whining with greater determination to get what she wants.

You will probably be tempted to change your mind and give in to her whining. Your child, being the thinking machine that she has become, may also be thinking, *I just talked in a whiny voice and Mom gave me a cookie. Hmm. I guess whining, crying, and nagging work. If I continue long enough, Mom will give me what I want.*

There lies the problem. Your child's interpretation of victory just put a tool in her box called *Getting My Own Way*. To avoid this, as soon as you hear whining, arguing, and nagging, *stop* the conversation immediately.

Say, "We can talk about this when you use your three-year-old voice." If she continues with the same whiny voice, say, "I'm not willing to listen when you whine." You will probably find it necessary to walk away and begin doing something else.

It may not seem like a big deal. Why not give in, just this one time? What can one time hurt? Be aware that if your youngster believes, *If I get really annoying, Mom will give in and let me have what I want,* she will repeat the behavior in other situations and with other people. Magnify that to the teen years.

I am convinced that parents today navigate the most challenging situations any of us have ever faced. Following the COVID pandemic, more is at stake for the physical, social, and emotional health of children than ever before. Setting reasonable limits requires enormous courage and strength. Lack of adequate finances, being a single parent, and the necessity for both parents to earn money compound the difficulties. And yet, no responsibility outweighs the importance of parenting well. Setting limits and guiding decisions, regardless of difficulties, cannot be set aside.

Tattling: An Opportunity to Learn

As annoying as tattling can become, this too can be a learning opportunity. A little background may help shine some wisdom on the situation. According to Conscious Discipline, children ages eight and under are conditioned by nature to go to adults when they need help.[58] Rather than be irritated about nature's

---

58   Bailey, *Conscious Discipline.*

programming, parents and grandparents can view this as a time to reinforce the idea that asking adults for help can be a wise action for a child to take. If you still feel annoyed, the good news informs us that tattling is developmental and will eventually end. (Many of the critical words and phrases below come from Conscious Discipline.)

Story: Can Tattling Be Used to Create Growth?

A child tattles by saying, "He took my helicopter."

Parent: "Did you feel happy when he took your helicopter?"

Child: "No."

Parent: "Tell him, 'I did not like it when you took my helicopter.' Practice saying this with me."

Child: "I did not like it when you took my helicopter."

Listen to the child's voice. Did she say the sentence passively, aggressively, or assertively? (Assertive statements speak with power. Aggressive comments promote increased agitation. Passive voices tend to be ignored.)

Parent: "I'm going to say the words again. Listen to my voice and then repeat the message by matching the way I say the sentence."

Child, speaking assertively: "I did not like it when you took my helicopter."

Getting the child to repeat your words while matching your assertive voice will be an amazing accomplishment. However, you have one more important step. Now, you must coach her to explain exactly how she wants to be treated.

Once again, you first teach and model what to say and how to send the message. Next, ask the child to practice until she can state exactly what she wants and can communicate her desires assertively.

Parent: "Repeat this statement one more time before you meet with your friend to solve the problem."

Child: "I did not like it when you took my helicopter. I want us to take turns. Maybe we can find an airplane so we can play together."

You may have to model speaking assertively many times as you encourage the child to attempt to match your tone. Repeat as many times as needed for her to catch your intonation, assertiveness, and volume. As with all new language skills, you will probably need to repeat the steps several times before mastery is achieved. Consider the lifelong importance of a child learning to end unwanted behavior and then knowing how to state what she wants. This is a critically important communication tool that many of us lack. What a victory!

Do Not Accept Blaming Others

Don't we all want to blame others when things go wrong? "It's not my fault, he was rude to me," can easily become a default refrain. Children learn this early. Conscious Discipline suggests asking the question, "Who is the boss of you?"

Story: Blaming Others

After Mary pushes Juan, he pushes her back. Mom notices and intervenes. Some phrases from the conversation below come from Conscious Discipline.

Juan: "It isn't my fault. Mary made me push her because she pushed me first."

Mom: "Does that mean Mary is your boss?"

Juan: "No.

Mom: "So, what could you have done instead of pushing her back?"

Juan: "She made me do it."

Mom: "That is so sad. You probably feel bad that Mary can boss you."

Juan: "No, she can't boss me."

Mom: "How can we solve this problem?"

Juan: "I don't know."

Mom: "Can you tell Mary how you feel? What could you say?"

Juan: "Mary, I do not like it when you push me."

After listening to Juan practice speaking assertively, Mom adds, "What do you want Mary to do instead of pushing you?"

Juan: "Mary, I do not like it when you push me. I want you to keep your hands off my body."

The hope of parents and grandparents is for each child to take responsibility for her behaviors and choices. A child who blames others gives her power away. How many times have we witnessed adults who continue to give power away by blaming their parents, siblings, schools, governments, or political parties? Claiming power requires taking responsibility for one's feelings, choices, and decisions to take positive and productive actions to improve situations. Research shows that a child who receives a consistent dose of punishment and shame for poor choices becomes an adult who lies about issues out of fear. To avoid this outcome, maintain a focus on teaching your child to assume responsibility by finding solutions and solving problems. One child at a time, you can contribute to changing the world into a more caring environment.

Any time a child stops blaming others and begins to cooperate and comply with your requests, offer a sincere, "Thank you," along with a small celebration such as a high five, fist bump, quick dance, large smile, pat on the back, smiley face, or short written note of appreciation. Buying a material reward is not needed or even wanted. Recognize that a child who cooperates uses willpower to honor your request. That willpower can be destroyed or strengthened by responses from parents and grandparents who love the child.

Teach Apologies and Amends

Although it is possible to force a child to say words you want to hear, a two- or three-year-old will not understand apologies. Your best way to teach this concept will be to model it by making your own apologies when you make mistakes. Making amends will be even more beneficial than the words of an apology. By demonstrating and then explaining, you begin to form a foundation for these two concepts.

What does it mean to make an amend? The term was made popular by Alcoholics Anonymous (AA) and is used with recovering alcoholics and addicts who seek to restore relationships. The concept goes beyond words and is based on taking positive actions to correct damages. A recovering individual may ask, "What can I do to make this mistake up to you?" To restore trust, the alcoholic may need to make significant changes.

How amends can be used with children depends on the age of the child as well as the situation. Consider the following example.

Story: Help Mend Aunt Janey's Hurt Leg

Two-year-old Daisy bit her Aunt Janey. "Janey, did that hurt?" asked Daisy's mom.

Janey: "Yes, Daisy's teeth hurt my leg."

Dad: "Daisy, can you apologize to Aunt Janey?"

Daisy: "No."

Dad: "Maybe tomorrow."

Dad realizes that forcing an apology when Daisy feels upset might teach his toddler to be insincere. At age two, Daisy doesn't grasp the meaning of the word "apology."

Knowing that Daisy likes to help, a second option might have been to ask, "Daisy would you be willing to get an ice pack or a drink of water to help Aunt Janey feel better?" Taking action to help Janey would qualify as making an amend.

Another Example for Making an Amend
Mom says, "Earlier, you refused to play with Ella. She cried and felt disappointed. Do you remember when that happened? Would you like to make sure Ella feels better?" Mom will need to make some suggestions, such as, "I think you can help Ella feel better by. . ."

• Eating lunch together
• Playing with Ella

- Giving Ella a hug
- Sharing a book with Ella

Nothing will be gained from shaming or punishing your child. Once she feels calm, you can encourage (but not force) her to repair the hurt feelings her actions created. Initially, you will have to take the lead in this effort. Making an amend by doing something positive carries more importance than merely saying the words, "I'm sorry." At times, the words are the best we can do.

How Can We Change Feelings? Change Actions First!

Changing angry actions to kinder ones will usually result in happier feelings. Previously, we believed we had to first change our feelings before we could choose different behaviors. Now, we learn that the opposite is true. Psychologist Noam Shpancer specializes in clinical and developmental psychology. His research has focused on home daycare and parent-caregiving. Shpancer wrote, "Recent research in clinical psychology has shown that the fastest way to change an emotion is to first change the behavior attached to it."[59] You want to change your own stormy behavior? A smile while quietly saying the word *yes* may be enough physical change to alter your negative feelings. Imagine the power of knowing that changing a negative action to a positive one (even if doing so feels somewhat fake at the time) will heal the underlying feeling.

Daisy's parents can also arm her with the information that when she is unkind to other people, they will usually respond by being unkind to her. Usually, we are motivated by two dominating feelings—fear or love. The power lies in understanding that treating others badly will perpetuate a cycle of unkind actions. Thus, fear is also continued without relief. Not a pleasant prospect.

Scientific research tells us that anger produces a hormone called cortisol. Research also suggests that excessive cortisol from anger kills brain cells. Even complaining about the terrible state of the world impacts individual self-esteem and values. Fortunately, love and kindness generally enhance brain health.

---

59   Shpancer, Action Creates Emotion.

Part IV

Parenting Anger Resourcefully

Drumming in high school band

Chapter 16
Types of Tantrums

Sometime between the first and fourth year, your sweet baby may melt into a puddle of uncontrolled chaos, throwing herself on the floor with her back arched, legs kicking, and fists pounding while she screams nonstop. You may wonder, "What happened to our sweet little child?" Whether considering a baby tantrum or an adolescent one, paying attention to her behaviors will determine how you react. Two major types of tantrums are usually witnessed: manipulative and temperamental. These two major types of tantrums and others will be described below.

A Manipulative Tantrum

A manipulative tantrum is contrived for the purpose of the child getting her way. To have a manipulative tantrum, she must be mature enough to believe she can trick you into giving in to her behavior. Babies do not begin with this kind of tantrum. However, if you give in, even some of the time, she will quickly choose this powerful method of getting what she thinks she wants.

Avoid saying, "I'm sorry."

Keep your voice calm and firm.

If this tantrum is contrived to manipulate you, calmly and quietly say, "You may not have _____. You will be okay without _____ ."

Ignore the child if the behavior continues. Do not negotiate the issue.

If you suspect a child is engaging in a manipulative tantrum, you may decide to move a short distance away. Although the manipulative tantrum is usually less intense than a temperamental one, you still need to be close enough to monitor and make certain the child does not hurt herself or break things.

How do you differentiate a temperament tantrum from a manipulative one? Notice what happens if you move a short distance away. If she picks herself up, follows you to a new location and starts the tantrum again, you will know that she is attempting to pressure you into giving her what she wants. Remind yourself: *She is trying to get her way, and I cannot reward this negative behavior by giving in to her.* The only exception is if you decide you were being unrealistic in the first place. If you know you were being unreasonable, admit your mistake.

Temperament Tantrum

Sometimes a sensitive baby or child has a temper tantrum because she truly loses control. This type of tantrum is called a temperament tantrum. She may have become frustrated with a toy or game. She may be too tired or hungry to cope with disappointment.

A temperament tantrum is not an attempt to manipulate. Once a baby, child, or teen exhibits frantic temperament behavior, she needs help to change her actions. Stay close enough to make certain she does not harm herself. Use your self-talk to mentally remind yourself, *She can't help this behavior and needs my understanding to break out of this tantrum.*

- Stay with her physically and protectively.
- Hold her lovingly.
- Speak softly, calmly, and reassuringly.

At any age, avoid delivering a long speech. Once she calms down, thank her for quieting herself and let the issue go. During a temperament tantrum, your baby or child will respond to your gentle and loving attention. Once you realize that being too hungry, tired, or stressed spins her out of control, you will fully comprehend the importance of avoiding triggering situations.

Gluten or Food Allergy Tantrums

Frequent rages accompanied by problems with diarrhea, gas, bloating, or constipation may be signs of a gluten intolerance and require a physician's assistance. Older children may also exhibit fatigue (sometimes referred to as brain fog), headaches, dizziness, or joint pain. Symptoms such as these coupled with extreme self-harming tantrums warrant seeing a gastroenterologist for celiac disease testing. Additional causes could include intestinal parasites, irritable bowel syndrome, bowel bacteria overgrowth, lactose intolerance, wheat allergy, or sensitivity to food additives. Tantrums due to digestive problems are not contrived for manipulation and require your understanding and patience.

Story: A First-Grade Tantrum

While teaching special education at a public school, I had a cute, quiet, first-grade student whose mother tearfully confided that when her daughter, Rita, was an infant, she had clawed and scratched herself bloody while standing in her crib.

Usually, Rita remained pleasant. However, if something or someone upset her, Rita would abruptly slam her desk to the floor before systematically slinging her books, binders, pens, and papers around the classroom. Knowing Rita would take careful aim at her peers, the other children learned to quickly duck behind their chairs as soon as Rita's desk hit the floor. Within a few seconds, the normally calm classroom would erupt into total chaos. By the time her tantrum reached its peak, her curly dark hair would be flying in different directions.

One morning, after dismissing Rita's special education class, I asked Rita to stay for a few minutes. I asked, "Rita, do you know ahead of time when you are headed for trouble?"

She nodded, indicating that she usually knew when she was about to lose control.

I prodded: "What would you think about asking Mrs. Green if you could come to my room anytime you knew you were starting into a meltdown?"

Rita: "I would like to do that. But Mrs. Green probably won't let me."

It turned out that Mrs. Green, being a sensible woman, enthusiastically embraced any possible way to get Rita out of her room prior to a tantrum.

Rita and I devised a plan. If I was working with other students when she entered the special education room, Rita selected a secluded spot behind some bookcases, where she could begin processing her feelings. I made two promises to her. "Rita, if you do not hurt anyone or break anything, you can show and tell me how you honestly feel. You will not be in trouble, and you will not upset me. If I think you are planning to hurt yourself or someone else, I will have to call someone who can help prevent this."

In addition, I shared, "Rita, if I am working with other children when you come to the room, I will need to continue. I'll get to you as quickly as possible. In the meantime, you have some choices about how to express your feelings." The ideas below describe Rita's options.

She could talk softly into a tape recorder.

She could express her feelings through modeling clay.

Rita could begin by drawing or painting a picture to depict her most recent upsetting event.

Using her own picture to guide her thoughts, Rita could write about her feelings.

The simple actions of calmly leaving her classroom and walking quietly down the hall to my room altered Rita's feelings enough that she could begin to breathe deeply and calm her thoughts. Rita could "break state"[60] or free herself from the negative feelings that were taking over.

Usually, when Rita reached my classroom, she started drawing. Writing often followed her art expression. As soon as the other special education students returned to their regular classes, Rita

---

60   Dills, *Neuro-Linguistic Programming*.

shared her work with me. Knowing she had a safe place to be and someone who would listen provided enough stability that Rita was able to wait until the class I was teaching left the room.

After Rita shared her drawing and her words, I would ask, "Rita, do you want to release those angry, hurtful feelings? Would you like to tear the paper into small pieces and throw the bits of paper into the trash?"

Together, we also discussed possible solutions she might try in her classroom. The words and thoughts Rita shared were not pleasant. However, the freedom to say, "I hate _____ and am furious that I have go back there" allowed her to express her feelings without threatening to harm anyone. Once she felt calm and armed with a plan, Rita would return to her room.

I share this true story from public school to suggest that parents and grandparents can use the same types of options provided for Rita. Some children feel safer talking, others want to model with clay. Most want to draw and then write about their feelings. One of my older students processed grief by running. We are all different. What works well for one may not be the best method of expression for another. It is critical to respect each person's needs.

Conscious Discipline Suggestions About Tantrums

Conscious Discipline, a highly respected program for children, makes similar suggestions for dealing with tantrums. Dr. Becky Bailey states that tantrums are normal up to age three.[61] With children below three, tantrums happen when the child needs something, feels too tired, has become frustrated, or is hungry. Bailey explains that tantrums typically begin between the ages of 15 months and three years. During this time span, a toddler grapples with concepts of dependence and independence. Outbursts generally reflect the child's inner struggle. Parents' responses determine whether tantrums end or continue beyond the toddler years. Problems can occur due to:

- Inconsistency with routines or daily practices
- Expectations that are too demanding
- Rigid strictness
- Overprotectiveness

---

61   Bailey, Handling Temper Tantrums.

- Overindulgence
- Lack of firm limits (boundaries)
- Inability to be realistic about the expectations of the parents
- Distress over divorce, inadequate childcare, death in a family, or depression

When children over three have tantrums, Bailey claims it is usually because tantrums have worked in the past. Parents may have been too permissive.

Some children seem easygoing from the beginning, while others become stressed easily. Either way, a tantrum is a nonverbal communication. Some tantrums occur when a child becomes overwhelmed, too tired, or too hungry. At other times, the tantrum happens because the child has gotten her way by throwing a tantrum.

Helping a child gain greater control has the potential to rewire her brain. Parents can help a child become calm by doing the following:

First, the parent must calm herself or himself.

The parent must also teach the child to be aware of her body. "Your arms are flailing (demonstrate), your face is red, your feet are kicking (demonstrate)."

Next encourage inner awareness by naming what seems to be the emotion being expressed by the body. "Your body seems to be telling me that you are frightened."

Usually, a child will be able to affirm the feeling or make a correction. "No, I am not scared. I am angry that I didn't get what I wanted."

Clearly and firmly, tell the child what you want her to do. Offer two positive choices by saying, "You may choose to sit quietly while I read a story to you, or you may ask Daddy to take a short walk with you. It's up to you."

Conscious Discipline believes there are two ways to respond.[62] Either walk away and leave the child alone or pick the child up and hold her close. Deciding which action to take depends on the child. Some children immediately calm down when held and comforted. Others fight for independence. If you decide to pick the child up, hold her close as you say, "Breathe. You are safe. You can handle this. I am with you. I've got you." In addition, honor the child who

---

62   Bailey, Handling Temper Tantrums.

does not want to be touched. Even the child who prefers to be left alone can be taught to breathe deeply.

Encouraging a child to breathe provides a learning tool for future upsets. As a parent, you will decide which action to take based on your personality, your child's preferences, and previous successes or disappointments with tantrums. Regardless of the type of tantrum, when it ends and all is calm, Conscious Discipline encourages you to avoid giving in to whatever triggered the initial conflict. Even if you must endure another tantrum, do not give in because of a meltdown. Please remember, if tantrums continue beyond age three it is usually because parents give the child what she wants. Once a child decides, *I can get what I want if I make my parent miserable enough*, the tantrums will continue.

Chandler and baby rabbits

Chapter 17
Teach Control of Anger

Avoiding tantrums provides more peace and comfort than ending them. By listening to her words and watching your child's body language, you will often be able to help her avoid a meltdown. Specialists in science and medicine vouch for the benefits of using breath to calm agitation and heighten feelings of calmness. Sharla Kostelyk, author and mother, claims, "Calm-down breathing is a skill that is effective when a child is under stress, struggling with anxiety, or having a meltdown."[63] Kostelyk suggests that at a time when deep breathing would help restore peaceful feelings, babies and children resort to shallow breaths. As soon as babies gain enough receptive understanding of language, demonstrate the steps below.

If your baby has seen or played with balloons, show her a blown-up balloon and compare it to her tummy.

Model as you say, "Use your nose to breathe into your belly balloon as I count to four."

Say, "Put your hand on your tummy."

Model holding your breath for two seconds. Maintain eye contact.

Model and ask your baby to exhale through her mouth. Kostelyk claims this step provides the release needed to prevent or reduce a tantrum.

---

63   Kostelyk, Calm Down Breathing.

Continue to guide your baby to keep her hand on her tummy, breathe in through her nose for four seconds, hold the breath for two seconds, and then release through her mouth.

Story: Teach Breath to Calm

Although Daisy is still calm, Margie can see her toddler heading for a meltdown. Quickly, Margie turns her total attention to the baby.

Margie: "Daisy, look at Mommy. I am putting my hand on my belly. Can you do that?"

As Daisy copies her mom's hand placement Margie touches her own nose and adds, "I'm going to breathe through my nose into my belly balloon while I count to four. Can you do this with me?"

As Daisy copies, Margie adds, "I am going to hold my breath. Can you do this while I count to two?"

Reminding Daisy to watch her, Margie asks, "Is your hand still on your tummy? Thank you." Touching her own mouth, Margie says, "Now I am going to blow the air out through my mouth." After modeling a loud shh sound, Margie asks, "Can you make a shh sound?"

Teach the breathing procedure at a time when your baby feels calm. Repeat the procedure with your baby often enough for her to establish "muscle memory." By practicing during calm times, you increase your chances of preventing a tantrum. According to Kostelyk, even blowing bubbles through a wand will be helpful.[64]

Control Anger by Naming It

Michaeleen Doucleff, PhD, shares the idea that during a calm time, before your child gets angry, you can prepare her to control anger by using the steps on the following page.[65]

---

64   Kostelyk, Calm Down Breathing.
65   Doucleff, Got Anger?

First, give the anger a name such as annoying anger, hurt feelings anger, or raging anger. Another possibility might be to call the various types of anger kitten anger, house cat anger, wild cat anger, or tiger anger.

Next, put anger into a category such as mild, moderate, or serious.

Psychologists use the term "emotional granularity" to communicate the idea that there are many types of anger. When describing emotional granularity, you can create your own names and categories. Doucleff reports that one individual came up with the following examples:[66]

• Exuberant anger when watching sports
• Sad anger after being rejected
• Illogical anger when someone else does something that seems totally silly
• Hurry-up anger toward pokey drivers

One couple created their own name to represent times when more than one issue simultaneously complicated anger. For example, the dog clawed the door to go outside at the same time the baby cried for a fresh diaper.

Analyzing your feelings thoroughly enough to identify your various types of anger can be a useful strategy for parents. Once you name an anger, you can categorize the feeling as "mild anger, moderate anger, severe anger, or ragingly nuts anger."

Consider the possibility of sharing your new insights with children ranging from elementary-school age through the teens. Even some younger children will be able to identify an angry feeling as being a "tiny baby anger, child anger, teen anger, or BIG GIANT ANGER."

Help Children Locate Their Feelings

Ask an upset child, age three or older, to place a hand over her heart before asking her, "Is your heart fast or slow? Are your shoulders tight or relaxed? How does your belly feel right now?" Relaxing the body may help reduce emotional stress and fear. If elementary-school-age children can match body reactions with feelings, they will be taking their first steps toward managing emotions.

_____

66   Doucleff, Got Anger?

Help Children Release Anger Through Art and Writing

When emotions spill over and feelings become too overwhelming for a breath exercise or for naming, invite a pre-writing child to draw what she feels. Depending on the age of the child, the outcome may resemble scribbling more than an actual drawing. Regardless, following the steps below will help the child defuse negative feelings.

Begin by inviting the child to show you how she feels through art. Supply large blank paper and markers or crayons. Allow her the freedom to determine what to draw without your suggestions. Even more important, *always avoid asking*, "What is this?"

When the child finishes, say, "Tell me about your art." This phrase is important. Accept whatever she says, even if she changes the description in a short time.

Next, ask an action question such as, "What is happening?" You may extend by asking, "What is she doing? How does she feel? What does she want?"

Continue the child's thinking by encouraging her to share additional information such as, "How do you feel about this? What makes you feel angry? Does anything make you feel sad or frightened?"

Ask, "What would you like to have happen? Would that help you feel better?"

If a child knows how to write, invite her to add a written explanation about her art. Tell the child, "Let it all out. Do not worry about spelling or how your letters look. You may want to write a letter. However, if your art or writing will hurt someone else, please do not share with that person."

When the child finishes, ask, "Would you be willing to read your story aloud or talk to me about your art or writing?" If she shares her work with you, say, "Thank you." Never insist that a child share.

After the child reads her written work to you, say, "It seems like you are really feeling _____. Do you want to tell me more about this?"

Ask, "Would you like to let go of these yucky feelings? If so, you can tear up the art and the writing." If the child wants to keep her finished work, allow her to do so.

Say, "As you tear up your art or your writing, imagine that all those angry feelings are being released into the air where they can be recycled in positive ways. Letting your feelings go will help you feel better."

Once the work has been torn into small pieces, ask, "Would you like to throw these pieces of paper into the trash?" If the situation is safe, you can even invite her to burn her work.

Art, talking, writing, and reading can be integrated or used separately. The purpose of these expressive activities will be to release feelings before they erupt into inappropriate behaviors. Nothing more needs to be done. If you encourage an angry or upset child to express negative feelings, you must accept the message as well as the delivery. In addition, accept her words, spelling, pictures, and emotions. Unless you get permission from the child, protect her privacy. This level of sharing must be viewed as personal and private.

Stress Balls, Exercising, Walking, or Running

Not only can stress balls relieve tension, but squeezing exercises also develop strength in hands, fingers, wrists, and forearms. Balls with different levels of resistance can be provided to the child.

During stressful situations, slow walks in nature can bring peaceful release. Some people benefit more from creating a flow of endorphins by running. Endorphins, produced by the pituitary gland and the central nervous system, increase feelings of pleasure and well-being. Additional ways to release endorphins include eating dark chocolate, creating music or art, dancing, getting acupuncture, and laughing.

De-Escalate Big Anger

A push/pull activity provides a method to help your child release anger. As you stand and face your child, ask her to place both of her palms against your hands with fingers pointing toward the ceiling. Next, you and your child will use your palms to push against one another as both of you exhale loudly through your mouths.

Finally, clasp hands and pull one another while inhaling deeply. Once your child understands how to do the activity, increase the intensity of the pushing and pulling. You will, of course, never use your greater strength to overwhelm your child.

Once your child demonstrates understanding, you can teach her to push and pull the knob on a closed door. By encouraging deep breathing while pushing and pulling, you will provide your child with a way to release intense feelings as she grows older.

Story: Use a Push/Pull Activity

Dad: "I can tell that you feel very angry right now. Would you be willing to do an activity with me that may help you feel better?"

Child: "I guess so. What do you want me to do?"

Dad: "First, let's stand up and face each other."

After they both stand, Dad continues: "Now, we will both put our hands up with our fingers pointing to the sky. Our palms will touch." While explaining, Dad demonstrates.

Dad: "As our palms touch, we will both exhale and push against each other. Let's try it with a gentle push to make sure we both understand."

After the dad and child press their palms together, Dad continues, "That worked well. This time, instead of pushing, we will inhale as much as we can as we hold hands and pull one another. Do you want to try it first?"

Child: "I'm ready to give this a try."

Promote Calmness with Quiet Times

Time-outs can be punitive. Taking time to breathe and restore calmness can become a lifelong skill. Parents can use calm times to redirect and soothe a baby or child. Recently, as we were finishing dinner with our grandson's family, we realized that our great-granddaughter, Daisy, was heading for a meltdown. My first thought was to get something interesting and redirect her attention. While I was searching for a distraction, our grandson headed upstairs, carrying his unhappy toddler. At the top of the stairs, Lane turned to me and said, "Grandma, we are not up here to play. Daisy and I need a quiet time for a few minutes."

Instantly, I understood his purpose. The young dad and his baby girl slipped into an empty room and shut the door. Quiet talking quickly replaced tears. Within minutes, the two opened the door, ready to calmly join the family. The next day, I asked, "What did you do during your quiet time? What did you say?"

Lane replied, "I showed her a bookend shaped like a goose's head, and we looked at some pictures on the shelf." By redirecting Daisy's attention, her dad was able to alter her negative feeling to a positive one. The combination of experiencing a calm time with her dad and redirecting her attention to items of interest improved Daisy's feelings and avoided an upset.

Adult-Child Space for Conflict Resolution

Instead of sending a child to sit in time-out alone, consider the benefits of sharing a quiet, reflective experience with your child. Say, "You seem to be getting upset. Let's go someplace quiet together." Often, a change of location is all that is needed to break out of a negative emotional place. Once your child has mastered expressive oral language well enough to articulate clearly, a quiet conversation based on the following questions from Conflict Resolution may be helpful.

- "What do you want?"
- "Why is this important to you?"

Restate what the child said for clarity. The purpose of this important step is to make certain you understand what your child wants. For example, "You just told me this is important to you because _____. Did I understand correctly?"

Work together to find a solution by asking, "How can we solve this? What can I do to help? What can others do? Are you willing to . . .?"

There may be times when new behaviors or words are rehearsed together. You can say, "I understand that you are upset about sharing your book with your brother. We can begin at the beginning and act out what we might do to find a solution."

Story: Use Conflict Resolution

Dad: "I can tell by the way you are treating your brother that you feel upset. Please tell me what you want."

Child: "I want the book that my brother is pretending to read."

Dad: "Why is that book so important to you?"

Child: "I need that book for my homework."

Dad will add the clarifying step below to be certain he understands exactly what his child needs.

Dad: "You are telling me you really want that book. You feel upset because you need the book to get your homework done. You want your brother to give the book to you now. Am I understanding correctly?"

Child: "Right."

Dad: "Let's work out a way so that you can get what you need and your brother can get what he wants. We want to find a win-win solution."

Child: "How can we do that?"

Dad: "How about we choose a different book for your little brother? Would you be willing to try trading books with him?"

Child: "I am willing to try. But, Dad, if this doesn't work, will you play with him so I can use the book to finish my assignment?"

Dad: "Good thinking. Thanks for helping me solve this problem."

Calm Corner or Cool-Down Space

While helping me with some revisions, John S. Williams, editor and revisionist for WriteByNight, told me his ideas about establishing a space for his children to cool down. He refers to the area as the Calm Corner. In the Calm Corner, the child will find the following items:

- A bean bag chair
- A small rug
- Two posters, one with facial expressions representing anger, sadness, fear, or other emotions, and a second showing ideas for self-calming
- A small bin with a notebook and writing utensils
- A stress ball
- A child-size yoga mat
- Two stuffed animals to cuddle for comfort
- A jigsaw puzzle
- Plain paper and crayons or markers
- Small bookcases placed to provide privacy.

Ana resting at a soccer game

Chapter 18
Hazards of Punishments

Any time you communicate with babies or children, you have everything to gain from an attitude of "Let's grow and learn together." Conversely, you have everything to lose from thinking, "It's them against me." An attitude of conflict between you and your child often leads to punishments. Punishments delivered while angry tend to be painful.

Proponents of Conscious Discipline insist that "punishments don't work."[67] If punishing others worked, why would the same kids be the ones frequently in trouble? Why are the return rates for prisons so terrible? Here are some reasons why leaders in Conscious Discipline believe punishment fails.

Punishments come from making judgments rather than asking, "Why is this child behaving this way? What is the fear driving this behavior? How can we comfort her and solve this problem?"

Punishments rarely ask a child to think about her actions or to take responsibility for them. Without careful thought, a learning opportunity may be lost. Consider the negative example of the father who yells, "Stop crying or I'll give you something to cry about." Nothing in this dad's warning leads the child to consider her mistake or set a personal goal for improvement. The lesson remembered by the child in later years will be the unreasonable and uncaring attitude of an angry parent.

---

67   Bailey, Why Conscious Discipline.

- When we punish, we do not encourage children to consider managing their own feelings.
- Punishments do not teach coping skills.
- Punishments do not tend to motivate those being punished to improve.
- Punishments build on intimidation.

Story: Teach Instead of Punish

When Jim jumped into the pool, he realized that the robot that cleaned the pool was going to be in his way.

Jim: "I'm going to pull the robot out of the pool."

Suddenly the door jerked open, and an angry grandpa stepped out.

Grandpa: "Stop pulling that cord. You're going to break the machine."

Jim's dad: "Grandpa, tell him what you want him to do. Teach him. He's a smart kid. He can learn."

Immediately the grandpa complied. Hopefully, the young boy learned what to do and added a new skill to his collection of assets. Hopefully, with time, the punishing feeling of being yelled at will be replaced by the intrinsic value of gaining a new level of competence.

Yelling typically does not appear logical. Often, a child decides that a parent or grandparent is mean. Unresolved childhood memories of being treated unfairly can erupt into rage in later life.

Abuse or neglect that takes place prior to language and conscious memory may cause even more substantial damage throughout a lifetime. A consequence, if used well, demonstrates a relationship between an action and a result. A child generally accepts an outcome if it seems fair.

Unfortunately, resentments often manifest as additional negative behaviors. In an adversarial position, a parent may initially exert control and win the small battle, but in the bigger picture, the offending adult probably will not feel successful. Children are faster, more energetic, and in many cases more intelligent than the adults in their lives. Following, you will find examples of behaviors, commonly used punishments, and natural or logical consequences for toddlers.

Toddler Behavior	Punishment	Consequences Can Be Natural or Logical
A toddler bites her dad while playing.	Dad bites her back or slaps her hand. Without understanding her dad's actions, the toddler feels frightened and unloved. Her dad, whose job is to teach and protect her, has become unsafe in her eyes.	As a natural consequence, Dad immediately says, "Ouch. That really hurt," as he pulls the toddler away from his body. As a logical consequence, Dad may say, "Look at the marks your teeth made. I'm not going to play until the marks stop hurting." As Dad puts the toddler down, he adds, "We can play later."
A toddler insists on eating sand, Play-Doh, and paint.	A parent yells at the toddler until the baby cries. To a toddler, yelling feels like withdrawal of love.	Mom says, "You ate the Play-Doh. That is so sad. We will need to put the Play-Doh away until another time. Tomorrow, we will try again." Removing Play-Doh seems logical to the mother and to the toddler.
A toddler refuses to share a toy at day care.	The day care attendant makes the toddler stop playing and forces her to sit alone on a bench until the class goes inside. The toddler does not understand why she is not allowed to play. She sobs with sadness and frustration.	The attendant quietly removes the toy while redirecting the attention of both children to two new toys. The attendant solves the problem.

On the chart below, you can compare punishments for preschool-age and early elementary-school-age children with natural or logical consequences.

Elementary-School-Age Behavior	Punishment	Consequences Can Be Natural or Logical
Bob yells rude words in Tom's face.	Bob's teacher gets in Bob's face and yells at him. What did Bob and Tom learn? Both boys learned that if you are big enough, you can yell at others.	As a natural consequence, Tom refuses to play with Bob. As a logical consequence, the teacher decides the boys will not play together the rest of the day.
Juan, a second-grader, leaves his sweater at home on a cool day.	When Juan gets home, his parents make him sit in time-out for 20 minutes. As a result, Juan misses his favorite TV show.	Without his sweater, Juan feels uncomfortable during recess. Feeling too cold is a natural consequence. Mom will be tempted to deliver the sweater. If she rescues him, what will Juan learn? (He will decide that Mom will always take care of him. Think about the ramifications of this in a few years.) Logically, Juan will write a note to remind himself about his sweater, or he will place the sweater next to his books for school.
Betty, a first-grader, rolls her eyes and sighs loudly while talking to her mom.	Betty loses her allowance for that week. Betty does not see a connection between her allowance and her rude behavior. Her anger increases.	As a natural consequence, Mom silently walks away. As a logical consequence, Mom says, "I am not willing to talk to people who are rude to me. We can try again later." Another logical consequence might be for Betty to work with Mom to list three alternatives that will be courteous ways to show disagreement.

While natural or logical consequences seek to avoid anger, the delivery can make a difference. Consider the child's conclusion if delivery of the consequence sounds factual and calm, as opposed to being announced through clenched teeth with an angry face. Keep in mind that the goal is to learn and grow together.

What About Spanking? You Know, "Spare the Rod and Spoil the Child"

Two types of parents exist. Both types are basically good people who want to parent well and guide their children to become responsible adults. The types described below go beyond Christianity and can be applied to any religion or to those with no religion at all. One type, grounded in a stricter philosophy often resembling the Old Testament, believes the father's job includes governing the behaviors of his wife as well as their children. Just as God often seems harsh in the Old Testament, the father maintains a strict environment. This type of parent believes that allowing his wife or children to "get away" with anything will lead to their corruption. Parents who believe punishment must be used to teach also assume that the wife and children will not learn without pain. This attitude sometimes opens the door to emotional and physical abuse.

A second type of parent, who believes nurturing and teaching take priority, adheres more closely to the philosophy expressed in the New Testament teachings of Jesus, as well as the words of Buddha. Love and security come first. These parents teach by modeling integrity and honesty. The mother and father share equal responsibility for guiding their children. Although misbehaviors are always met with consequences that have the potential to teach, neither parent seeks to make a child suffer.

Between the two philosophies, arguments abound over whether to spank. As you think about potential outcomes from spanking, consider the following:

Good parents and grandparents teach more by demonstrating desired behaviors than by talking or punishing. If you control through coercion, the fear of punishment settles into your child's mind as resentment and anger. Your child will instinctively do as she sees you do. Your words may say, "We don't hit people," or "People are not for hitting." However, if you hit, the action suggests that hitting others works if you are bigger, stronger, and have more power.

Intelligent parents have the capacity to link consequences that are logical to a child's behavior. Hitting requires minimal thought.

If a moment of stress finds you unable to think logically, ask for time to determine an appropriate response. Better to wait than to make a harsh decision out of frustration.

I believe that only parents who are unhealthy ever seek to harm a baby or child. The problem arises when generation after generation perpetuate cruelty on family members, which then becomes a way of life. Only a parent who has been terribly damaged by his or her own upbringing can possibly believe this is a good idea.

True Story: Tragic Losses

I recall a tragic story of a father who threw his crying infant against a wall. Police discovered a hole behind a poster the same size as the infant's head. It is conceivable that a very ill father thought he was teaching his infant son a lesson. The real-life consequences of this father's action were the death of an infant and life in prison on a murder charge for the father.

A healthy parent will never believe that creating scars or brain damage can be good for guiding behavior. It is unfortunate that even with the intention of spanking moderately, anger can sometimes cloud rational thinking. It will be safer to never put that possibility into play. Hitting tends to increase the desire to hit. I have read that within each one of us is the capacity to behave like the most heinous criminal, while at the same time, each of us has the capacity to love like Mother Teresa. Something savage relishes the power of taking total control.

Intrinsic Values

Some parents seek to be strict but do not want to be cruel. I too seek firm standards for appropriate family behaviors. The word "firm" seems more accurate than the word "strict." Sample guidelines might include:

- Telling the truth
- Admitting mistakes
- Repairing the damage

- Attempting to understand what caused the mistake
- Apologizing and repairing damages
- Speaking courteously
- Mediating disagreements
- Finding solutions
- Living with integrity
- Seeking justice for all human beings
- Giving and receiving love
- Remembering that every individual is precious

Standards and Expectations

Children thrive with routines and external expectations regarding health. Although not every family will be willing or able to maintain all the standards listed below, we can embrace these ideas as values most parents seek to provide. Family values related to health include the following:

- We eat food that provides the nutrients needed to maintain strong bodies.
- Personal cleanliness is important. We take regular baths or showers, shampoo our hair, brush our teeth, and wear clean clothes.
- We encourage learning and support getting a good education.
- We live in a comfortable, well-organized home.
- We work together to keep our home clean.
- We sleep in beds with clean sheets.
- Our yard is uncluttered and safe.
- Our cars are maintained for safety.
- We value nature and take care of plants and animals.
- We recognize the difference between needs and wants.

Thinking about things we want is part of life. Although no one can expect to get all their wants met, everyone should get their needs satisfied. Expecting to get all we want could easily contribute to being spoiled or developing feelings of entitlement.

Differences Between Consequences and Punishments

Consequences, sometimes called "corrections," that are either natural or logical always connect the problem behavior with an outcome. Although many people use the word "correction" for consequence, both words seek to demonstrate cause and effect. Consequences/corrections are not designed to make a child miserable. In fact, some of the best consequences with the longest-term results are pleasant. Consequences require thinking and logic on the part of parents and grandparents. Punishments are designed to make a kid suffer (at least a little). No effort is made to meaningfully connect offensive behavior to a punishment. Little or no thought is needed. For that reason, children usually gain nothing other than resentment.

Offensive Behavior	Natural Consequence	Logical Consequence	Punishment provides little or no connection to the behavior
A two-year-old toddler hit the family dog.	The dog was allowed to take a nap in a safe place away from the child.	The child needed to repair damage done to the dog. She could either take him on a walk or give the dog a snack. Although the child enjoyed both activities, the point was to help the dog feel better. It was not necessary for the child to suffer to receive the lesson about kindness.	Parents scolded the child using words such as "mean," "bad," and "stupid." Using derogatory words created a negative self-image. Prolonged guilt damaged the child.
A child failed to brush her teeth before bedtime Monday evening.	Cavities were found at the next dental visit.	All candy was removed. (Rationale: If we can't count on you to brush, we fear there will be too much build-up of sugar).	The child was not allowed to watch a movie with the family on Saturday night. What was the problem with this? The teeth were not brushed on Monday, so a punishment on Saturday came too late for the child to recall the reason for missing the movie. In addition, there was no connection between teeth and a movie.

A five-year-old boy rode his bicycle across the street.	The boy put his bike away for the rest of the evening.	The following day, his parents asked the boy to wait until either his mom or his dad could monitor his bike riding. In a short time, the child regained their trust.	The dad spanked the child. Years later, a grown man continued to complain about how unfair his dad was. Some actions stick in a grown child's memory.

Questionable Strictness

Strictness must be reconsidered when it results in the following types of outcomes:

A father told his son that unless the boy played rough sports, he was a sissy. His father's disapproval became so painful that even before leaving elementary school, the boy was sniffing glue and investigating additional methods of escaping feelings of rejection.

A child taught to strictly obey house rules without question fails to develop higher-level critical thinking. Without critical thinking, what do we have? Not much meaningful thought is what we have.

An almost religious obedience to laws, even when the laws are cruel to some groups, destroys the courage to take compassionate actions. Some city, state, and federal laws need to be challenged.

A curious toddler stopped wanting to learn after being slapped for interrupting.

Emotional Abuse

Strictness (firmness) can be applied with compassion or with a rigidity that damages the heart, mind, and soul. If you walk a path built on being strict, please walk gently and talk carefully lest you destroy the very goals you seek to accomplish. Substituting the word "firm" may shift rigid thinking toward compassion.

Keep in mind that emotional abuse has the potential to be even more damaging than physical battering. Emotional abuse includes the parental behaviors on the next page.

- Fighting through the night as children listen
- Allowing infants to cry without feeding or changing them
- Slapping or hitting others while children watch
- Getting drunk or high on drugs
- Keeping children home for the convenience of parents
- Failing to protect children from abuse by other family members or friends
- Yelling at others while children listen
- Yelling at children

Lies Are Abusive

Adults confuse children by twisting words taken out of context, lying through omissions, denying truth, or refusing to answer questions. Parents who use these tricks of deceit do so in spite of knowing they are causing emotional harm. Consider the strange examples below.

Saying to a healthy child, "You look sick. I think something is wrong with you. You need to see a doctor." The child silently wonders, *Am I sick? I feel great.*

Complaining to a child wearing clean clothes after her bath, "You smell bad." This statement may cause the child to silently ask, *What's wrong with me? I just took a bath and put on clean clothes.*

Saying, "You thanked me, but what you really intended was to hurt me. You are being passive aggressive." The child feels guilty even though the accusation is incorrect.

Insisting, "I never said that to you." This creates doubt about the child's sanity as she thinks, *Wait! I know I heard him say those exact words. Am I losing it?*

Accusing, "You did not tell me you were going to your friend's house." The child feels confused when she remembers a conversation about going to see her friend.

Insisting, "When you say you love me, I do not believe you do. I do not feel loved by you." Hearing this, the child (who is the victim) begins to feel guilty for not showing love correctly.

Saying, "I don't know if I love you or not. I'm not sure I know what the word means."

Chapter 19
Toxic Parents

Whether at the time of their baby's birth or soon after, most parents experience a release of oxytocin, a hormone and neurotransmitter produced in the hypothalamus that triggers feelings of love. Some parents report that the moment they look into the eyes of their newborn infant, a burst of love floods their emotions. Many parents who adopt a child report experiencing the same loving attachment when meeting the child for the first time. Although a burst of amazing love often fails to manifest at the time of birth or adoption, most parents quickly become aware of loving and protective feelings toward their new baby.

A few parents seem incapable of loving a baby or a young child. The term "toxic parents" fits individuals who either lack the capacity to provide loving care, or who do not care enough to improve. The four examples of unhealthy parental behavior described below strongly impact and damage babies and older children into adulthood.

Shaming a child of any age creates damage. Shaming might look like a parent's frowning face and angry voice. Children also feel shamed when a parent talks negatively about the child in front of others. A mother who tells friends, "Ashley is failing math because she refuses to study" embarrasses and shames her daughter. The author of *Four Examples of Toxic Parents and How to Fix Them* suggests that parents who catch themselves shaming should teach themselves to counter negative talk by repeatedly saying, "Yes!" to themselves while smiling.[68] Even increasing the number of times a parent smiles may make a significant difference.

Toxic parents fail to encourage a child to express feelings and ideas. Refusal to pay attention to a crying baby clearly fails to encourage. Saying, "I wasn't asking for your input" sends a message of unacceptability to a child. Even conversations with infants should not be one-sided. As infants begin to babble, parents can pause to listen. When the babbling ceases, the adult can say, "Tell me more." As babies grow into toddlers and young children, listening to their oral expressions becomes even more important. Failure to listen and allow a child to express her feelings inhibits the development of her self-worth and personal value. When a parent decides to stop talking and to listen patiently to a child's communication, the effort suggests a loving acceptance.

Sarcasm falls into the category of unhealthy parenting. Often, sarcasm attempts to be funny but falls short because the remark feels like a put-down to the child. There is no amusement if a parent says, "You run like a streak of lightning" to a child who runs slowly. Even words the baby cannot understand, when uttered harshly, sink in at some level of a baby's consciousness. Mocking results in the same kind of self-rejection or destruction of personal value. Authors of an article about sarcasm claim such remarks are rooted in the parent's own insecurity. Parents can decide to replace sarcasm with kindness: "You seem to be having a hard time with your jacket. Would you like a little help getting the zipper started?"

Toxic parents tend to communicate with gruff voices, angry looks, rough behavior, and negative words. Children who have heard too much negativity often press their hands over their ears or go to their rooms and put a pillow over their heads. Babies respond by crying for no obvious reason.

Without realizing it, parents set a tone with their emotions, words, and actions. When parents think negative thoughts, they tend to say hateful words. Once toxic parents understand the damage they cause, they can decide to pay attention to their own thoughts and to make deliberate changes.

Many parents who learn to listen for their unhealthy words and behaviors can choose to change their actions and communication methods. Many will benefit from individual and/or group therapy. Asking physicians, social workers, and school counselors for appropriate reading material may be beneficial. Most

---

68   Butler, Four Examples of Toxic Parents.

of all, unhealthy parents can learn by carefully observing and listening to parents they admire.

Abusive parents usually grew up being abused as children. When others realize that an abusive adult is probably copying behaviors experienced during childhood, the insight often provides an avenue for understanding. However, the safety of babies, children, and even teens must take priority. A parent who is incapable of gaining insight or who lacks the courage to self-assess and change will need to lose custody of their children and possibly even visitation rights.

An Initial Disconnection Differs from Failure to Ultimately Bond

Although feeling disconnected from a newborn is normal and occurs frequently, parents who do not soon begin to relate to their babies can obtain help from hospitals, medical professionals, counselors, schools, churches, and community centers.

If a parent's love does not develop over time, grandparents, friends, day care workers, and ministers must get involved. In cases of neglect or abuse, staying quiet cannot be an option. In fact, staying quiet is not even legally acceptable. Act by gently confronting parents, locating a therapist, modeling appropriate behaviors, suggesting specific articles to read, recommending classes to take, and providing breaks for the parents.

Interventions can be powerful but usually require guidance from someone trained to lead the procedure. The basic idea of an intervention is for family, friends, and those who love the unhealthy couple to meet with the parents in order to provide observed, factual feedback and first-person accounts of unacceptable behaviors or words. A trained leader will ask questions to guide the sharing.

Story: Child Abuse

Results of abuse can often be observed. Connecting a bruise to parental abuse requires maturity as well as strength. The first year I taught, I believed that abused children came from ramshackle homes, ate unhealthy foods, dressed inappropriately, and came to school dirty.

In my first-grade class of 36 children who had not attended preschool or kindergarten, I had a lovely little girl who never gave me any problems. Gloria skipped into the classroom each day with her shiny, waist-long black hair swinging from hair clips and bows. Each day she arrived dressed beautifully and was always clothed appropriately for the weather. As I noticed what children brought to school for lunch, I was pleased at the healthy assortment Gloria's mother sent. The mother presented herself well and seemed interested in her daughter's education.

One morning, Gloria came to me and asked, "Do you have any medicine for my hands?"

As Gloria opened her small hands, I saw quarter-inch-wide raw spots on both palms. Concerned, I sent Gloria to the school nurse, who bandaged her hands after doctoring the places where the skin had been broken. The nurse said nothing.

I asked, "Gloria, how did you hurt your hands?"

Gloria: "Oh, a bully hit me with a ruler. He lives on my street. He was mean to me."

That sounded strange to me, but I weighed the bully story against Gloria's good lunches, clean hair, and more than adequate clothing. Much later, I learned that when Gloria's mom saw the bandages and medicine, she threatened Gloria with a beating if she ever let the school know about her abuse at home again.

Time passed. Early one morning, the bus driver left his bus running outside our school while he walked in to talk to the principal. The big, burly bus driver leaned on the principal's desk as he said, "I've been driving Gloria to school all year. Usually, she gets on the bus happy and excited. This morning was different. She climbed on crying." He straightened up as he continued, "Gloria kept crying, so when we got to your school, I walked back to check on her. As I placed my hand on her back, she yelled. I thought her back felt squishy. When I unbuttoned the top button, I saw blood. I've left her with your school nurse." The outcome was that Gloria was removed from the parents and placed in a home for abused and neglected children.

210

After many decades, I still grieve when I think of this child who sat in my classroom unattended. Yes, I was young. Most certainly my life had been sheltered. Identifying abuse was foreign to me. I should have recognized it. When other neglected and abused children came through my life after Gloria, I did my best to be aware and alert enough to make referrals to Child Protective Services.

Identify Signs of Neglect

Neglect may be harder to identify than abuse. Although not as dramatic as physical abuse, neglect can be equally damaging. Even parents who care about their children can fail them due to the parent's depression, stress, illness, alcohol or drug use, or lack of resources. Below are some signs of neglect.

- Regression in babies or children may offer important clues. Regression refers to times when babies or children use less-mature behaviors than they have demonstrated earlier. Examples include baby talk, temper tantrums, or loss of skills such as the ability to dress herself.
- An infant may become clingy or needy and may cry more.
- Infants lacking care sometime fail to reach standard milestones.
- Older children who are much too young to do so sometimes become responsible for younger siblings.
- Children may be dressed inappropriately for the weather conditions. For example, a child may wear shorts and sandals in the winter.
- Educational abuse occurs when children frequently arrive late or miss school.
- In the worst cases, children become malnourished. They may steal or beg for food from peers or cafeteria workers.
- Parents leave children alone, locked in parked cars. Being left in hot cars has caused heat stroke and death.
- Frequent illnesses or injuries may be signs of abuse or neglect.
- Some parents withhold food to punish children.
- Sometimes, children display anxiety disorders and depression after experiencing abuse or neglect.
- Obesity often occurs when children fail to eat nutritious diets and gorge on junk food.
- Cruelty to peers often suggests that abuse or neglect has been either experienced or witnessed.
- Children who use inappropriate sexual terms or who demonstrate sexual behaviors may be suffering from molestation.

Story: A Neglected Infant

Many years ago, a lawyer called my husband and said, "I've been working with a young couple at the army base. Before the couple married, the woman got pregnant by another soldier. The young private thought he would be able to accept another man's baby. It turned out that he could not. I am afraid the baby may not last another day. Would you please take him until I can find foster parents?"

Later that same day, the lawyer brought the infant to our home. Before giving her baby away, the teen mother had put every single item of baby clothing she owned on his emaciated body. As I peeled the layers away, I began sobbing. Although older than my own baby, the little guy made my baby girl look enormous. His limbs amounted to skin stretched over tiny bones. Puss and mucus drained from his eyes. A raw, inflamed rash covered his thighs and genitals, and puss drained from his penis. Although most of his head had a rounded look, one side had become totally flat. Through my tears, I tried to comfort the baby boy. "Your little eyes must be bothering you. We will take you to the doctor to get some medicine. We will get help for you."

As soon as I bathed and dressed the baby, we took him to our pediatrician. Examining the baby, our doctor speculated that the boy had probably turned his head toward sounds from an adjoining room. After turning his head and crying for weeks, the bones in the baby's head had flattened. Untreated diaper rash had advanced into an infection that not only covered his genitals but had crawled up his penis to infect internal organs.

When the doctor gave the little guy a shot, the baby barely whimpered. The doctor explained, "This baby has cried without relief so many times that he has given up. In his short life, no matter how much he cried, no one came to help."

Foster parents accepted the baby within a few days. We moved to another city. Over the years, I have wondered if a baby who gives up during his first six or eight weeks of life will ever trust anyone. Our pediatrician assured me that the baby's head would eventually round out and that the infections in his eyes and penis would heal. Knowing the impact of trauma on early brain and psychological development, I assumed he had been emotionally damaged. Too young to retain memories for talk therapy, I imagine he has struggled with the lasting emotional impact of neglect.

I have also wondered about the teenage couple who first neglected and then gave their baby away. Any individual who can listen to an infant cry in distress without responding needs emotional assistance.

As awkward and even painful as it will be, if you suspect a parent simply cannot or will not rise to a child's needs, you must confront the situation. Changes must be made quickly. Later may be too late. Unfortunately, in many cases, the child must be removed from the parents.

Part V

Parenting Challenges

Families and technology

Chapter 20
Technology Challenges: A Brave New World

Many experts fear that babies, teens, and adults spend too much time passively engaged with technology. Devices surround us. On one hand, we realize that our children need to gain technical competency to prepare for their present and future realities. In fact, our children who are growing up using technology are considered native speakers of the tech language and skills. Grandparents usually find mastering technology to be challenging. We who are not natives must now tread on unfamiliar territory. We learn what we can and often ask our grandkids to provide help and guidance.

Yet even though we understand the importance of technology for the younger generation, questions come up. An organization called First Focus on Children posted an article asserting that many children and teens are being negatively impacted cognitively, socially, and emotionally by too much technology.[69]

When considering appropriate limits for technology, you will be wise to remember that your words count far less than your actions. If you bring cell phones or devices to the dinner table and ignore your family, you are modeling an action you do not want children to copy. I realize there are emergency situations. Anytime you model what you do *not* want, please consider explaining the reason. It is preferable to leave the phone and other devices turned off and in another room. Concerns such as the ones listed below are legitimate for the health and well-being of all of us who use computers.

---

69   Todres and Wright, A Healthy Digital Environment.

Concerns with Technology

In some cases, even babies spend hours each day poking on devices. How can they possibly develop in healthy ways?

If you begin to set limits at an early age, the resistance will not be as terrifying as it will become later. Waiting for a better time to set limits on technology will probably result in even more intensely passionate and angry scenes. Setting limits from the beginning may create a smoother path for future negotiations.

It seems reasonable for you to select a few quality programs for your young child. An occasional movie can be a good idea, especially if you view the movie with the child. Viewing together may result in a valuable opportunity to answer questions and to discuss the movie afterward.

You can also say, "You may use your device for _____ (amount of time). After that, take a break and enjoy some active play." When the time for being on a device ends, muster your strength to get your child moving and doing.

If your child refuses to stop using her device when the time ends, you need to establish a consequence. A logical consequence might be, "You spent so much time on your device today that your allotted time for tomorrow is now gone. I will keep your device until the following day."

When possible and safe, most growing children benefit from exploring, running, climbing, and moving. Although being outside offers the important benefits of noticing nature, exploring science, and having fun with animals, children can also move and play active games inside.

One summer, while staying with grandsons during a time when their parents were out of town, I rearranged the living room furniture to create climbing, crawling spaces. With a little imagination, you too will invent ways for your children to move their bodies, even if going outdoors is not an option.

Older children often seem glued to technology. Are they building strong bones and muscles? What about social skills? Is any time being set aside for family activities or conversations?

Hopefully, when parents establish limits by age two, the process of discerning and selecting will feel more natural as your child matures. Even if your child is long past the age for an early start (as recommended above), you must work with your child to set priorities and to establish limits. Claim your strength by saying, "I'm not willing for you to sit passively with your computer all day. I'm not willing to watch your muscles waste away and your creativity atrophy." Below, you will find a tentative plan to consider when working with an older child.

Tentative Plan
Begin by asking your child to create a list of her favorite technology programs or apps.

Next, create two written lists. On one list, write the values you want your family to promote. On list two, record potentially damaging impressions. For example, consider whether scenes with excessive violence will possibly plant thoughts or fears that you do not want your child to entertain. This list could possibly include cruelty to animals or humans, sexuality, curse words, or even inclinations toward disloyalty to the country or to your personal values.

Together, share lists of values and concerns with your child.

Armed with your child's names of favorite programs along with your lists, analyze her selections for quality, potential lessons, and establishment of values. If your child is mature enough, analyze each of her programs together.

With your child, agree on the amount of time she will spend passively with devices. You may even consider the amount of time she can spend on questionable programs. For example, you may decide to allow one violent show a week.

When possible, seek technology that teaches and inspires values.

It is your responsibility to determine whether programs or apps threaten healthy emotional development. There will be situations when a firm "no" is the only sensible response.

To avoid the unpleasant task of policing your child, stress the importance of trusting one another. An agreement to turn devices off after an agreed amount of time or at a specific time of day may establish a reasonable guideline. Build trust by modeling your own dependability.

Insist on physical movement every day. Inspire movement by joining your family in outdoor activities such as taking walks or riding bikes. Indoor activities can include activities such as target practice with balls and trash cans, a stationary bicycle, an egg and spoon race, yoga, or dancing. Your example will be more relevant than your words.

You have the hard task of insisting that your child engage in physical activity, time outdoors, and exercises that build grit and stamina every single day. No parent wants to see their children grow up with weak, undeveloped bodies, minds, or social skills.

Common Courtesy Does Not Go Out of Style

What about basic courtesy? Consider a different situation regarding technology. Grandparents yearn for quality time with their grandchildren. Imagine their frustration when a grandchild spends the entire visit glued to her phone or iPad. Not only does this deprive the child or teen of gaining potentially insightful ideas from her grandparents, but she is also treating them with blatant rudeness. A conversation prior to the visit may be helpful. Consider the conversation below.

Story: Courteous Behavior to Grandparents

A mother could not help but notice that during a previous visit with her parents, her child refused to look at or talk to the grandparents. Instead of providing even the most cursory replies to questions, her child's eyes and attention remained locked onto her small iPhone. Hoping to prevent a repeat performance, the mother set aside time to talk with her child.

Mom: "The last time we were with your grandparents, you scarcely paid any attention to them. I imagine they felt disappointed by your lack of interest. I would like for us to have a plan that will take care of your wants as well as your grandparents' needs."

Child: "They are old. They don't understand my life at all. I think they are boring."

Mom: "Yes, they are old. It is true that they struggle to understand your life. That does not mean they are not interested in you. I think they want to know about your friends, school, band, and your job."

Child: "I don't want to sit there bored the entire time."

Mom: "I understand. I know they do not want you to be bored either. How can we solve this?"

Child: "Maybe we stop going?"

Mom: "Refusing to see them is not reasonable. Let's look for a way that you can amuse yourself some of the time and show kindness and courtesy at other times. What would be a logical amount of time for you to escape to your phone?"

Child: "Maybe you could carry the conversation for about 30 minutes while I am on my phone. After half an hour, I'll put my phone down and talk to the old folks."

Mom: "That sounds like a good plan. The exception will be if the grandparents ask you a direct question. I expect you to respond with basic courtesy. Are you willing to do this?"

Child: "As long as you can take over from time to time, I will agree to stop using my phone some of the time. I will also look at my grandparents and answer their questions."

Parents have always set limits. Being challenged as a parent is not new. However, without a doubt, many of your issues are new and frightening. You face threats of COVID variations, climate changes, rampant technology, insecurity about education, and crippling inequity. Although you cannot solve all the complex issues that you face, your courage must now match the love you have for your child. Claim your strength, seek guidance, and bring your best to this enormous challenge.

Consider the Rights of Children

Although there are ample concerns about safety, courtesy, and health regarding technology, parents must remember that kids also have rights. They have the right to:

• Learn from technology
• Develop needed skills
• Enjoy the excitement and challenges of technology

- Improve their eye/hand coordination by playing video games
- Solve mental problems with Minecraft
- Have fun alone and with friends

It is conceivable that a family's guidelines for technology use could be so rigid that the rights listed above will be lost. As we look to the future, it seems evident that all of us need a new vision for society and technology. Who better to help create that vision than our young people?

When possible, a partial solution might include spending more time exploring nature and playing with animals. In addition, encourage children to participate in sports or other group or school activities.

Elliott making a friend

Chapter 21
Children with Challenging Behaviors

Whether you are teaching a preschool child the names of colors, strengthening beginning reading for a first-grader, or helping with high school algebra, you may face one of four challenging behaviors. William Glasser claims children choose behaviors with the expectation of getting their needs met.[70] Both Lee Canter, an expert on classroom management, and Rudolph Dreikurs, who discovered that human behavior stems from having one's basic needs met or unmet, describe four types of challenging children.[71, 72]

Each type of challenge has a mistaken goal, which provides a cover for the child's genuine need. For example, a mistaken goal might be to get out of work. Taken at face value, you may believe your child is simply lazy. The hidden (and true) problem is the child's belief in her inadequacy.

Most of us realize that no baby, child, or teen will act the same way all the time. For that reason, we need to be cautious about labeling anyone. From day to day, the behavior, and thus the label, may change. However, when thinking about specific behaviors, we may be more sensitive to a child by asking ourselves, "What need does this behavior truly indicate? What is her mistaken goal, and what is the genuine need beneath it?"

---

70   Glasser, *The Quality School Teacher*.
71   Canter, *Assertive Discipline*.
72   Dreikurs, *Children*.

Canter and Dreikurs describe a sequence of deep needs ranging from feeling inadequate, needing self-love, wanting safety, and requiring emotional healing. Each type is examined below.

The Child Who Feels Inadequate

A capable child, who has everything she needs to achieve success, may believe she is inadequate. Whether a baby learning to walk or a teen mastering a major part in a play, imagine your frustration, as her parent, when she avoids a task because she believes it is too difficult for her. This child does not have a learning disability, low intelligence, a physical disability, or an emotional problem. You know she can achieve success. Her mistaken goal will be to either get out of work or to solicit help. Her real need is to build inner confidence. Until that need has been satisfied, Canter and Dreikurs believe, in almost every situation, the child who feels inadequate typically exhibits the following behaviors:

- Avoids getting started on a task or job
- Gives up quickly
- Says, "I'm stupid" or "This is too hard for me."
- Whines or cries

As her parent or grandparent, you will often feel frustrated. Most days you feel sad for her. Sometimes you will help too much and do most of the work for her. When this happens, she decides, "Yep, I'm hopeless. Mom knows I can't do this work, and that's the reason she took over for me." Once your child latches on to a feeling of hopelessness, you will probably feel equally discouraged for her.

Before your child becomes so upset that she refuses to try, say, "I know you feel discouraged. Let's get started together." Now comes a critically important action. Follow each step carefully.

- Cover or remove all but one small part of the assignment or task. Covering most of the work will reduce feelings of crippling insecurity and will provide a little hope—maybe even a small burst of courage. For a baby, you might encourage one single step. If your teen feels hopeless about memorizing her lines in the school play, work on one short part at a time and cover everything else.

- Say, "I am only asking you to do this small part that I did not cover. I will help you get started."

- Following completion of the first short task, acknowledge her achievement. Say, "I knew you could do it. Give yourself a pat on the back."

- Uncover one small part at a time. Feelings of inadequacy probably did not appear suddenly and will not disappear instantly.

- Always acknowledge her successes and celebrate her small victories.

If your child continues to resist, you may decide to say, "Do it anyway" or "You can do it now or during _____." As you work with this child, avoid expressing pity. There is a difference between "I understand that you do not want to do this" and "You poor thing, this is too hard for you."

Dr. Madeline Hunter, a famous teacher, warns that a child who constantly fails becomes unmotivated. For this reason, do everything possible to ensure a series of successes for the child who feels inadequate. One successful achievement will not fill a need for confidence. Only regular, long-term, daily successes will reprogram her attitude. When you work with your child's teacher, suggest the following ideas, which you hope the teacher will allow.

As a parent, you might say, "Maybe you could alter the assignment by reducing the amount required. Instead of 20 math problems, ask my daughter to complete 10 or 15 out of the 20. She may not require as much repetition as many other students."

The teacher might be willing to allow your daughter to choose five problems to eliminate from the assignment. Continue to ask the teacher to adapt the work until your child's confidence increases. This is a recognized and reasonable request.

If your child is old enough, invite her to join in solving the problem. Ask, "How can we make this work?" If possible, give her ideas a try.

Teach her to use self-talk such as "I can do it."

Nagging will escalate the behaviors you do not want. When encouraging a child who feels inadequate, avoid the following:

- Expressing pity
- Doing the work for her
- Nagging or asking, "What's wrong with you?"
- Punishing
- Comparing the child to others

The Attention-Needy Child

Many children have deep and painful needs to accept and love themselves. Their behavior, designed to get your attention, becomes irritating and annoying. Although the only true healing is self-acceptance, the first step toward inner healing may come from your love for the child and your positive affirmations. In her effort to gain your interest and your help, an attention-needy child may employ any of the following behaviors:

• Constantly interrupting others
• Losing pencils, papers, and books
• Pulling on your sleeve
• Getting jealous when you pay attention to others
• Demanding your attention when you are busy

Even though you understand your child's real need is to love herself, you may often feel annoyed. When behaviors occur at a time when you cannot stop and give her your total attention, the following sequence may make a significant difference. Once again, follow the steps precisely, even if they feel uncomfortable.

Without looking at the child or saying her name, gently rub her back. Although this sounds easy, doing it is challenging. You will need strong willpower not to look at her or say her name while initiating a gentle back rub. In fact, you may need to practice with someone who will role-play with you. Congratulate yourself each time you can achieve this critical step.

Make certain to touch this attention-needy child calmly and slowly. Your goal is to send the message, "Although I am busy, I care about you."

Avoid patting. You are not burping a baby. Avoid ruffling hair, pinching ears playfully, or moving quickly. A child who needs to feel lovable will respond more positively to gentle touch and slow movements. Touching playfully has a place and time, but not when promoting self-love while you are busy working.

Teach this child to use positive self-talk. An appropriate example might be for the child to say to herself, "I love and respect myself and am loved by others." Although not a magic fix for a child who needs to love herself, an affirmation provides a start toward self-healing. Your assurances of love will also help the child accept that, in fact, she is worthy of being accepted and loved just as she is.

During a calm time, say, "There may be times when I need to concentrate on what I am doing. Let's think of a secret signal, which you and I can share. My signal to you will mean, 'I really love you, and I'll spend time with you as soon as I can.'"

Always appreciate positive behaviors, such as times when she remembers the signal you both agreed to use. If positive behavior is ignored, it will go away.

Frequently, a child seeking attention will get negative feedback because of her behaviors. The negative feedback gains attention but feeds her mistaken goal for the wrong reason. In fact, children who desperately need love would rather be scolded or even punished than feel ignored. Negative feedback also increases feelings of need and reinforces thoughts about not being lovable. For these reasons, avoid:

- Saying, "Don't interrupt me. I hate it when you are rude to me."
- Giving up on feelings of love for her
- Yelling at the child
- Looking at the child when she seeks attention in negative ways or when you cannot stop what you are doing

The Bossy, Controlling Child

Nothing you say or do satisfies the bossy, controlling child. The bossy child demonstrates an outward need to correct and control other children and adults. Although the mistaken need is to correct others, the real inner need is to feel safe.

Possibly the child believes no adult in her world handles life responsibly. Some children learn early to switch roles with one or both parents and assume more responsibility than a healthy child should carry. Typically, the bossy child exhibits the following behaviors:

- Defies authority and argues
- Says, "No, I won't, and you can't make me."
- Confronts and talks back
- Tells others what to do
- Refuses to comply
- Makes rude comments
- Says, "You are doing it wrong!"

You feel angry. The bossy child is not pitiful and wants much more than your attention. This child needs to feel safe by running the show and challenging your authority. Following the suggestions below will help.

Remove the bossy child from an audience. If confronted in the presence of others, especially in front of peers, the child will save face by either continuing the same action or accelerating negative behavior in the hopes of gaining control over those watching.

You will be tempted to whisper or talk softly with her. Please remember this important fact: Talking softly when others are in the area will not work. Even if other people do not hear what you whisper, the controlling child will assume her peers can hear your message.

Once you and the bossy child have a private place to talk, communicate by touching the child on her arm or shoulder, looking her in the eye, saying her name, and adding, "I'm not willing for you to refuse to do what I ask of you."

Add, "Any time you strongly oppose something I want you to do, we can communicate privately. Usually, you will be able to make choices."

As a parent, if you are challenged in front of your friends or family, you may feel embarrassed. You may find it helpful to say, "I want to be certain I understand. You are telling me you will not do what I asked. Is this correct?" If the child says, "Yes," you will reply, "That is useful information. We will handle this later. Try not to worry about it now." At a private time, return to the conversation.

Depending on each family's needs, as well as the age and maturity of a child who bosses others, you may find it useful to place the child in charge of an important job. Possibilities include:

- Feeding and caring for a pet
- Taking dishes from the table to the kitchen
- Watering a plant
- Helping plant a small garden
- Setting the table for the evening meal
- Making her bed each morning
- Helping to cook something for the family
- Putting dirty clothes in the appropriate place
- Practicing a musical instrument or physical skill

However, the most important way for parents to help children feel safe is to take their adult responsibilities seriously. When meals are served at obvious intervals, naps occur, teeth get brushed, toys are put away, and the atmosphere remains calm most of the time, children will not feel a need to take charge and maintain vigilance for personal safety.

Remember that to a child who wants to boss you and take control, a struggle will amount to a powerful payoff. If you show anger or let the child know you feel challenged, she wins the battle. Avoid doing any of the following:

- Arguing with the child
- Forcing compliance
- Threatening the child
- Embarrassing her in front of others

For most children, learning a new social skill will take time. In fact, it may take as many as 2,000 repetitions in context before the aggression ends. The good news is that change is possible. Never give up.

Usually, we address the bossy child by saying useless things such as these:

Useless Things to Ask or Say to a Bossy Child	Reasons They Are Useless
"Was that nice?"	Avoid adjectives such as "nice" or "bad." The aggressor will not change but will attach the words "not nice" to herself. Instead, say, "Did that work well? Did your action solve the problem? What else might you do?"
"Why are you doing this?"	This question invites blame. In the blame-game, no one wins. She may say, "He was mean to me first." Useless! Instead, consider, "What was the result of your bossy words?"
"Go to your room for the rest of the evening."	When possible, link negative behavior to a consequence. A natural consequence would be, "Since you were bossy to your brother, he does not want to play with you." A logical consequence would be, "We do not want you to be rude to your brother. Let's take a short walk to cool down."

The Hostile Child Who Wants Revenge

Humans, being messy creatures, sometimes find that feelings spill over, and new behaviors emerge. When a child who feels incapable struggles without assistance or improvement, she may add a desperate need for self-love to her increasing beliefs of inadequacy. Children who do not love themselves may become bossy due to fears of lost safety. Feeling a lack of safety may transition into rage and acts of hostility. With each change of a deep need, behaviors are either added or modified. For that reason, if you ignore a child at one level, her behaviors may eventually evolve to represent an even more pressing need.

If needs remain unmet through the first three levels, the child may ultimately seek revenge. A child who feels hostility toward her parents and siblings probably demonstrates behaviors that frighten neighbors, teachers, and peers. Standard behavior management tools will not work with a child in a fit of hostility.

The outward and mistaken manifestation of the hostile child is to get revenge. The child thinks, "I'll give them a lesson they won't forget. If I can show them how angry I am, my parents will pay attention to me, and things will get better." The deep need is for emotional healing. The amount of pain a child creates is a measure of the pain she carries inside. The hostile child who needs emotional healing demonstrates her need by hurting others. She may engage in the following behaviors:

- Willfully destroying property
- Deliberately hurting other children
- Engaging in substance abuse
- Pouting and throwing tantrums that continue into preteen years or beyond
- Being rude to parents and teachers
- Screaming, spitting, cursing
- Using self-destructive behavior
- Fighting, lying, stealing
- Participating in or even instigating sexual behaviors

Living with an angry, hostile child will leave parents feeling deeply hurt, enraged, or both. Your instinct will be to fight back. Hurting the child by being angry or punishing will only add to the child's pain, which, in turn, will increase her desire to hurt others.

Peers or siblings who witness an out-of-control situation rightly feel frightened.

Even if they are not involved, the young witnesses will absorb intense anxiety, which will not dissolve easily. As a parent, you need to ask for assistance.

Actions *Not* to Take

In a moment of crisis, you may find it challenging to think clearly. If possible, do not:

- Show anger
- Argue, debate, or bargain with the child who is upset
- Hurt the child, or allow the enraged child to hurt you

Actions to Take

In a moment of crisis, use your own self-talk to stay as calm as possible. If other children are in the area, keep them safe by separating or removing them from the child who is raging. Send the other children outside, to another room or to a neighbor's house. Call for help. Sources of help may come from:

- Your partner if you share parenting responsibilities
- Another person in your family, or a friend or neighbor
- Your pediatrician
- A child therapist or school counselor

While waiting for help to come, stay with the upset child. Your goal will be to calm the child and to prevent her from harming herself or anyone else. Damage to property will be a secondary and lesser concern.

Later, once the child is not with you, spend time thinking and writing. Document everything that was said or done. If there were witnesses, ask them to sign and date the document after adding to your account.

- Write, "Three things I love about this child are . . ." You must think of qualities about the child that are important. Do your best to go beyond "She's so cute." Dig deeper for inner qualities you can love.
- Look for patterns of events that precede outbursts. These prior events, called antecedents, can sometimes be altered or avoided to prevent future outbursts. For example, does the angry child tend to lose control at predictable times of the day, after or before eating, or when meeting other children?
- Ask yourself, *Do some areas of life seem too stressful for her? Are there games in which this child cannot control her emotions? Are there friends who seem to upset her?*

Start the Healing Process

Keep in mind that in some cases the major difference between a punishment and a consequence is your intention. This mental and emotional shift requires inner work in your mind and in your heart. Say to yourself, *This child hurts badly. How can I love this one who seems so unlovable?*

If things were broken during the rage, say, "We can repair the damages together. We may even have some fun in the process." Since you are not trying to punish the child, you and she may enjoy completing the job together. Although the point is for the child to assume responsibility, you can encourage success with a little fun and laughter. This is not to imply that you do most of the work. You are there to motivate and to assist, but not to do the job for her. Usually, when you offer an invitation to work together, she will be less resistant to the task. If you keep the job pleasant, you provide a way for the stress and tension to leave. Model a positive work attitude by including music, some jokes, and a bit of fun.

- When asking the child to repair damages, offer two positive choices by saying, "You may either sweep up pieces of the broken vase, or you may transfer this plant into the new container. You decide."
- If you believe it is appropriate for the child to pay for damages, help her find a way to do so. You may choose to hire her to complete a task for you. If she gets an allowance, you might suggest using some of her own money to pay for the cost of repairs.
- Get counseling for the entire family. Although the emphasis will be on healing the angry child's emotional damage, counseling must include all family members. It is tempting to shift blame to one child. Real healing comes only when each person involved in a broken family system is honest enough to own their mistakes and to change.

For no special reason, have a one-on-one lunch with the child who has demonstrated hostility. During lunch, make eye contact as you listen to what she has to say. Avoid using the time to lecture or discuss negatives about the child. You may be surprised at how much your heart will open when you sit eye-to-eye and heart-to-heart with a troubled child. Eye contact with pets, as well as humans, releases hormones that make animals and humans comfortable, relaxed, and trusting. Although you cannot expect a miracle, you will make a difference. For some children, you are the difference they yearn to find.

Chapter 22
Additional Challenges

In addition to the four challenging behaviors above, other situations sometimes confuse parents and grandparents.

Are the Words "I Hate You" Normal?

When a child says, "I hate you," reply appropriately by saying, "You seem terribly angry at me. You were hoping to get _____." Validate the child's feelings by adding, "I understand that you are feeling upset. Disappointment feels awful. You can handle this. I will help you."

It is possible that if your child says, "I hate you," she is expressing a fear that you do not love her. Once she matures enough to label her feelings accurately, she can learn to speak honestly and resolve conflicts. Like developing cognitive intelligence, learning to resolve conflicts requires time, good examples to copy, and the experiences that ultimately result in maturity. Let's be honest. Many adults lack this level of control.

If you repeatedly lose your temper during conflicts, you are not modeling healthy behaviors for your child. Instead of beating up on yourself, seek help. Every parent makes mistakes. We all get angry at times. We forgive ourselves, get the help we need, and continue to learn. One of the finest ways you can help your child is to take care of yourself. That means taking care of your own physical, emotional, and mental needs. Love yourself and you will be better equipped to love your child.

A major job of parents and grandparents is to help your child deal with the stresses of life. You want your child to notice and manage stress instead of stifling or denying her feelings. You also want her to identify the feelings of others. Helping your child begins with helping yourself.

As an adult in the situation, you do not want to either give in to inappropriate expressions of emotion or respond at the child's level of immaturity. If getting personal therapy seems out of reach, consider contacting your local YWCA or United Way for guidance and assistance.

My Child Says, "I Don't Care What You Think!"

If you give your child a consequence and she defiantly yells, "I don't care," be aware that she just gave you important information. If you hear these words, take a deep breath, and pause. The deeper message may be that she does not believe you care about her. Her words probably indicate that she needs something more significant than simply getting her way with the issue at the heart of your struggle. She also needs something much more important than a gift money can buy. Avoid attempting to buy your way out of this. The most important way to respond to "I don't care" is to increase the quality of time together and deepen family relationships.

Perhaps she needs more of your time to share fun activities such as reading a book, playing a game, taking a walk, drawing, painting together, or baking something to eat. She may also need loving rituals such as making eye contact, talking, holding hands, getting a gentle back rub, or playing games with you.

When you feel upset, pausing and focusing on what you want from your child provides an important example for her. Speaking slowly, tell her, "I want you to _____." When you say exactly what you want, you may be able to refocus your child so that she can provide the action you desire. Nothing works 100% of the time. However, always err on the side of modeling what you want, using eye contact, and stating your wishes succinctly. Saying and then demonstrating, "I will show you what I want you to do," can be helpful.

Your Child Steals—Now What?

When a child steals, she is communicating that she feels deprived in some area of her life. Years ago, my husband and I were asked to become unpaid foster parents for a 13-year-old boy from a family with ten children. Jimmy's father was an alcoholic who sometimes broke bottles and slashed the children's mother. We agreed to accept Jimmy, who arrived late one evening without so much as a toothbrush.

Story: Feelings of Deprivation Create Stealing

After school the following day, my husband and I took Jimmy to a store and bought appropriate clothes for school. He seemed proud of his new wardrobe and carefully hung his clothes in our son's closet. In about a week, the police arrived at our door saying that Jimmy had stolen cigarettes from the corner store. For Jimmy to earn money to reimburse the store, we hired him to do some light work for us.

After a few additional incidents, the police skipped the talks at our house and took Jimmy to the city jail, where my husband bailed him out. Our family talks and logical explanations did not seem to register with Jimmy. Yes, we felt discouraged, but agreed to continue. I insisted, "Jimmy wants more cigarettes, Cokes, or candy than the allowance we provide will buy, but he would never steal from us."

One evening we threw a party for some of the clergy in the area. Included on our guest list was the Jewish rabbi and his wife. Shortly after leaving our party, the rabbi called to tell us that $24 had been stolen from his wife's purse. About the same time, our small son announced that he had looked everywhere and couldn't find Jimmy. After my husband and I joined the search, we discovered that all of Jimmy's new clothes were missing. We alerted the police, who found Jimmy at the train station waiting to hop onto a railway car.

When my husband talked to Jimmy, he asked, "Jimmy, didn't you realize we would be embarrassed when you took money from one of our guests?" Jimmy replied, "I thought it was Barbara's purse."

Today, I realize that living in poverty with an alcoholic dad for 13 years had created deep deprivation in Jimmy. It did not matter that we furnished all his needs and most of his wants. The deprivation lived within Jimmy, waiting to be remedied by stealing things he believed he needed.

Stealing can represent a lack of love, lack of attention, or even an inability to accept personal worth. A healthy individual can give love as well as receive love. Stealing is a desperate scream for help. The needs may also be due to a lack of family attention, or lack of needed or coveted material items. Although a child who steals must experience logical consequences, the child will only heal if deep internal needs are met. Without healing inner needs, the child will probably continue stealing.

When the child is your own, say, "I notice money missing from our family fun jar. I suspect that something must be bothering you. We love you and want to help." Instead of threatening or accusing, show empathy. Above all, do your best to identify the underlying need. Listen to the child's story. Avoid lecturing, pointing out faulty thinking, or describing her terrible choices. Together, create a way for her to repay the stolen money. Your most important action will be to address the inner needs that may be represented by her outer expressions of pain.

My Child Is Mean

Once again, ask yourself, "What is my child communicating? Is she saying she is angry? Does she need attention? Do her words imply that she thinks I am being mean to her?"

The second step is even harder. Cease concentrating on the child's mean behavior. Remind yourself that when you attempt to end any behavior, you are focusing on the behavior you do not want. Instead, emphasize what you want your child to say and do.

Focusing on ending her mean behavior requires you to enter a power struggle with your child. Instead, focus on modeling and then teaching new behaviors, so the child learns different ways to express kindness as well as needs. Good modeling is critical. Always remember the power of showing a child exactly what to do and how to speak.

Teach your child to tell you how she feels. Demonstrate this type of verbal communication repeatedly. Your most important task will be to build or rebuild a relationship with your child. Jessica Mattern shares four ideas she has successfully used to change mean behavior in one week.[73]

Mattern recommends that parents stop responding to negative behavior. She claims that when most parents react, they provide negative attention to the misbehaving child, which may seem better to the child than no attention at

---

73   Mattern, How to Change.

236

all. Once Mattern's son realized he was not going to get her attention, he calmed down.

She wants parents to believe in the child. Using an assertive voice and matching facial expression, Mattern tells her son to "fix it (change his negative attitude or behavior)." Her tone indicates that she believes he can do this.

She reminds parents that children will live up or down to expectations. Mattern also reminds parents to set good examples for kind and loving behavior. She claims that when her attitude improves, her children also become kinder and more positive.

Speak So Your Child Will Listen

Usually, parents and grandparents use one of four types of voices to communicate with children: aggressive, assertive, passive, or passive aggressive. Children usually respond to an assertive voice much better than to the other three.

Aggressive messages tend to be loud and carry an attitude of "I'm the parent and I'm right. You are my child and therefore you must do what I say." Aggression promotes defensiveness and even fear. Aggressive statements are generally not considered healthy.

Passive communications seek to avoid conflict. For example, even when you do not get what you need, you fail to speak up for yourself. If you sound weak and uncertain when talking to a child, she will probably ignore your request. Although passive communications avoid conflicts, they usually result in disappointing outcomes.

Rather than communicating with either aggressive anger or passive meekness, the passive-aggressive parent may initially say nothing but later complain endlessly. The parent may allow the child to behave badly but spend hours nagging the child. Passive-aggression also fits the category of unhealthy communication. Other examples of passive-aggressive behavior include:

- Criticizing
- Being irritable
- Procrastinating
- Being forgetful
- Acting stubborn
- Blaming others

- Complaining
- Feeling unappreciated

Assertive comments are delivered with a firm but neither loud nor angry voice. "Please do this" can be stated with respect. For best results, use the following steps when speaking assertively.

Get on the child's level and make eye contact. Move close until she notices you. Children who get distracted easily may need for you to get as close as six inches.

State your expectation clearly and simply. Make sure your request is positive and focuses on what you want, rather than what you want her to avoid doing. An example might be, "Hold my hand when we cross the street so you will be safe." If going swimming, you could say, "We will put your life vest on before you get in the pool. I want you to have safe fun in the water."

When your verbal and nonverbal communications are given slowly and suggest certainty and firmness, your child will usually comply. If a statement or request feels aggressive (such as a loud, "Do it now!"), she will probably rebel.

Celebrate success even before the task is accomplished. Even a slight start can be followed with, "Thanks, I see you getting started," or, "Thank you," as she accepts your hand.

If she chooses not to comply, say, "I'm going to show you how to do this." Modeling generally provides a message that is easy to understand as well as nonthreatening.

Slow Down and Demonstrate

Usually, eruptions begin when you give a command the child does not like, or when she feels too tired or hungry to cope. In the early years of a child's life, she processes thoughts 12 times slower than adults. That information informs us that we must speak ... more ... slowly and limit instructions to only one or two ideas for the child to process. Avoid saying, "After your nap, we will have a snack, choose a few toys, and go to the playground to meet some friends." Too much information has been shared for her to process. Try, "After your nap, we will go to the playground."

Also, as has been mentioned before, children do not process the word "don't." If you say, "Don't run," your child will hear only the word run. Off she will go, thinking she is doing exactly what you want. Instead, say, "Walk slowly like this." Demonstrate exactly what you want.

Children between the ages two and seven do not have the ability to engage in inner self-talk.

To clarify your request, act out your words. Showing is more powerful than telling.

Match your actions to your words by demonstrating as you say, "Walk slowly by putting one foot in front of the other."

Another important consideration is that the brain seeks patterns. Thus, routines become important for children of all ages. The more consistently you maintain schedules, the easier it will be for the child's brain to develop and make use of the routine. Patterns enhance feelings of safety. Neurological resources are then used for learning rather than for protection and power struggles.

Motivation to behave comes from routines and from healthy relationships. Consider taking time each day to share activities such as reading a book, playing a game, cooking, taking a walk, talking about one's day, or laughing with your child. Ten minutes of loving rituals such as making eye contact, touching, being present, cuddling, reading stories, singing, holding hands, sitting close, or putting your child on your lap will also help to decrease power struggles. Think of these loving times as bonding experiences.

To remain calm when your child or grandchild confronts you in a power struggle, take deep breaths and affirm to yourself, "I am calm. I can handle this." These words are designed to disconnect you from your survival (reptilian) brain. Teach this technique to your child.

Part VI
Parents as Teachers

Catherine painted with markers for the joy of creating

Chapter 23
Creativity: Art, Music, and Dancing

Wren has some thoughts to share about experiences in art.

> *Dear Dad,*
> *I see you working on art activities with my sister, Daisy.*
> *Wow! It looks like you two are having such a good time,*
> *even though you are working hard. Daisy gets paint or glue*
> *all over the place. She even gets sticky art materials on*
> *her legs and in her hair. I notice that you are very patient*
> *about helping her clean up her art messes. I can hardly wait*
> *to join you two. If the goal is to get art stuff on almost*
> *everything, I know I can do this as well as Daisy. I already*
> *have ideas that will dazzle you with my style and pizzaz.*
> *When will I be old enough to work at this art thing?*

Although discovery plays an important role in all areas of learning, many academic subjects, such as math, rely less on intuition and more on mastering skills. On the other hand, creativity usually works better if we initially avoid all "how to" steps and allow more creative expression simply for the love of doing the activity. Creativity turns out to be a wonderful gift that can be nurtured or discouraged. Parents, grandparents, and teachers sometimes want to teach the correct way too soon.

Introduce creativity early. Before babies engage in interactive play, they enjoy parallel play. Art activities fit comfortably with the parallel stage of development. Babies younger than a year old can enjoy smearing thick paint across a page or surface, listening to and pretending to play music, and moving with dance-like motions to rhythm or tunes. These early experiences fit perfectly while babies enjoy playing side by side with another child or an adult.

Parallel Play

Parallel play happens when a baby and another child or an adult engage in the same general activity but interact minimally. Although close together, each usually plays or works alone. For example, Dad may play his guitar and sing while a baby either ignores his music, pretends to play her own toy instruments, or tries to join Dad on his guitar. Although her dad may be playing the best he can, he does not attempt to teach his baby where to put her tiny fingers on the strings.

Daisy likes to play along with her dad

Wren does his best to join the fun with music

Parallel play with art might look like Mom and baby working together by using their hands to put thick paint on paper. Mom may create a picture while baby smears paint randomly. However, it is important for Mom to resist the temptation to teach a baby how to create any specific object. A baby can see what her mom is doing. She can hear her dad playing music. At the same time, she experiences her own pleasant feelings and movements. Any effort to teach her correct procedures for guitar playing or painting would be lost on her. Worse yet, the pressure could easily destroy her interest in continued creative play.

Dancing for the Joy of Moving

The same holds true for dancing. A baby who begins to move when she hears music creates fun for herself and for others. She moves for the joy of responding to the melody and rhythm. Although you will often hold her and move in rhythm so she can feel the beat, you should not attempt to teach her specific steps or movements. As with music and art, your baby moves with her own joy.

Much later, the day will come when she says, "Show me how to do that." As she matures, she may even ask you to locate an art, music, or dance teacher for her.

Process Art

Process art provides an experience that is "child-directed," "choice-driven," and based on discovering what can happen when a variety of objects combine with various types of paper and paint. The process of doing the activity outweighs the final product in importance.

- Process art enables a child to think creatively and work independently.
- The child learns about physical limitations and the possibilities of materials. Critical thinking skills are reinforced by discovering what she can do with various materials.
- Motivation and interest often generate many curious questions from children.
- Children will embrace experimentation.

Examples of process art activities

Making collages with leaves, glue, and thick paper

Placing stickers within a hand-drawn frame

Making handprints and footprints on a cookie sheet with tempera paint.

Possible Items for Process Art

Although the materials a child can use for process art seem to be endless, a few commonly used items are listed below.

- Paper in various sizes, textures, and colors
- Sponges cut into a variety of sizes and shapes
- Paint brushes
- Finger paints
- Tempera paints in primary colors and white
- Popsicle sticks
- Glue sticks
- Crayons
- Squeeze bottles (to hold paint that children can squirt on thick paper or cardboard)
- Strings
- Sequins
- Oatmeal (for texture)

Organize art supplies
for easy use

Meri Cherry owns an art studio where she teaches classes and produces birthday parties for toddlers. She also makes the following suggestions.[74]

- Keep art supplies in containers that children can access easily.
- Protect surfaces.
- Protect children's clothes as much as possible.
- Arrange a place for art to dry.
- Establish a way for art to be displayed.
- Remember that although the result may or may not be beautiful, the emphasis remains on the act of creating.
- Model appropriate amounts of glue, paint, or other materials to use, and allow children to experiment.
- Do not attempt to teach the child how to create anything specific. Just allow the process to unfold.

The following page shows the result of two-year-old Daisy's first process art experience. She added yellow paint to the yellow paper, which can't be seen. Quite a bit of non-permanent yellow paint was also spread on the concrete

---

74   Cherry, *Meri Cherry*.

floor of the back porch. Although she showed little interest in the final product, she enjoyed the process.

The Problem with Children's Coloring Books

I recall watching a three-year-old draw a beautiful bird one afternoon. He knew his bird looked good and he smiled happily. Suddenly his mom, with good intentions, swooped in to teach him how to draw a very primitive symbol for a bird. His little face scrunched up with confusion as he said, "I can't draw a bird like Mommy's." Although I assured him that his bird looked much better than the one his mother drew, he believed he had failed. His confidence in his artistic ability vanished.

Christine McLean, who works for the Department of Child Youth and Family Services in Newfoundland, says the same damage occurs when parents or grandparents insist that a child use coloring books.[75] McLean believes that just as potato chips and Pepsis are not good substitutes for a healthy meal, coloring books do nothing to promote healthy growth. "If used to excess, they can actually have a negative effect on children's overall development," McLean says. She hopes that children will be given crayons, markers, paint, pens, pencils, chalk, and lots of blank paper of various sizes. Given these art supplies, children will experiment. "To rob them of these opportunities of discovery and expression is to deny them the chance to realize their full potential as artists, writers, readers, and critical thinkers," McLean says. "Freedom of expression in art leads to creative expression in other areas as well."

Tanja Mcilroy, an experienced teacher, claims that although children are naturally creative, coloring books are the least creative activity parents or teachers can provide.[76] On the next page you can see a picture of a glorious peacock from Tanja's site. Her wise suggestions for parents can be located at www.empoweredparents.com. Visit her site to learn many ways to guide your child's creative development.

---

75   McLean, What's Wrong.
76   Mcilroy, The Negative Effects.

This big, colorful bird was created by a child before using coloring books

After using a coloring book for several weeks, the same child was once again asked to draw a bird. Her new bird looked like the drawing below. The peacock above is much like the bird my grandson originally drew. The version below is almost identical to the one his mother wanted to teach him to produce. What a loss. What a terrible shame. Who knows what he might have been able to do in art without his mother's demonstration?

This is the same child's bird after using coloring books

In reply to those who claim children love coloring books, McLean states that the products are designed to attract the attention of children.[77] She says children love coloring books the same way they love BBQ chips and Pepsi. To those who say, "I colored with coloring books, and I turned out OK," she responds by wondering how much more imaginative and able to solve problems you might have been if you had reached your full potential.

Young children love art. They love to create and should do a free-drawing activity every single day. Gradually, at their own pace, children's drawings will change and expand. Creative expressions come from within, with no expectations or limitations on a child's artistic outcomes. Let the child be. I

---

77   McLean, What's Wrong.

believe this is one of the times when less help produces greater benefits. For several years, I taught a course to preservice teachers called *Art for Children* in which we studied the work of Lowenfeld as my students created activities for children. After being involved with children and education for over forty years, I have found that research has consistently discouraged use of coloring books.

Appropriate Procedures

Supply babies and young children with materials that are totally safe. Check the ingredients of paint, markers, and crayons. This is especially necessary during the time children chew and taste everything. As children grow and develop language, art can be used to enhance communication.

Many teachers and parents insist that a child age four or older tell or write a story before allowing them to draw or paint as a reward. However, experts suggest that children usually tell or write more if they draw or paint first. You will help the child become more creative and expressive if you follow these guidelines.

- Provide plain paper without lines or designs, which may get in the way of creativity.
- When working with young children, do not insist that colors match real life. Joyfully accept her purple cows. Artistic realism will come later.
- Avoid asking a child at any age, "What is this?" The random marks made by babies do not represent anything. As children develop, they may be insulted by the question. Instead, say, "Tell me about your art." When the child tells you about her work, she builds confidence as she strengthens oral language skills.
- As the child talks about her drawing, ask questions that require verbs. For example, if the child tells you some mark in the picture is her dad, ask, "What is Daddy doing? Where is he going? What might happen next?"

When your child identifies a mark as something specific, you may want to write the word on a small Post-it® Super Sticky Note. Get the child's permission to add the Post-it® to the piece of art by asking, "May I put the word "tree" next to the tree you created?" However, do not be upset if the next time she tells you about the same art piece, the "tree" becomes something totally different.

Stages of Art Development

Viktor Lowenfeld was a Viennese artist and educator born of Jewish parents. In 1939, he fled to the United States, where he taught at Pennsylvania State University. He is remembered for his work in art education. In 1947, he wrote *Creative and Mental Growth*. The information, examples, and names of the art stages below originated from Lowenfeld's work.[78] Although you will see estimated ages when stages occur, these can vary. Children develop individually. For this reason, consider all age estimations with flexibility. Each stage is worth celebrating since each represents a milestone in a child's mental and physical development.

Scribbling Stage
The Scribbling Stage occurs between ages one and three. Initially, the child enjoys making marks on paper for the joy of copying adults. Her enjoyment is not based on artistic discovery, but on the realization that she can do something new. The image below shows approximate grasps children often use. Keep in mind that the ages associated with different ways of holding the pen will vary.

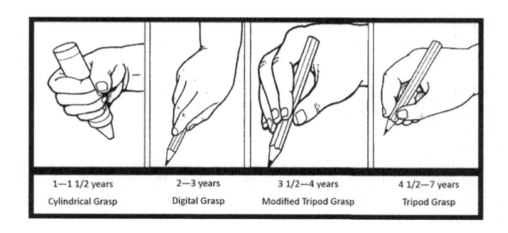

1—1 1/2 years	2—3 years	3 1/2—4 years	4 1/2—7 years
Cylindrical Grasp	Digital Grasp	Modified Tripod Grasp	Tripod Grasp

---

78   Encyclopedia of Education, Lowenfeld.

The first efforts at drawing or writing happen around one to three years and are called *Random Scribbling* or *Disordered Scribbling*. Marks may look like random combinations of lines and circles. The child has very little control and her marks may be bold or very faint.

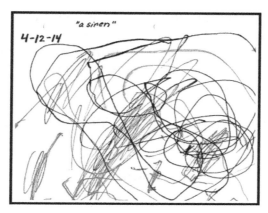

Disordered Scribbling

Between ages two and a half and three and a half, a pattern emerges called *Controlled Scribbling* or *Longitudinal Scribbling*. This change indicates new control with a series of lines. Circles soon follow.

Two examples of Controlled or Longitudinal Scribbling

Soon, the child begins naming her marks. During *Named Scribbling*, the appearance does not change but the child begins to tell stories about her art. Remember that the names and stories may change each time the child tells the story. The child continues to lack understanding of space, and objects seem to float around in a random way without established spatial relationships. Although the child uses color, the color choices lack realism and appear to be associated with emotions. Thus, people may be green. Always accept the child's use of color without questioning or attempting to teach reality. *Named Scribbling* indicates an important change from simply making marks to thinking about pictures.

Please enjoy the poem below, written by Alexis Rotella.

PURPLE

In first grade Mrs. Lohr

said my purple teepee

wasn't realistic enough,

that purple was no color

for a tent,

that purple was a color

for people who died,

that my drawing wasn't

good enough

to hang with the others.

I walked back to my seat

counting the swish swish swishes

of my baggy corduroy trousers.

Parents as Teachers

With a black crayon

nightfall came

to my purple tent

in the middle

of an afternoon.

In second grade Mr. Barta

said draw anything;

he didn't care what.

I left my paper blank

and when he came around

to my desk

my heart beat like a tom tom.

He touched my head

with his big hand

and in a soft voice said

the snowfall

how clean

and white

and beautiful. [79]

---

79   Rotella, *Purple*.

Preschematic Stage

Between three and four years of age, a child's drawings begin to combine circles and lines to depict people or animals. A visual idea is beginning to develop based on what the child sees as the most important features about a person or animal. Space remains a mystery, with objects floating around the page. Colors also continue to be unimportant in terms of realism. It will be critical to accept the child's lack of understanding about spatial relationships and the unimportance of color. Do not attempt to teach realism at this time.

Preschematic Art

Schematic Stage

Space and color now become meaningful and are rigidly important. Between ages five and six, objects relate spatially to the ground or the sky. The ground, referred to by teachers as the base line, will probably be green (maybe brown). Toward the top of the page, a blue skyline will often appear. The child now has a plan (a schema) for how to draw people, houses, the sun, trees, and flowers. People in the drawing below also relate to one another. For example, a family will have parents and children lined up with amazingly identical "genetic" characteristics.

However, the sizes of family members will often express strong emotional attachments rather than ages or actual sizes. For example, if the young artist includes herself with a group of friends or family members, she may draw herself larger than the others. Although she is not making a conscious decision

Schematic Art

254

to draw herself larger, her increased size indicates her emotional feeling of self-importance in the drawing. Probably, at this time, all of her drawings of people will be similar to the previous example. This child will repeat her schema until she enters the next art phase.

*Schematic Art
with x-ray and folding over*

The art to the left also belongs in the *Schematic Stage*. The child imagines seeing an object on the inside of the house from the outside. Drawings may show internal parts of a house or internal body parts. The inside-out perspective is called *x-ray drawing*. Another interesting technique, sometimes called *folding over*, happens when a child turns the page around and draws both sides of a street. Notice the flowers on both sides of the path in front of the house.

Dawning Realism

Dawning Realism begins to appear between ages seven and nine. This is also known as the *Gang Age*. Peers become important, and drawings clearly represent boys and girls or men and women. Details in drawings often create a feeling of stiffness.

Dawning Realism

In the drawing at left, the child begins to perceive and draw perspectives. Items no longer need to stand on the base line. Dimensions are indicated with size, shading, and color. In the drawing, the sun and birds remain in the *Schematic Stage* of development. Perspective is shown with a tree clearly drawn in front of the mountain. Notice that the tree has individual characteristics with a dark hole and small stub. Both mountains show perspective with slopes.

Pseudo-Naturalistic Stage

Around the ages of 10 to 13, more sophisticated changes can be noticed. For the first time, the product becomes more important than the process of creating.

Pseudo-Naturalistic boy

Pseudo-Naturalistic owl

Chapter 24
Bonding Language, Writing, and Reading

I have composed another imaginary note from a future Daisy.

> *Dear Mommy and Daddy,*
> *I have been told that many years ago, my daddy and his grandma did an experiment with eggs· His grandma let him crack raw eggs and then, after boiling a few additional eggs, they cracked cooked ones· When my daddy was little, he thought the entire idea was to crack the eggs· When he went on an Easter egg hunt, he broke each and every egg before putting it into his basket· Later, my daddy described the egg hunt to his grandma, who carefully wrote down what he said· Wasn't he silly to break his Easter eggs? I wish his grandma had saved the story they wrote together· I think she was also silly not to keep their story·*

Language Experience Approach

Language Experience Approach (LEA) combines oral language, art, storytelling, reading, and comprehension. The process has been around a long time as both a reading and writing strategy.[80]

---

80   Taylor, *The Language Experience.*

A now-retired teacher named R. Van Allen from Harlingen explained the value of the strategy in the following way:

> What I can think about, I can say.
> What I can say, I can write, or someone can write for me.
> What I write, I can read.

Parents, grandparents, and teachers can co-write stories as soon as children are able to talk well enough to participate. Initially, when co-writing a story, you will guide your child's thoughts by asking questions. If you do not have good handwriting and the child dictates to you, use your computer to copy the story. Even before your child begins to read, it will be helpful for her to see print that is like the letters she sees in books. Follow the steps below to incorporate the entire LEA experience.

Share an Exciting Experience: Provide an exciting experience such as a field trip, a story you read, an art piece, music, clouds, puppies, or retelling a memory. Keep in mind that to young children almost any activity can be considered an exciting experience.

Talk About the Experience: First, talk about the experience to help the child become familiar with words needed for the story.

Ask Specific Questions: The chart below shows how to use questions to develop vocabulary needed to create a story about a field trip to a bakery. Various experiences will require different formats and sequences.

Guiding Questions	Child's Response to Questions
We had an exciting trip to the bakery. Tell me what you remember.	Jot down any words or phrases the child voluntarily says. Usually, younger children will have only a few words and will need your help.
What did we see?	We saw flour, sugar, eggs, vanilla, and butter.
What did we smell?	We smelled vanilla, cookie dough, and baked cookies.
What did we touch?	First, we felt the dry flour and sugar. Next, we cracked an egg. After we mixed everything, we felt the damp dough.
What did we taste?	Although we smelled the vanilla, we did not taste it. We tasted butter, sugar, raw cookie dough, and the baked cookies.

As you ask questions, jot down words and expressions used by the child. Although the example above implemented several senses, you will neither be limited to nor expected to use this many questions. You will probably not get as many examples as listed in the previous chart. Many experiences follow a sequence, such as:

- "First, we drove to the bakery."
- "Next, we got to help measure each ingredient."
- "As we measured, we also got to touch, smell, and even taste each item."
- "After measuring, we mixed everything in a big bowl."
- "Next, we rolled out the dough and used cookie cutters to create raw cookies."
- "Finally, the cook helped us put our raw cookies into the oven."

At other times, random questions may solicit more interesting information. The basic steps will be repeated below with a slightly different emphasis.

<u>Suggest Writing a Story</u>: After jotting ideas on paper, say, "Let's write a story about our experience." You can take dictation from younger children or allow older kids to write their own accounts.

<u>Extend Ideas</u>: While writing, ask questions that extend thinking. For example, after each category, ask, "What else did you see, touch, smell, or taste?"

If you write the story by hand, later you will want to type it using a large font to make the print easier for the child to read. Font choice and size will depend on the age of the child. Through age eight, many children need a font size as large as Times New Roman size 24. After fourth grade, use Times New Roman size 16 to 18. Larger sizes protect young eyes. You will not damage a child's eyes with larger print. Smaller letters may cause vision loss.

An experience does not need to be complicated or elaborate to be worth writing about. An activity as simple as taking a walk with a baby brother can become a stimulus for writing, and later reading.

An older brother walks with his baby brother from the bus

Read aloud as the child listens and follows visually. While reading to the child, use your hand to track the line of print. Avoid pointing to each specific word. This approach benefits beginning readers, children whose primary language is not English, and children with dyslexia.

Co-reading
After you have read the story aloud enough times for the child to understand the vocabulary and be familiar with the sequence, ask if the child wants to read with you. Read slightly louder than your child. Again, guide the pace by letting your hand move smoothly under the line of print.

Following many experiences with co-reading, the child may want to read the story by herself. Your job just shifted to being a good listener. Instead of correcting mistakes, allow the child to proceed if she basically captures the meaning. Do not worry about word-by-word accuracy. In time, she will begin to read each word. If the child "reads" the basic idea but not the actual words, thank her when she finishes. You may want to ask questions to check her understanding. Continue to read the story to her.

On the other hand, if the child totally misses the meaning of your shared experience, wait till she finishes before thanking her. Review your shared experience and read the story to her again. The next day, return to the story. Again, read to her several times before inviting her to read along with you. Soon, she will be able to pretend-read by correctly recalling the basic meaning. Word accuracy will soon follow.

Once the child masters reading the words aloud, ask her to repeat the story often to build confidence and pleasure. Fluency improves with repetition. When a child can read smoothly with good understanding, teachers refer to this as Independent Reading.

Who Benefits from LEA?
A Language Experience Approach is a strategy or plan that uses reading and writing to record a child's experiences. The strategy works beautifully for children who do not speak English, as well as for children with a learning disability such as dyslexia. Let this activity be a delightful experience for you and for a child with special needs as well as for beginning readers and writers.

Avoid Ruining the Experience
Although the experience is intended for young pre-readers and pre-writers, I have witnessed teachers insisting that the child help edit and make corrections. Avoid ruining an enjoyable experience with your need for perfection. Editing

and revising will come much later. LEA is meant to connect reading and writing with positive feelings.

Story: LEA with a Nonreader and Nonwriter

When our granddaughter Catherine was three years old, she came to spend the day with us. At that time, we lived near a small creek. In the afternoon, Catherine and I walked hand in hand to the creek to enjoy the water. We spotted small fish, colorful rocks, and cool shade from large cypress trees with slender branches drooping almost to the water. Dappled light from the sun streaming through tree limbs warmed our skin. By the time our creek adventure ended, it was time to return Catherine to her parents.

As Grandpa drove, Catherine and I sat in the back seat. We used our time in the car to talk about some of the things we had done that day. Looking at her delicate features, wispy blonde hair, and serious expression, I said, "Catherine, let's write a story about our adventure at the creek. You can share our story with your parents." Gravely, she nodded in agreement.

After locating a piece of scrap paper and a pen, I asked, "What did we do first?"

Catherine recalled, "When we got to the creek, we took off our shoes and waded in the cold water."

To be certain I understood, I repeated, "We waded first? Did the water feel cold?" After clarifying, I wrote her words. I then asked, "What else did we do?"

After responding to a few questions, Catherine surprised me by saying, "Now Grandma, you talk, and I will write what you say."

Catherine and Grandma had fun at the creek

261

Recalling the experience, I find it interesting that from the beginning of Catherine's efforts at spoken language she preferred not to talk. That afternoon in the car, she handled her preference by turning the tables on me. I talked and she wrote. The other interesting fact? Catherine did not know how to write a single word.

With an exaggerated air of confidence, Catherine reached for the paper and pen. Next, after rearranging herself in her car seat, she began asking questions. As soon as I started responding to her questions, Catherine began making copious scribbles. I could not miss the fact that she copied my previous actions by 1) asking a question, 2) listening to my reply, 3) repeating what I said for clarity, and 4) scribbling my reply on paper.

Once we finished, Catherine looked at her own scribbles and accurately "read" our story aloud. I imagine she also used her scribbles to read our story to her mom and dad.

Pretending to read and pretending to write demonstrated that Catherine had been read to many times. She had also watched her parents as they wrote lists, paid bills, and answered letters. Even at age three, she had absorbed the concept of words on paper. Contrast her preparation with that of a child who has never listened to stories or put pen to paper to create glorious marks.

Daisy is only pretending to read Brown Bear, Brown Bear

Pretend Reading

When parents spend time reading to babies and toddlers, these young children often begin to pretend to read. Called approximation reading, the activity demonstrates a healthy understanding of what reading is all about. In the picture, Daisy cannot read the words, but she has heard the story enough times that she remembers what each page says. She also knows how to hold the book, move her eyes from top to bottom, and turn the pages.

Catch Reading by Repeating Short Passages

Dr. Guszak, a retired professor from the University of Texas in Austin, promoted the concept that reading can be "caught."[81] To guide a child to catch literacy, begin reading to her from before birth and continue until she grows up. Reading to and writing for her will provide examples of literacy. These actions are the first steps toward catching literacy.

When a child begins to read words, one of the best ways to prepare her to "catch reading" and become a lifelong reader is to ask her to re-read familiar paragraphs or short parts many times. Repetition creates confidence. Confidence creates love of reading. Keep in mind that success breeds success. Conversely, forcing a child to read material that is too difficult breeds discouragement. Discouragement breeds dislike of reading. Dr. Guszak recommends using predictable books, such as Bill Martin Jr.'s *Brown Bear, Brown Bear, What Do You See?* [82]

If you want your child to master other languages in addition to English, begin early. When possible, read books in English and in Spanish (or another language). Each time you read a book to or with her, point out and mention the following:

- "The title of this book is _____."
- "The author, who is the person who wrote the book, is _____."
- "The artist (or illustrator) who drew the pictures is _____."
- Sit side by side so you and the child can both see the pictures and text.
- Gesture as you say, "We read from top to bottom."
- Let your hand track from left to right under each line of print. Avoid pointing to each word.

Research suggests that teaching two languages to babies at the same time often delays initial oral language. The payoff comes a few years later when your child becomes proficient in both languages.

81   Guszak, *Diagnostic Reading.*
82   Guszak, *Diagnostic Reading.*

Letter Sounds and Letter Names (For Adults Only)

Sometimes an author wants the reader to say the name of a letter. At other times, the emphasis will be on saying the sound a letter makes. The following information is intended to guide you as a parent or grandparent. The markings that follow are not intended for the child.

When *naming* a vowel, underline the letters a, e, i, o, and u. When asking for the *sound* of the letter, surround the letter with parentheses (o) or with slashes /o/. For example, the letter a begins the word *ape*. In the word *at*, the sound of the letter a is pronounced /ă/. Indicating whether you are talking about the name of the letter or the sound is only important when communicating with other adults. The underlines, parentheses, and slashes are not relevant for children.

When parents or grandparents shop for an educational chart that shows pictures, words, and letter sounds, it is important for the sounds of the letters to be correct. Often, a word will begin with the correct letter but not the right sound.

Teaching Letter Sounds

For beginning readers, start with the names of vowels, which are also called long vowel sounds. See examples of words that begin with long vowel sounds below.

- *Ate* begins with the name of the letter a.
- *Eat* begins with the name of the letter e.
- *Ice* begins with the name of the letter i.
- *Ocean* begins with the name of the letter o.
- *Unite* begins with the name of the letter u.

Instruction about the most common sounds of vowels, referred to as short vowel sounds, follows quickly. Pictures to demonstrate the short or long vowel sounds should be items that most children recognize.

Always begin teaching a vowel sound by placing that vowel as the first letter in the word.

- Apple is the correct picture for the sound /ă/.
- Egg is the correct picture for the sound /ĕ/.

- Iguana is the correct picture for the sound /ĭ/.
- Octopus is the correct picture for the sound /ŏ/.
- Umbrella is the correct picture for the sound /ŭ/.

Ask yourself what would be wrong with a picture of ice cream for the short vowel sound /ĭ/? (Ice cream is not the correct picture for the short sound /ĭ/. Ice cream begins with the sound of the long ī, which says the name of the letter. An example for the short sound /ĭ/ could be igloo.)

What about the picture of an owl for short sound /ŏ/? (Owl is not the correct picture for the short /ŏ/ sound as in octopus. The /ow/ sound also does not represent a long ō as in ocean.)

In the TREND chart above, pictures for the vowels represent short sounds

Ways to Start Teaching Vowels

When teaching children and again while preparing preservice teachers at a small university, I presented ideas from *Project Read*. I found the *Project Read*[83] lessons the best available. Materials can be ordered at projectread.com.

- Show the child an alphabet chart with stars above each of the five vowels.
- Tell her that these letters have stars above them because they are very special and important; a, e, i, o, and u are the star letters.
- Why are the vowels so important? These special letters are important because you cannot make a word in the English language without a vowel—a starred letter.
- When teaching a young child, write the vowels on each of the five fingers of her left hand. Begin with the letter a on the child's thumb. If you use the left hand, the sequence will be correct when the child turns her hand over to look at the letters.
- Sing, "I've got the vowel sounds in my hand. . ." to the tune of *He's Got the Whole World in His Hand*.

___

83   Project Read, Project Read.

Additional Teaching Possibilities

Incorporating additional senses will strengthen anything you teach.

Use a picture or object along with each written form of the letter to strengthen visual identification. (Notice the correct pictures for vowels on the previous TREND alphabet chart.) Using index cards or sturdy paper, create puffy paint letters by outlining handwritten lowercase letters with glue. Write the tall letters about two inches in height and the short ones one inch tall. Outline the letters with glue. Be sure to give the glue time to dry before asking a child to trace over the puffy letter. As the child traces the letter with her fingers, say, "The name is a and the sound is /ă/ as in apple." Tracing adds the sense of touch to the lesson.

If you add a motion for each short vowel sound, you will be using the kinesthetic modality. One way to add motions is with puppets. Notice the handmade sock puppets for the sounds /ě/ and /ŏ/ below.

The kinesthetic movements below are from Project Read.[84] With each movement, use a correctly printed lowercase letter.

For a, ask the child to locate her Adam's apple. First, she touches the spot at the front of her throat, then brings her hand forward in a gliding motion as the two of you say, "The name is a. The sound is /ă/ as in Adam's apple."

For e, show a puppet representing Mr. Ed, the talking horse. The child can pull on the reins as the two of you say, "The name is e. The sound is /ě/ as in Mr. Ed."

A sock puppet of Mr. Ed will make his short /ě/ sound when his reins are pulled back

The letter i comes with his own story. His name is Icky. Each time his mother gives him something to eat that he does not like, he touches his chin with his thumb and dots his nose with his pointer finger of the same hand as he says, "The name is i and the sound is /ĭ/ for Icky." Pretend to feed the child something awful (such as boiled bugs) so she can touch her chin and her nose as she says, "/ĭ/—Icky." The child adds, "This food is icky."

------

84   Project Read, Project Read.

When teaching o, tell the story of Miss Odd, the opera singer. Miss Odd admits that even though she wants to be an opera singer, she gets too frightened to open her mouth when she sees all the people in the audience. A child promises to attend the concert and to open her own mouth to encourage Miss Odd. Miss Odd, with help from the child, finally succeeds by singing, "/ŏ/ as in Odd." Together say, "The name is o. The sound is /ŏ/ as in Miss Odd."

Miss Odd

Finally, to teach the letter u, ask the child to pretend to be a weightlifter. As she lifts an imaginary weight to her knees, her chest, and finally above her head, she says, "/ŭ/–/ŭ/–/ŭ/p!" Together say, "The name is u. The sound is /ŭ/ as in up."

Label Important Items

When your child reaches about age three, you may want to label a few items in your child's room, such as her bed, lamp, toy box, or desk. If you do so, use large, correctly written lowercase manuscript (printed) letters. If you want to promote another language, write words in the second language as well as in English.

Mom, pointing to a label: "Daisy, this word is bed. Can you say bed?" If Mom wants her child to also learn Spanish, she will gesture to a second word and say, "In Spanish, the word is *cama*. Can you say *cama*, the Spanish word for bed?" Mom then adds, "Daisy, can you point to your own bed?"

Avoid any attempt to drill or memorize. Instead, keep your approach gentle and without any pressure. Plant the seeds, which will come to fruition in a short time.

Creating Word Cards

When creating word cards, please print using manuscript (printed) letters. Unless the word requires an upper-case letter, such as a proper name, avoid writing the word, or even the beginning letter of the word, with an uppercase letter. For example, do not write BED or Bed.

A sample printed word card

A writing program called D'Nealian promotes a writing style that implements characteristics of both manuscript and cursive. Proponents of D'Nealian claim that their program is easier for children to master than more traditional methods.[85]

When a parent or grandparent writes words or sentences for a preschool or school-age child, the adult needs to become familiar with the writing program used at the child's school. If uncertain, use either block manuscript or D'Nealian. Other companies, such as TREND, create alphabet letters in traditional print or modern printed manuscript. If an uppercase letter should be called for (as in a child's name), use the capital. Otherwise, stay with lowercase letters. Markers or crayons can be used to print words.

Create One-Sentence Stories

Using sentence strips and markers, you can begin to create short, personal sentences for your preschool child to read. Each strip of paper has one sentence. Initially, you may substitute a picture of the child instead of the child's written name. You can purchase blank sentence strips with lines to guide the size of your print.

Two-word sentences are an easy way to start reading. If you want, the same sentences can be printed in Spanish (or any other language) as well as English.

• Rhett runs.	Rhett corre.
• Rhett eats.	Rhett come.
• Rhett sees.	Rhett ve.
• I see Rhett.	Lo veo Rhett.

Any time you show typed letters from a computer to a preschool child, keep the size of the letters large. Keep the sentences short. Young eyes have not matured enough to view small objects or letters, and you do not want to risk causing any damage to a child's eyesight. If a child of any age has trouble reading, first try enlarging the print. Sometimes that is the most beneficial action you can take.

---

85   Wikipedia, D'Nealian.

To teach a simple sentence, follow these steps:

- Show the child a sentence strip with a simple two-or three-word sentence written in large, correctly formed lowercase letters. Use an uppercase letter only at the beginning of the sentence and to capitalize the child's name.
- Say, "This is a sentence. A sentence can be read. This sentence says, 'This is a bed.'"
- Repeat the sentence, with your hand tracking the line of print.
- Ask, "Would you like to read this with me?" If the child agrees, read together. If the child is not ready, put the sentence away and wait for more maturity. If the child doesn't read the words in the sentence but recalls the message from memory, consider this a win. Continue to model reading until the child can read the words with you.
- Ultimately, your child will be able to read the sentence alone. You can say, "You just read a sentence. You must feel good that you are becoming a reader."

If you think, *She's just memorizing the sentence*, do not worry. Memorizing is a worthwhile starting place for a beginner.

Although I created the sentences below, the idea for the short stories comes from Dr. Guszak, a retired professor from the University of Texas in Austin.[86] Substitute the name of your child to complete each story below.

See, see (This is the title of story.)_
See Wren.
I see Wren.
Wren, see, see, see.

Go, go
See Wren go.
Go, Wren, go.
Go see Wren.
Wren, go, go, go.

It, it
Go see it.
See it go, Wren.
Wren, see it go.

---

86   Guszak, *Diagnostic Reading.*

Can, can
Can Wren go?
Can Wren see?
Can Wren see it?
Can it see Wren go?

Graduate from simple sentences using your child's name to slightly longer sentences, such as the one below.

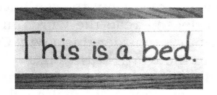

Chapter 25
Using Sensory Input to Strengthen Learning

Below is a note from great-grandson Wren a few months before his first birthday.

Dear Mom and Dad,
Even though I am not one year old yet, I often hear you asking me to look at interesting objects· You do not need to worry one bit· I am absorbing all kinds of information in my own clever ways· I am learning by tasting my toes, smearing food on the table, looking at new colors when you paint the walls, listening to Dad's guitar, and eating the cat's food· I am one cool little guy! My great-grandma tells me I am learning new things every day! See? It's all going well·

Learning by Integrating Senses

Except for individuals with limited visual or auditory acuity, most people benefit from integrating as many senses as possible into a learning experience. Ideally, new information can include visual references, such as pictures, graphs, or print, or auditory input such as explanations, discussions, and music. When possible, include hands-on application of ideas. Touching objects and moving will help many children. Ideally, a child can learn through any sensory modality. If a new idea or concept seems challenging, integrate as many senses as possible. Each one is described below.

Story: Visual Learning Preference

When our grandson Dalton was an infant, he and I attended Cradle Gym. Each week, I drove the baby to their location to enjoy the class. Each week focused on a different sensory modality. For example, during the first week of the class, I showed Dalton black and white toys and pictures, along with a few items in primary colors. Week two emphasized touch. Using feathers, rough and soft materials, and various objects, I rubbed his chubby little arms and legs.

And then we came to week three, when the sensory modality happened to be auditory. A variety of sounds at different volumes failed to gain his interest or attention. Looking at the teacher, I whispered, "Do you think he can't hear?"

The teacher suggested that I say his name. "Dalton, look at Grandma."

He immediately turned his head and looked at me with a smile. He simply had no interest in the bells, rhythm sticks, or tambourines. As a school-aged child, seeing a picture or reading a printed description worked better for him than hearing instructions. However, this did not imply that Dalton could never learn from auditory input. Through his school years, he encountered many teachers who relied on lectures. Dalton may have preferred reading print, seeing videos, or using pictures, but he also had the ability to learn by listening.

Story: An Auditory Preference

As a little boy, Lane responded more eagerly to auditory communication. After his family moved to another state, Lane and I carried on lengthy conversations.

Many times, Lane and I sang songs over the telephone. I soon realized that anything attached to music or rhythm not only maintained his attention but also cemented mastery within a short time.

Like most children, Lane wanted to listen to the same story many times before indicating that he was ready for a new book. This is not unusual. Most children will ask for a story to be repeated so many times that parents begin to consider hiding the book. If parents skip a page, the child will usually insist on a correction. Once all the input from pictures and words has been integrated, the child will be ready to move to something new. Be patient and repeat as many times as requested.

As a university student, Lane preferred lectures and class discussions. Situations in which conversations were shared, thoughts were expressed orally, and debates were presented suited him well. Fortunately, when faced with a need to learn solely from print or graphs, Lane could do so successfully. Although parents will want to respect a child's preferences, never limit learning to one sensory modality.

Story: A Kinesthetic Preference

Chandler enjoys action

Even as a toddler, our grandson Chandler showed tendencies of learning differently. He continues to be oriented toward action and movement and prefers to learn by doing rather than by listening to a lecture or reading a book.

While in elementary school, Chandler enjoyed walking around the classroom to check on his friends. Now that he is in high school, no one is surprised that Chandler plays football. Although he enjoys moving, Chandler can also read a text or sit quietly and listen attentively when that is the appropriate behavior.

Tactile Benefits

When working with infants, parents are wise to develop kinesthetic paths to learning by using tummy time and activities that develop motor skills. Touch and texture also strengthen a baby's motor abilities. Encourage gripping, holding, squeezing, stacking, pouring, or scooping to strengthen muscles and help develop hand-eye coordination.

Elliott continues to explore gadgets

Research indicates that touch improves brain function. Movement and touch improve memory, perception, language, attention, and emotional development.

Different Ways of Thinking

Different ways of thinking also impact learning possibilities. Regardless of which term you use, you are seeking to find beneficial ways to communicate with and teach your child.

Type of Thinker	Explanation
Reflective Thinkers	Reflective thinkers, who are usually quiet and thoughtful, need time to consider an idea before deciding what to do. These thinkers begin with the big picture and like to ask questions. They enjoy writing summaries, reading, and journaling.
Intuitive Thinkers	Intuitive thinkers frequently ask "why" questions. They also want to look at the big picture before breaking the task into details. When studying, intuitive thinkers like to divide work into small parts, read the directions before starting, and check their work often.
Sequential Thinkers	Sequential thinkers start with small, logical steps and build into the whole. They frequently ask, "Why is this information important?" They prefer taking notes in an outline format. Learning happens in small chunks.
Global Thinkers	Rather than carefully going through all the logical steps before deciding what to do, global thinkers make choices quickly. Studying in small groups, playing hands-on games, and seeking feedback help global thinkers learn. Global thinkers also begin by combining the whole picture with details included.

Multiple Intelligences: Sometimes Called Learning Preferences

Howard Gardner developed a theory he called Multiple Intelligences.[87] It is important to remember that the most successful learners are the ones who can switch gears for learning. Either using senses sequentially or integrating several senses at the same time will benefit most learners. The chart below names each type of preference and describes the characteristics.

Type of Intelligence or Preference	Description
Verbal	Language and vocabulary are important to children who like to work with verbal skills. They enjoy definitions, grammar, poetry, and plays.
Logical	Logical learners like to play with numbers, quantities, and math operations. They tend to be critical thinkers who enjoy abstract reasoning and organization.
Visual	Art and even science appeal to children who enjoy visual presentations. Good control of their bodies and strong eye-hand coordination develop success in shop, labs, games, skits, and plays.
Kinesthetic	Children with a strong need to move like to use their whole bodies, or even body parts such as hands, feet, fingers, and arms, to physically solve problems or be creative. They do well in shop, labs, games, and plays. Usually, they are strong athletes.
Musical	Not only do these children enjoy music, but they also hear and remember rhythms and patterns. Once they hear something they like, they can't get it out of their minds. Sensitivity to rhythm, pitch, jazz, rap, and songs fill their needs.
Interpersonal	These children understand people. This could be called social intelligence for children who are outgoing and interactive. They usually show sensitivity to the moods and feelings of others.

---

87   Gardner, *Frames of Mind.*

Intrapersonal	Some children seem to know and understand themselves at deep levels. They recognize who they are and what they need to be happy. They also understand what to avoid in life. They understand what they cannot do and when they need to ask for help.
Naturalistic	Children who love nature want to study living things and are sensitive to all aspects of nature, such as clouds and rock formations. They care deeply about Earth and are aware of changes in plants, seasons, weather, animals, and unusual conditions on and beyond our planet.
Existential	Children with existential interests like to consider deep questions such as black holes, the meaning of life and death, and human existence. They see philosophical connections and push mental boundaries. Often, they become scientists, philosophers, and theologians.

Learning experts assert that no evidence supports the idea that students should focus on only one type of intelligence. These educators claim that people who focus on one specific modality are as foolish as those who go to the gym and exercise only one body part while allowing other parts to atrophy.

What Does Good Learning Look Like?

Good learners tend to be persistent. They usually like to read, research, and ask questions. When searching for answers to probing thoughts, they frequently reflect on their uncertainties while going to bed, working out, or listening to others. New claims describe what good learning looks like. Consider the examples below.

Name	Explanation
Adaptive and Flexible	Regardless of subject matter, good learners seek to be adaptive and flexible. They hope that what they are learning will apply to a wide variety of needs. Ideally, each area of mastery should benefit all other areas of study.
Multimodal	Good learners also want to use many senses and modalities to master material. Communicating with a combination of visual, auditory, and life experience strengthens learning.

Repetitive	Repetition is important and must be included as a critical component of learning. Some experts believe gifted students require one to four repetitions, general education students need 8 to 18 repetitions, and children with learning disabilities may require 600 repetitions to obtain mastery. Keep in mind that you must consider your child's individuality, as well as the content being considered.
Meaningful and Personal	Finally, any time learning can be related to personal interests or meaningful situations, the material becomes more interesting and relevant.

Even though our neurons work collaboratively in groups, brain neurons tend to forget new information quickly. Connecting new learning to previously mastered material helps a student remember important information. A phenomenon called "the forgetting curve" suggests that the most significant loss occurs in the first twenty minutes, with additional reductions occurring during the first hour. Fortunately, even forgotten information can be mastered more easily when relearning occurs. To increase recall, use the following ideas.

- Learn simple facts in a familiar location. For example, studying in a part of your house that is familiar and comfortable for you will support your efforts to recall new information.
- Record new material in many forms, such as with associations, auditory input, visual representations, and repetition.
- Use spaced repetitions, which can be generated on computer programs that use flash cards. Spaced repetitions involve reviewing material at intervals following breaks. Initially, the intervals are close together. Gradually, the reviews occur farther apart. The purpose is to establish new information in long-term memory.

Ed Cooke, Grand Master of Memory, recommends the following strategies to increase memory.

Memory Suggestion	Explanation
Guess at the Meaning	When meeting someone for the first time, silently guess the person's name before hearing it. Although the initial guess will probably be incorrect, the act of considering the possibility increases recall.

Repeat, Repeat, Repeat	Mega-drilling adds power to ordinary repetition. Cooke suggests that learners repeat information 30 times to establish long-term memory. (Review the explanation of spaced reviews above.)
Create a Mnemonic Aid	Connecting the information to previously mastered material will increase memory.
Think Spatially	Picture a room and relate the new word and its meaning to a place in the imaginary room.
Relax	Take a one-minute break in the middle of memorization. Although taking a break feels like wasting time, the change will relax your brain and create a space for the new information. Resting your brain will speed up learning in the long run.

A successful author shared a story. When struggling to locate a missing jigsaw puzzle piece, she finds that taking a break will often speed up the process. Following a break, the missing piece will usually show up, along with a few other "hard-to-find" puzzle pieces.

Mnemonics

Mnemonics are memory aids that provide easy ways to remember information.

- Wherever there is a Q there is also a U.
- The word r**hyth**m helps your two **hip**s move.
- Never be**lie**ve a lie. (lie in believe)
- The princi**pal** of a school is a **pal**. A princip**le** is a ru**le**.
- An image mnemonic may exaggerate a hard-to-remember letter as in sep**A**rate.
- **LONG**itude refers to the lines that run north–south on a globe. **LAT**itude rhymes with **flat** and flat runs horizontal or east–west.

Acronyms

Acronyms use the first letter of a series of words to help with recall.

- FANBOYS stands for conjunctions: for, and, nor, but, or, yet, and so.
- ROY G. BIV represents the colors of the rainbow spectrum: red, orange, yellow, green, blue, indigo, and violet.
- "HOMES" stands for the Great Lakes: Huron, Ontario, Michigan, Erie, Superior.

Chapter 26
A Brief Look at Dyslexia and Dysgraphia

Although every single child brings unique qualities to the learning process, there are some who deserve all the patience and faith parents, grandparents, and teachers can provide. The passages below are limited but encourage you to understand and accept children with learning disabilities such as dyslexia or dysgraphia. It is critical to remember that special learners have tremendous potential. With loving guidance, they can achieve happy and fulfilled lives.

Can a Child with Learning Disabilities Also Be Gifted?

The mother of a child with learning disabilities requested a teacher conference when her child was placed in the gifted program. The mother hoped to explain the accommodations her daughter needed for her learning disabilities. The teacher in the gifted program informed the mother that no child could be identified with both labels. Sadly, many teachers and parents share this incorrect belief. A child with learning disabilities may struggle to read but grasp the functions of calculus with mathematical genius. An expert in science may be unable to write a logical paragraph. The goal of educating children with multiple labels must remain focused on meeting the needs of each area in the child's path to learning.

A child with dual labels usually has high intelligence but faces challenges with academic requirements. Often, the child also has a lack of executive processing ability. Executive functioning includes skills such as working memory (the ability to work on learning without losing track of what is happening generally), flexible thinking (the ability to cope if the schedule changes), and self-control. Lack of executive functioning creates problems with focus, following directions, handling emotions, and many daily tasks.

As parents and grandparents, one of our many responsibilities is to accept each child unconditionally. That means enjoying the child's strengths while also respecting her challenges.

Dyslexia

The following definition of dyslexia is provided by the International Dyslexia Association: *Dyslexia is a specific learning disability that is neurobiological in origin. It is characterized by difficulties with accurate and/or fluent word recognition and by poor spelling and decoding abilities.*[88]

Broken down, the definition above suggests the following:

- *Specific disability* refers to a problem in a particular area of the brain such as the section that handles language. The disabilities that fall into this term include dyslexia, dysgraphia, dyscalculia, auditory processing disorder, language processing disorder, nonverbal learning disabilities, and visual perceptual disabilities.
- *Neurobiological disorder* has to do with a problem in the nervous system. The cause may be genetic, metabolic, or biological.

Children with dyslexia often find reading easier if the print is enlarged (Times New Roman size 24 point). Although larger letters help children visually decode words, older students often feel embarrassed by print that looks different from that used by their peers.

It is critical to understand that children with dyslexia typically have higher IQs and greater creativity than average students. Although reading materials and instruction must be adjusted to promote literacy success, content areas such as math, social studies, and science must be taught at the child's ability to think and master information. Even if a fourth-grade child can only decode words at a first-grade level, the child should be taught concepts at the level of the child's cognitive proficiency. A multisensory approach may also help children with learning disabilities.

The importance of presenting instruction at the child's level of mastery is to avoid dumbing the child down to her reading level. When a child realizes that

---

88   International DYSLEXIA Association, Definition of Dyslexia.

her peers with less intelligence are passing her up in reading and writing, the frustration and pain become overwhelming. One grandson with dyslexia asked, "What's happening, Grandma? I'm smarter than _____ but he reads well, and I can't read at all."

Bewildering and agonizing. And yet, this grandson is an amazing thinker who will achieve remarkable, but probably unconventional, successes. One key is to promote and safeguard the child's self-esteem. A second key is to emphasize the child's strengths. This grandson who has struggled with decoding print has become an expert with drones and robots.

Teachers and parents who seek to help must remain open-minded about a variety of strategies, such as:

- Making print larger
- Using all acceptable accommodations and modifications
- Individualizing instruction when needed
- Teaching concepts at the level of the child's thinking ability
- Engaging the child in many more repetitions than are usually needed
- Using a minimum of three senses to teach
- Teaching the child to analyze word patterns
- Encouraging the child to create visual memory aids such as mental pictures
- Reminding a child of the importance of effort

Effort has the power to become even more important than intelligence. The will to persist can carry the day.

Technology Assistance for Dyslexia

In the last decade, technology has gained tremendous power. Opportunities are available for students struggling with dyslexia, including the following:

Students with dyslexia may find it helpful to record lectures and tutorials. For recorders to be useful, they must include digital counters to locate specific information. It will be even more helpful for teachers of older students to provide handouts at the beginning of class.

The inability to read at a normal pace can be a severe challenge for students with dyslexia. Listening to books read at a more normal speed allows for easier assimilation of information, which may help with comprehension.

If the technology also includes the ability of the student (or a teacher) to highlight important information, the technology's value to a student will be more significant.

A free program called "Read Please" was first published in 2003.[89] The program allows the student to hear what is written on the screen. The program will read the text while highlighting words as they are read aloud.

Microsoft Windows and Mac systems offer their own versions of text-to-speech programs.

Dysgraphia—Written Expression Disorder

Reading Rockets provides the following definition of dysgraphia: *Dysgraphia is a learning disability that affects writing abilities. It can manifest itself as difficulties with spelling, poor handwriting and trouble putting thoughts on paper.*[90]

Reading Rockets suggests the following materials for young writers.

- Paper with raised lines (such as Pacon Multi-Sensory Raised Tablets)
- Different pens and pencils to try for comfort
- Pencil grips and writing claws
- Multisensory instruction
- Word processors

An amazing program called Open Dyslexic: A Typeface for Dyslexia can be found at https://opendyslexic.org. Additional resources on the site include applications, books, and devices. Even a new keyboard for dysgraphia is presented. The program is based on related research and several follow-up studies can be read.

- Using graph paper for math calculations
- Allowing extra time for written assignments
- Beginning by drawing or talking, followed by writing
- Teaching many types of writing, such as expository, personal essays, short stories, poems, and other types
- Allowing a child to use a spell checker
- Using alternative ways to assess knowledge

---

89   Softonic, Read Please.
90   National Center for Learning Disabilities (NCLD), *What is Dysgraphia?*

- Reducing emphasis on neatness
- Suggesting that students take breaks before proofreading

Although not always the case, I have known students diagnosed with dysgraphia who achieved remarkable success with keyboarding mastery. Those children who cannot achieve success with pen-to-paper activities often demonstrate amazing progress when typing on computers.

Story: A Technology Success for Dysgraphia

Many years ago, I got a sad phone call from a fourth-grade grandson. "Grandma, my teacher told me my essay was like a paper written by a first grader." Before our telephone call ended, I asked the child to have his dad telephone me that evening. Later, a conversation with the boy's father followed.

Grandma: "Your son called me this afternoon upset about an essay. Can you tell me about this?"

Dad: "I'm not surprised since I know he is struggling. I'll send a copy of the essay he wrote." (The essay looked like the written work of a first grader.)

Grandma: "We can determine whether he simply doesn't have any good ideas or if the problem revolves around putting a pen to paper. Ask him to dictate a story to you."

The result was a story dictated with good ideas, interesting characters, and lively dialogues. A computer and some keyboarding lessons made a tremendous difference. The same grandson recently earned a master's degree. He can think and he can express himself when free of paper and pens.

Accommodations

An accommodation provides an alternative way to learn. Although the level of difficulty remains the same as for other children, a task may be accommodated in the following ways:

- Allow the child to type rather than write answers by hand.
- Highlight the most critical ideas for the child to read in the textbook and encourage her to skip the unmarked sections.
- Permit extra time for assignments or tests.
- Read tests aloud for the child and allow her to verbally dictate answers.
- Enlarge the print.
- Use audio books.

Modifications

Modifications allow a child with a learning disability to reduce the amount of work required or to master less-challenging information. Examples may include the following:

- Reduce the length of an assignment.
- Substitute easier word problems in math.
- Allow the child to use a calculator or draw pictures to support understanding.
- Create shorter or easier spelling lists.
- Grade on a pass/fail basis.

Although the terms *modification* and *accommodation* usually apply to children with disabilities, many other learners need to be considered for these concepts. Some children require both. Although modifications usually lower the level of difficulty, a requirement to complete a shorter assignment at the same level of difficulty might rightfully be considered an accommodation. Accommodations make small changes to allow a child with a disability to succeed at the same level of challenge as the rest of the class.

Children rarely benefit from the fair practice of providing identical teaching methods or materials. Usually, identical assignments result in boring lessons for a gifted student while overwhelming the child with disabilities. A child living with terrible deprivation as well as one who speaks English as a second language will probably also benefit from considerations of their individual needs.

Parents as Teachers

The higher goal gives each child what she needs to eventually be as successful as her peers. One child may move through learning objectives very quickly. Another may need shorter lessons, more repetitions, and expanded time. Instead of looking at a child as a typical third grader, we must view each one as a unique learner. Ask, "What does this individual need in terms of interest, difficulty, time, number of repetitions, or type of instruction? What will help her be successful?"

I have two grandsons, who are currently in their late teens. When the boys were younger, we usually gave them identical Christmas gifts. As they boys matured, it became evident that one liked sports and the other enjoyed music. No more identical gifts. In some cases, that translated to different amounts of money spent. The different gifts did not indicate favoritism. We simply wanted each boy to get a gift that would be meaningful, maybe even helpful.

Education must adopt a similar view of children as individuals. Although it appears that buying the same learning materials and spending the same amount of money is a demonstration of fairness, this practice will miss the mark too many times. Instead, when educators, parents, and grandparents focus on providing each child with what that child needs to achieve success, we may buy different programs, and even spend varying amounts of money, to help each one achieve academic, social, and emotional success.

The children in the picture above represent the universal desire to master reading

Grandson Rhett sits with his kindergarten friends

Chapter 27
Final Thoughts

Teaching beginning reading will probably not be a job most parents want. Never feel guilty if teaching pre-reading does not feel like a good fit for you. On the other hand, you may long to introduce reading to your child. For those of you who feel compelled to venture into this area, please consider using the ideas expressed earlier. If your efforts are not fun for you and your child, it's better to set instruction aside than to instill negative feelings. If it's not fun, stop.

Keep in mind that teachers need help, and most welcome an eager parent. Even if all you do is read stories to children, you will be providing an enriching experience. Being read to is one of the most important ways to motivate a child to learn to read and write. Many children hunger for adults who will help them master new concepts. If the thought of working with children appeals to you, the experience may be extremely rewarding. Go for it!

In nations and cultures around the world, children yearn to read and find meaning in print. In addition, kindness is our natural state of being. No one hates others unless taught to do so. Unmarred, children will view racial and cultural differences with interest and respect. Our children will always be our greatest teachers.

Your Greatest Challenge

You brought a tiny baby into the world with every intention of helping her develop into a happy and productive adult.

I believe children grow and thrive when they know they are loved unconditionally. That level of love requires accepting your precious child at each stage of her development and through every behavior she tries on for size. "I love you, just as you are" remains the best gift you can give your baby.

Before you can love your child, you must love and accept yourself. Remember, you are always modeling. When you strive to fulfill your spiritual goals as well as your physical, mental, and emotional ones, you demonstrate a powerful truth. Seek to become all you can be, give all you can give, and love without judgment of others.

During your baby's early months, you were encouraged to listen to her. That meant sometimes remaining quiet as you listened to what sounded like gibberish from your baby. You were advised that when your child reaches her teens and twenties, she will sometimes talk in ways that will sound just as strange as the babble-language she spoke as a baby. In addition, even though your infant could not understand the words you were saying, you were urged to start talking early. Communication cushioned in love will continue to be a key ingredient from early days until parenting ends. Keep listening and speaking with love.

The text also encouraged you to eliminate punishment by establishing boundaries with a combination of natural and logical consequences. The experience of living in a home filled with unconditional love while also understanding that behaviors come with matching consequences will provide your child with a strong foundation for her future life.

I assure you that, despite your mistakes, you can parent your child lovingly. With that thought, I end by sharing a creed that my mother lived by. This creed is my hope for you and for your child. Your primary question will continue to be, "Can we raise this precious baby/child/teen to achieve all she can?" You want her to develop strong self-esteem and honest self-love laced with acceptance for others. If she can balance kindness with lessons learned by experiencing consequences, you will have achieved a valuable goal.

My Creed

To take what comes of good or ill,
To cling to faith and honor still.

To do my best and let it stand,
The record of my brain and hand.

And then, should failure come to me,
Still work and hope for victory.

To be the same when I'm alone,
As when my every deed is known.

To live without pretense or sham,
Exactly what men think I am.

—Edgar Albert Guest
(Taught to me by my mother.)[91]

Ana, Rhett, and Rylie look to the future with hope

---

91   Guest, My Creed.

Bibliography

Abdullah, Maryam. "How to Reset Your Family's Screen Time After the Pandemic." Greater Good Magazine, July 1, 2021. https://greatergood. berkeley.edu/article/item/how_to_reset_your_familys_screen_time_ after_the_pandemic.

Alaskan-Natives.com. n.d. "Eskimo, Inuit, and Inupiaq: Do These Terms Mean the Same Thing?" Alaskan-Natives.com. Accessed August 15, 2021. https://www.alaskan-natives.com/2166/eskimo-inuit-inupiaq-terms-thing/.

American Academy of Pediatrics. "Bedwetting." Pediatric Patient Education, 2021. https://doi.org/10.1542/peo_document012.

American Pregnancy Association. n.d. "Breech Births." American Pregnancy Association. Accessed August 15, 2021. https://americanpregnancy. org/healthy-pregnancy/labor-and-birth/breech-presentation/.

Angier, Natalie. "Deaf Babies Use Their Hands to Babble, Researcher Finds." New Your Times, March 22, 1991.

Arulraj, Nancy. n.d. "11 Pacifier Alternatives for Babies and Toddlers." All Natural Mothering. Accessed August 15, 2021. https://www. allnaturalmothering.com/baby/pacifier-alternatives/.

Avery, Justine. Everybody Poops! Suteki Creative, 2019.

Bailey, Becky. n.d. "Handling Temper Tantrums" (Video). Conscious Discipline. Accessed August 15, 2021. https://consciousdiscipline.com/videos/handling-temper-tantrums/.

———. "Why Conscious Discipline Consequences Work and Punishments Don't." Conscious Discipline, September 25, 2018. https://consciousdiscipline.com/why-conscious-discipline-consequences-work/.

———. Conscious Discipline: 7 Basic Skills for Brain Smart Classroom Management. Oviedo, FL: Conscious Discipline, 2001.

Barr, Matthew. "Video Games Can Develop Graduate Skills in Higher Education Students: A Randomized Trial." Computers and Education 113, October 2017.

Bates, Michael. n.d. "Glossary of Dyslexia Terms and Dyslexia Facts." The Reading Well: A Virtual Well of Dyslexia Resources. Accessed August 15, 2021. https://www.dyslexia-reading-well.com/.

Baumgardner, Julie. "How to Avoid Raising an Entitled Child." First Things First, October 3, 2017. https://firstthings.org/how-to-avoid-raising-an-entitled-child/.

Bertin, Mark. "How Parents Can Hit the Pause Button on Screen Time." Greater Good Magazine, June 5, 2018.

Bjarnadottir, Adda. "Breastfeeding Diet 101: What to Eat While Breastfeeding." Healthline, July 31, 2020. https://www.healthline.com/nutrition/breastfeeding-diet-101.

Blaine, Helwig. "Repetition and Practice—Necessary to Students' Learning and Mastery." The New 3Rs Academic Transformation, July 25, 2017.

Bierma, Nathan. "Nicaraguan Deaf Children Create Language of Their Own." Chicago Tribune, Oct. 14, 2004.

Bolinger, Dwight. Aspects of Language. 2nd ed. New York: Harcourt Brace Jovanovich, 2002.

Bibliography

Bonyata, Kelly. n.d. "Help! My Baby Won't Nurse!" Kelly Mom. Accessed August 15, 2021. https://kellymom.com/ages/newborn/nb-challenges/back-to-breast/.

Brain Balance Achievement Centers. n.d. "Nutrition for ADHD: Kid-Friendly Foods That Enhance Focus." Brain Balance Achievement Centers. Accessed August 15, 2021. https://www.brainbalancecenters.com/blog/nutrition-adhd-kid-friendly-foods-enhance-focus.

Brough, Devon. Get OVA It!: A real-life solution to get unstuck and break free. Independently published, 2021.

Buscaglia, L. Living, Loving and Learning. Thorofare, NJ: Charles B. Slack, 1982.

Butler, Cheryl. "Four Examples of Toxic Parents and How to Fix Them." Quick and Dirty Tips, May 3, 2020. https://www.quickanddirtytips.com/parenting/behavior/4-examples-of-toxic-parenting-and-how-to-fix-them.

Cahill, Gavin. n.d. "Why Game-Based Learning?" The Learning Counsel. Accessed August 15, 2021. https://thelearningcounsel.com/article/why-game-based-learning.

Canadian Broadcasting Company. n.d. "Never In Anger." Canadian Broadcasting Company. Accessed August 15, 2021. https://www.cbc.ca/ideas/popupaudio.html?clipIds=2263113692,%202263121091.

Canter, Lee. Assertive Discipline: Take Charge Approach for Today's Educators. US: Lee Canter and Associates, January 1976.

Carlson, Julia. "My Child Was a Victim of Restorative Justice. But It Doesn't Have to Be This Way." Education Post, October 21, 2019. https://educationpost.org/my-child-was-a-victim-of-restorative-justice-but-it-doesnt-have-to-be-this-way/.

Center for International Education. n.d. "Rethinking Education: A Conversation with Dr. Yong Zhao." College of Education at the University of Massachusetts Amherst. Accessed August 15, 2021. https://www.umass.edu/cie/news/rethinking-education-conversation-dr-yong-zhao.

Cherry, Kendra. "Authoritative Parenting Characteristics and Effects." Verywell Mind, September 17, 2020. https://www.verywellmind.com/what-is-authoritative-parenting-2794956.

———. "What Does the Acronym BIPOC Mean?" Verywell Mind, September 17, 2020. https://www.verywellmind.com/what-is-bipoc-5025158.

Cherry, Meri. n.d. "Meri Cherry." Accessed August 15, 2021. https://mericherry.com/.

Chertoff, Jane. "Guide to Tummy Time: When to Start and How to Make Tummy Time Fun." Healthline, May 28, 2021. https://www.healthline.com/health/parenting/tummy-time.

Chua, Amy. n.d. "Chua, Amy." Accessed August 15, 2021. https://www.amychua.com/.

Coldquads. "Baby's Conversation with Grandmother." YouTube, October 3, 2013. https://www.youtube.com/watch?v=9gsjGAW18rk.

Conover, Lynda. n.d. "Gifted and Learning Disabled? It Is Possible." LD Online. Accessed August 15, 2021. http://www.ldonline.org/article/6068/.

Coping Skills for Kids. n.d. "Deep Breathing Exercises." Coping Skills for Kids. Accessed August 15, 2021. https://copingskillsforkids.com/deep-breathing-exercises-for-kids.

Coppa, Christine. n.d. "How the 3-Day Potty Training Method Works." Parenting. Accessed August 15, 2021. https://www.parenting.com/toddler/potty-training/how-3-day-potty-training-method-works/.

Coppola, Marie and Diane Brentari. "Nicaraguan Sign Language." Serious Science, September 7, 2016.

Crider, Catherine. "What Are Breast Compressions, and How Do You Do Them?" Healthline, November 23, 2020. https://www.healthline.com/health/breastfeeding/breast-compressions.

de Bellefonds, Colleen. "Consequences for Toddlers: Fast Ways to Stop Bad Behavior." What to Expect, March 12, 2019. https://www.whattoexpect.com/toddler-discipline/consequences-for-toddlers.aspx.

Bibliography

Dann, Larissa. n.d. "Three Reasons to Avoid Saying, 'I'm Proud of You.'" Parent Skills. Accessed August 15, 2021. https://www.parentskills.com.au/blog/three-reasons-avoid-saying-im-proud-you.

Dannemiller, Scott. The Year Without a Purchase: One Family's Quest to Stop Shopping and Start Connecting. Louisville, Kentucky: Westminster John Knox Press, 2015, 238.

Debrito, Joannie. "Dads Parent Differently Than Moms." Focus on the Family, August 26, 2019. https://www.focusonthefamily.com/parenting/dads-parent-differently-than-moms/.

Dewar, Gwen. n.d. "Traditional Chinese Parenting." Parenting Science, 2011–2019. Accessed August 15, 2021. https://parentingscience.com/chinese-parenting/.

Dills, R., J. Grinder, R. Bandler, and J. DeLozier. Neuro-Linguistic Programming. Vol. 1, The Study of the Structure of Subjective Experience. Cupertino, CA: Meta Publications, 1980.

Doucleff, Michaeleen, and J. Greenhalgh. "How Inuit Parents Teach Kids to Control Their Anger." Goats and Soda, NPR, March 13, 2019. https://www.npr.org/sections/goatsandsoda/2019/03/13/685533353/a-playful-way-to-teach-kids-to-control-their-anger.

Doucleff, Michaeleen. "Got Anger? Try Naming It to Tame It." Shots, NPR, January 28, 2019. https://www.npr.org/sections/health-shots/2019/01/28/688180879/got-anger-try-naming-it-to-tame-it.

———. "How to Get Your Kids to Do Chores (Without Resenting It)." Goats and Soda, NPR, June 9, 2018.

Dreikurs, Rudolf. Children: The Challenge: The Classic Work on Improving Parent-Child Relations. New York: Penguin Publishers Group, December 1991.

Dweck, Carol. Mindset: The Psychology of Success. New York: Ballantine Books, 2006.

Eagle, Ruth. Medically reviewed by Darragh O'Carroll, M.D. "How Various Levels of Electric Shocks Affect the Body and How to Recover." Medical News Today. January 11, 2022. https://www.medicalnewstoday.com/articles/electric-shock.

Encyclopedia of Education. n.d. "Lowenfeld, Viktor (1903–1960)." Encyclopedia of Education. Accessed August 15, 2021. https://www.encyclopedia.com/education/encyclopedias-almanacs-transcripts-and-maps/lowenfeld-viktor-1903-1960.

Fastiggi, Will. n.d. "What Are the Biggest Myths in Education Today?" Technology for Learners. Accessed August 15, 2021. https://technologyforlearners.com/what-are-the-biggest-myths-in-education-today/.

Fay, Jim. n.d. "The Delayed or 'Anticipatory' Consequence." Love and Logic. Accessed August 15, 2021. https://www.loveandlogic.com/pages/the-delayed-or-anticipatory-consequence.

Foster, B. J. n.d. "Five Bad Kid Behavior Issues That You Need to Break Early." All Pro Dad. Accessed August 15, 2021. https://www.allprodad.com/bad-behavior-in-kids/.

Frandsen, B. Teaching Responsible Behaviors. Austin, TX: Family School, 2002.

———. Diversified Teaching. Austin, TX: Family School, 1993.

Fussell, Matt. n.d. "The Stages of Artistic Development." The Virtual Instructor. Accessed August 15, 2021. https://thevirtualinstructor.com/blog/the-stages-of-artistic-development.

Gardner, Howard. Frames of Mind: The Theory of Multiple Intelligences. New York: Basic Books, 1983.

Gaskins, Mahea. "A Village to Raise a Child . . . And a Community to Keep Parents Sane." The Village Method, June 16, 2015.

Gaszak, Frank. Diagnostic Reading Instruction. New York: Harper Collins, March 1985.

GenoPro. n.d. "Family Systems Theory." GenoPro. Accessed August 15, 2021. https://genopro.com/genogram/family-systems-theory/.

Bibliography

Ginott, Haim. Teacher and Child. New York: Macmillan, 1972.

Glasser, William. The Quality School Teacher. New York: Harper Collins, 1993.

Goldentouch, Lev. "How Many Repetitions for Long Term Retention?" Key to Study, December 27, 2014. http://www.keytostudy.com/many-repetitions-long-term-retention/.

Gomes, Mary. "Five Reasons to Take a Break from Screens." Greater Good Magazine, April 25, 2018. https://greatergood.berkeley.edu/article/item/five_reasons_to_take_a_break.

Gordon, Thomas. Parent Effectiveness Training. New York: New American Library, 1975.

Greenbaum, Everett, and Jim Fritzell. n.d. "M*A*S*H: The Kids." FANDOM: Monster MASH. Accessed August 15, 2021. https://mash.fandom.com/wiki/The_Kids_(TV_series_episode).

Greene, R. The Explosive Child. New York: Harper Collins, 2001.

Grinder, M. Envoy. Battle Ground, WA: Grinder and Associates, 1993.

Guest, Edgar Allen. "My Creed." Favorite Verse of Edgar A Guest. New York: Permabooks, 1950, 12.

Gushue, Lisa. "Eminent Anthropologist Jean Briggs, Inuit Language Expert Dead at 87." CBC News, July 29, 20216. https://www.cbc.ca/news/canada/newfoundland-labrador/anthropologist-jean-briggs-dead-at-87-1.3700470.

Gaszak, Frank. "Diagnostic Reading Instruction." New York: Harper Collins, 1985.

Haarer, Johanna. Die deutsche Mutter und ihr erstes Kind (The German Mother and her First Child). Verlag, Germany: JF Lehmann, 1938.

Hamilton, Kori, and Elizabeth Kessler. n.d. "Accommodations and Modifications: Wait, They're Not the Same?" National Association of Special Education Teachers LD REPORT. Accessed August 15, 2021. https://www.nast.org/publications/ld-report/accommodations-and-modifications-wait-theyre-not-the-same.

Harder, Eva. "6 Steps Toward Restorative Justice in Your School." Education Post, December 14, 2018. https://educationpost.org/6-steps-towards-restorative-justice-in-your-school/.

Hubbell, Elizabeth Ross. n.d. "Creating Your Own Destiny: Teaching the Importance of Effort." AMLE. Accessed August 15, 2021. https://www.amle.org/creating-your-own-destiny-teaching-the-importance-of-effort/.

Hunter, Madeline. Enhancing Teaching. New York: Macmillan College Publishing, 1994.

Hutauruk, Bertaria. "Children First Language Acquisition at Age 1–3 Years Old in Balata." Journal of Humanities and Social Science. Vol. 20, no. 8 (August 2015).

International DYSLEXIA Association. "Definition of Dyslexia." International DYSLEXIA Association, Nov. 12, 2002. https://dyslexiaida.org/definition-of-dyslexia/.

Jandu, Allison. n.d. "Expert Tips for Potty Training Success." Get Parenting Tips. Accessed August 15, 2021. https://www.getparentingtips.com/toddlers/development/expert-tips-for-potty-training-success/.

Jensen, E. P. Superteaching: Master Strategies for Building Student Success. Del Mar, CA: Turning Point, 1988.

Karp, Harvey. n.d. "The 5 S's for Soothing Babies." Happiest Baby. Accessed August 15, 2021. https://www.happiestbaby.com/blogs/baby/the-5-s-s-for-soothing-babies.

———. The Happiest Baby on the Block; Fully Revised and Updated Second Edition: The New Way to Calm Crying and Help Your Newborn Baby Sleep Longer. New York: Random House Publishing Group, October 2015.

Bibliography

———. n.d. "How White Noise Can Help Your Baby Sleep." Happiest Baby. Accessed August 15, 2021. https://www.happiestbaby.com/blogs/baby/white-noise-for-baby-sleep.

Kearns, Devin M., Roeland Hancock, Fumiko Hoeft, Kenneth R. Pugh, and Stephen J. Frost. "The Neurobiology of Dyslexia." TEACHING Exceptional Children, Vol. 51, No. 3, January 2019, 175-188.

Kelley, Tracey. "What Does It Mean to Make Amends?" Twin Lakes Recovery Center, April 8, 2019. https://twinlakesrecoverycenter.com/make-amends/.

Kennedy, Kristy. "Unwrapping the Controversy over Swaddling." American Academy of Pediatrics, 2013. https://publications.aap.org/aapnews/article-abstract/34/6/34/10796/Unwrapping-the-controversy-over-swaddling?redirectedFrom=fulltext.

Kostelyk, Sharla. n.d. "Calm Down Breathing for Kids." The Chaos and the Clutter. Accessed August 15, 2021. https://www.thechaosandtheclutter.com/archives/calm-down-breathing-for-kids.

Kratzer, Anne. "Harsh Nazi Parenting Guidelines May Still Affect German Children of Today." Scientific American, January 4, 2019. https://www.scientificamerican.com/article/harsh-nazi-parenting-guidelines-may-still-affect-german-children-of-today1/.

Kvols-Riedler, B., and K. Kvols-Riedler. Redirecting Children's Behavior. Gainesville, FL: INCAF Publications, 1993.

LD online. n.d. "What is Dysgraphia?" National Center for Learning Disabilities, 2022. Accessed August 15, 2021. https://www.ldonline.org/ld-topics/writing-spelling/what-dysgraphia.

Leman, Kevin. n.d. "Ten Ways to Establish Clear Boundaries with Children." All Pro Dad. Accessed August 15, 2021. https://www.allprodad.com/10-ways-establish-clear-boundaries-children/.

Leonard, Jayne. "What Is Dysgraphia?" Medical News Today, July 14, 2020. https://www.medicalnewstoday.com/articles/dysgraphia.

Liu, Lindsy, PharmD. n.d. "What Happens if My Child Eats Kinetic Sand?" Poison Control. Accessed August 15, 2021. https://www.poison.org/articles/what-if-my-child-eats-kinetic-sand-204.

Lowenfeld, Victor. "Creative and Mental Growth." New York: Macmillan Co., 1947.

Marcin, Ashley. "Guide to Baby Wearing: Benefits, Safety Tips, and How To." Healthline, July 31, 2019. https://www.healthline.com/health/parenting/baby-wearing.

Markova, D. How Your Child Is Smart. Berkeley, CA: Conari Press, 1992.

Marriage and Family Encyclopedia. n.d. "American-Indian Families: Boarding Schools." Marriage and Family Encyclopedia. Accessed August 15, 2021. https://family.jrank.org/pages/74/American-Indian-Families-Boarding-Schools.html.

———. n.d. "American-Indian Families: Family Life Today." Marriage and Family Encyclopedia. Accessed August 15, 2021. https://family.jrank.org/pages/75/American-Indian-Families-Family-Life-Today.html#google_vignette.

Martin, Bill, Jr. Brown Bear, Brown Bear, What Do You See? New York: Penguin, 2007.

Mattern, Jessica Leigh. "How to Change Your Kid's Bad Behavior in One Week." Woman's Day, September 15, 2016. https://www.womansday.com/life/a56309/how-to-change-your-kids-bad-behavior/.

Mayer, Sandra. "15 Signs the Baby Is Suffering from Neglect." Babygaga, December 29, 2016. https://www.babygaga.com/15-signs-the-baby-is-suffering-from-neglect/.

Mayo Clinic Staff. n.d. "Hip Dysplasia." Mayo Clinic. Accessed August 15, 2021. https://www.mayoclinic.org/diseases-conditions/hip-dysplasia/symptoms-causes/syc-20350209.

Bibliography

McCall, Ashley. "Criminalizing Students Isn't Helping Anyone, Here's How Restorative Justice Can Help." Education Post, May 30, 2017. https://educationpost.org/criminalizing-students-isnt-helping-anyone-heres-how-restorative-justice-can-help/.

Mcilroy, Tanja. n.d. "The Negative Effects of Coloring Books." Empowered Parents. Accessed August 15, 2021. https://empoweredparents.co/why-you-should-never-give-your-child-colouring-in-pages/.

McLean, Christine. "What's Wrong with Coloring Books." INTERACTION, Spring 2009. https://elf2.library.ca.gov/training/docs/whatswrongwithcoloringbooks.pdf.

Mental Health Foundation. n.d. "Kindness Matters Guide." Mental Health Foundation. Accessed August 15, 2021. https://www.mentalhealth.org.uk/campaigns/kindness/kindness-matters-guide.

Michigan Department of Health and Human Services. "Screen-Time Reduction Toolkit for Childcare Providers." Michigan Department of Health and Human Services, January 2013. https://d3knp61p33sjvn.cloudfront.net/2015/04/Screen-TimeReductionToolkit.pdf.

Miller, Susan, Ellen Church, and Carla Poole. n.d. "Ages and Stages: How Children Develop Self-Concepts." Scholastic. Accessed August 15, 2021. https://www.scholastic.com/teachers/articles/teaching-content/ages-stages-how-children-develop-self-concept/.

Morin, Amy. "The Difference Between Race and Ethnicity." Verywell Mind, September 21, 2020. https://www.verywellmind.com/difference-between-race-and-ethnicity-5074205#.

Moyses, Kendra. "Movement Can Increase Learning in Children." MSU Extension: Michigan State University, May 30, 2012. https://www.canr.msu.edu/news/movement_can_increase_learning_in_children#.

National Center for Learning Disabilities (NCLD). n.d. "What Is Dysgraphia?" Reading Rockets. Accessed November 15, 2001. https://www.readingrockets.org/article/what-dysgraphia.

National Geographic Society Resource Library. n.d. "Storytelling." National Geographic Society. Accessed August 15, 2021. https://www.nationalgeographic.org/encyclopedia/storytelling/.

Niala, J. C. n.d. "African Parenting: The Sane Way to Raise Children." InCultureParent. Accessed August 15, 2021. https://www.incultureparent.com/african-parenting-the-sane-way-to-raise-children/.

Noirdquist, Richard. "Holophrase in Language Acquisition." Thought Co, January 7, 2020. https://www.thoughtco.com/holophrase-language-acquisition-1690929.

O'Donnell, Lauren. n.d. "Disciplining Your Child." KidsHealth. Accessed August 15, 2021. https://kidshealth.org/en/parents/discipline.html.

Oaklander, Mandhy. "The 5 Best Ways to Improve Your Memory." TIME, September 29, 2015. https://time.com/4042569/how-to-improve-memory/.

Pappas, Stephanie, and Callum McKelvie. "What Is Culture?" Livescience, December 15, 2021. https://www.livescience.com/21478-what-is-culture-definition-of-culture.html.

Pearson, Catherine. "Want to Avoid Raising Entitled Kids? Don't Do These 4 Things." Huffington Post, March 29, 2021. https://www.huffingtonpost.co.uk/entry/4-things-parents-do-that-inadvertently-raise-entitled-kids_l_606208a1c5b67593e05b000b.

Positive Action Staff. "Social and Emotional Intelligence: An Introductory Guide." Positive Action, July 15, 2020. https://www.positiveaction.net/blog/social-and-emotional-intelligence.

Project Read. n.d. "Project Read." Language Circle Enterprises. Accessed August 15, 2021. https://www.projectread.com/.

raisingchildren.net.au. n.d. "Discipline and Guiding Behavior: Babies and Children." Australian Parenting Website. Accessed August 15, 2021. https://raisingchildren.net.au/toddlers/behaviour/discipline/discipline-strategies.

Bibliography

Reischer, Erica. What Great Parents Do. New York: Penguin Random House, 2016.

Rich, Mandy. n.d. "Child Regression: What It Is and How Can You Support Your Little One." UNICEF. Accessed August 15, 2021. https://www.unicef.org/parenting/child-development/what-is-childhood-regression.

Roberts, Lindsey M. "Less crying, more snuggling: Choosing the right baby carrier for you." The Washington Post, July 12, 2018. https://go.gale.com/

Rotella, Alexis. Purple. North Carolina: Rosenberry Books, 2011.

Schiller, Pam. Seven Skills for School Success. Lewisville, NC: Gryphon House, 2009.

Shafer, Alyson. "Why You Shouldn't Say, 'I'm So Proud of You'." Alyson Schafer, February 25, 2010. https://alysonschafer.com/why-you-shouldnt-say-im-so-proud-of-you/.

Shanahan, Timothy. "How Many Times Should Students Copy the Spelling Words?" Shanahan on Literacy. March 6, 2016. https://www.shanahanonliteracy.com/blog/how-many-times-should-they-copy-the-spelling-words.

Shpancer, Noam, Ph.D. "Action Creates Emotion." Psychology Today, October 25, 2010. https://www.psychologytoday.com/us/blog/insight-therapy/201010/action-creates-emotion.

Siegal, Kim. n.d. "Why I Love Raising My Children in Kenya." InCultureParent.com. Accessed August 15, 2021. https://www.incultureparent.com/why-i-love-raising-my-children-in-kenya/.

Siegle, Steve. "The Art of Kindness." Mayo Clinic Health System, May 29, 2020. https://www.mayoclinichealthsystem.org/hometown-health/speaking-of-health/the-art-of-kindness.

Silver, Katie. "Adolescence Now Lasts from 10 to 24." BBC News, January 19, 2018. https://www.bbc.com/news/health-42732442.

Softonic. n.d. "Read Please." Softonic. Accessed August 15, 2021. https://readplease.en.softonic.com/.

Solis, Marisa, "What Is a Lactation Consultant?" BabyCenter, March 3, 2021. https://www.babycenter.com/baby/breastfeeding/lactation-consultant_40008000.

Stanborough, Rebecca Joy. "Born This Way: Chomsky's Theory Explains Why We're So Good at Acquiring Language." Healthline, June 14, 2019. https://www.healthline.com/health/childrens-health/chomsky-theory.

Sterling, Christa. "Keeping Your Mind Sharp May be Easier Than You Think." Office of Continuing Education, Central Connecticut State University, January 4, 2017. https://ccsuconed.wordpress.com/2017/01/04/keeping-your-mind-sharp-may-be-easier-than-you-think/.

Stetka, Bret. "Extended Adolescence: When 25 Is the New 18." Scientific American, September 2017. https://www.scientificamerican.com/article/extended-adolescence-when-25-is-the-new-181/.

Taylor, Marcia. "The Language Experience Approach and Adult Learners." Joblink 2000, June 1992. https://www.academia.edu/15315515/LEA_Language_Experience_Approach_.

Taylor, Marygrace. "How to Swaddle a Baby." What to Expect, June 29, 2020. https://www.whattoexpect.com/first-year/baby-care/baby-care-101/secrets-to-swaddling.aspx.

The National Native American Boarding School Healing Coalition. n.d. "US Indian Boarding School History." The National Native American Boarding School Healing Coalition. Accessed August 15, 2021. https://boardingschoolhealing.org/education/us-indian-boarding-school-history/.

Todres, Jonathan, and Joseph Wright. "A Healthy Digital Environment for Children Means More than Protection." First Focus on Children, August 4, 2021. https://firstfocus.org/blog/a-healthy-digital-environment-for-children-means-more-than-protection.

Bibliography

TREND Alphabet Charts. n.d. "Alphabet Learning Chart." Trend Enterprises, Inc. Accessed August 15, 2021. https://www.trendenterprises.com/products/t38026.

Turecki, S. The Difficult Child. New York: Bantam Books, 1989.

Wallace, Guy. n.d. "What Are the Biggest Myths in Education Today?" Technology for Learners. Accessed August 15, 2021. https://technologyforlearners.com/what-are-the-biggest-myths-in-education-today/.

Watkins, Meredith. "Video Game Addiction Symptoms and Treatment." American Addiction Centers, Updated October 26, 2021. https://americanaddictioncenters.org/video-gaming-addiction.

Wikipedia. n.d. "D'Nealian." Wikipedia. Accessed August 15, 2021. https://en.wikipedia.org/wiki/D%27Nealian.

Young, Alexander. "How to Remember What You Learn with Spaced Repetition." Alexander Young. July 30, 2021. https://blog.alexanderfyoung.com/how-to-remember-what-you-learn-for-longer-with-spaced-repetition/.

Zaske, Sara. Achtung Baby: How to Parent Like Germans, An American Mom on the German Art of Raising Self Reliant Children. London, England: Picador, January 2018.

Zhao, Yong and Wei Qiu. "How Good Are the Asians? Refuting Four Myths About Asian-American Academic Achievement." Sage Journals, January1, 2009. https://journals.sagepub.com/doi/10.1177/003172170909000507.

Made in the USA
Las Vegas, NV
27 August 2024

94503397R00168